day *to* day cookery

fourth edition

I. M. Downes | Elaine Grant

jacaranda
jaconline.com.au

Fourth edition published 2002 by
John Wiley & Sons Australia, Ltd
33 Park Road, Milton, Qld 4064

Offices also in Sydney and Melbourne

First published 1980 by
William Brooks Queensland

Second edition 1985 by Brooks Waterloo Publishers

Third edition 1991 by Brooks Waterloo Publishers

© I. M. Downes 1980, 1985, 1991
© I. M. Downes and Elaine Grant 2002

National Library of Australia
Cataloguing-in-Publication data

Downes, I. M. (Isla M.).
  Day to day cookery.

  4th ed.
  Includes index.
  ISBN 0 7016 3621 1.

  1. Cookery. I. Grant, E. (Elaine). II. Title

641.5

Cover image: © 2002 PhotoDisc, Inc.

Internal design images: © 2002 Photo Disc, Inc and © 2002 Stockbyte

Printed in Singapore by
CMO Image Printing Enterprise

10 9 8 7 6 5 4 3

Contents

Preface

Day to Day Cookery goes into its fourth edition as a highly popular and successful collection of recipes that meets the needs of both novice and experienced cooks. Each successive edition has reflected the changing tastes and cooking habits of Australian people. This fourth edition has been revised with a view to retaining a balance between traditional favourites and contemporary recipes fast becoming favourites in twenty-first century, multi-cultural Australia.

For healthier living, and to follow dietary guidelines, salt has been eliminated from recipes, except where it is an essential ingredient (for example chutney, pickles and yeast doughs). Salt can be added to other recipes if desired.

The fat content has been kept to a minimum wherever possible. Margarine has been suggested instead of butter, except where butter is needed for a superior product (for example pastries, some cakes, shortbread and confectionery). Low-fat spreads are suitable replacements for butter or margarine provided they are 60 per cent or more fat. Vegetable oil, olive oil or cooking sprays have been used for sautéing and frying. The microwave section has been deleted and microwave recipes have been incorporated into the relevant sections. These are indicated by the ✳ symbol.

A selection of low-fat and gluten-free recipes has been included for those with special dietary needs. Many of the recipes in the book can be converted to gluten-free versions by substituting rice flour, maize cornflour (not wheaten), soy flour, potato flour or combinations of these for standard flour. It is recommended that a teaspoon of xanthan gum (available in powdered form at health food outlets) be added to each cup measure of gluten-free flour to prevent crumbling and improve texture. The gluten-free recipes are indicated by the ✕ symbol.

The authors hope that this book will continue to encourage 'budding cooks' and enthuse those of us who try to continually prepare new and interesting meals for family and friends.

Acknowledgements

The author would like to acknowledge the support of teachers, friends and family members who willingly made suggestions for change where necessary. Many assisted with recipe testing. This input has been invaluable for keeping in touch with modern trends in food preparation and assembly.

I. M. Downes

My thanks to Isla Downes for allowing me to update this 'classic' recipe book. There were times, as I worked on this project, when my enthusiasm could have waned as everyday life took over. That it did not is a tribute to my family. To my husband, proofreader and typist, Garry, and my children Rebecca and Georgia, my thanks for their patience, care and support.

Elaine Grant

The ✗ symbol is a trademark of Coeliac UK and has been reproduced with their permission. www.coeliac.co.uk.

Images
© PhotoDisc 2002, Inc (pp. 7, 22, 37, 39, 96, 111, 123, 128, 149, 159, 173, 196, 210, 212, 217, 223, 272, 281, 293, 305)
© 2002 Stockbyte (pp. 27, 56, 66, 104, 143, 185, 231, 260)

Weights and Measures

In order to simplify recipes, the need for scales has been kept to a minimum. Most of the recipes require the use of the following:

- Measuring jugs (1 litre and 250 mL).
- A set of four fractional cups (one cup, half cup, third cup, quarter cup).
- A set of measuring spoons (20 mL tablespoon, 5 mL teaspoon, 2.5 mL half teaspoon, 1.25 mL quarter teaspoon).

All measures are approved by the Australian Standards Association.

Approximate weights of the common commodities are given below.

1 cup sugar	Approx. 250 g
1 cup caster sugar	220 g
1 cup brown sugar	170 g
1 cup icing sugar	175 g
1 cup butter	250 g
1 cup flour	125 g
1 cup grated cheese	125 g
1 cup cornflour	130 g
1 cup coconut	95 g
1 cup mixed fruit	160 g
1 cup rice, barley	210 g
1 cup honey, golden syrup	360 g
1 × 20 mL spoon sugar	20 g
1 × 20 mL spoon caster sugar	20 g
1 × 20 mL spoon butter	20 g
1 × 20 mL spoon flour	10 g

Oven Temperatures

Most oven temperatures are given as slow, moderate or hot. As a general rule the following classifications apply.

Gas Oven — Celsius

Very slow	100°–130°
Slow	130°–170°
Moderate	180°–190°
Hot	200°–220°
Very hot	230°–250°

Electric Oven — Celsius

Very slow	130°–150°
Slow	150°–190°
Moderate	190°–200°
Hot	200°–230°
Very hot	230°–260°

Note: Oven should be preheated to required temperature before use.

Using the Microwave

Microwave recipes in this book have been tested in a 700 watt oven. For ovens of other wattages a slight variation in cooking time will have to be made, as the table at right shows.

Caution should be exercised during the cooking process. It is better to check foods just prior to minimum cooking time stated and then reprogram in 30-second or 1-minute intervals. Undercooking is advisable to allow the further cooking of the food during the standing period.

Elevate dishes on a plastic stand during cooking to allow more efficient cooking.

It is recommended that salt not be used in microwave cooking. Should it be required, add just before serving.

Output power	Cooking time	% of increase/ decrease in cooking time
800 watts	50 seconds	Decrease 10%
750 watts	55 seconds	Decrease 5%
700 watts	1 minute	Standard
650 watts	1 minute 5 seconds	Increase 5%
600 watts	1 minute 10 seconds	Increase 10%
550 watts	1 minute 15 seconds	Increase 15%
500 watts	1 minute 20 seconds	Increase 20%

Terms Used in Cookery

accompaniment – a sauce or food served with a dish, e.g., pork and apple sauce

au gratin – food coated with white or cheese sauce, sprinkled with breadcrumbs and browned in the oven

baste – to spoon hot oil over joints while baking

blanch – to whiten, i.e., food is placed in cold water and raised slowly to boiling point, then strained

blend – to mix a dry and a cold liquid ingredient to a smooth paste

boiling point of water – 100°C

bouquet garni – a bunch of herbs consisting of two sprigs of parsley, one sprig of marjoram, two sprigs of thyme and one bay leaf, tied together

braise – to cook meat or poultry very gently, with a minimum of liquid, in a covered pan

canapés – small pieces of fried bread, toast or pastry used as a base for savouries

cannelloni – tubes of pasta for filling with savoury mixtures

casserole – an ovenproof dish with a lid

caviar – the salted roe of the sturgeon

clarify – to remove impurities from food

compote – pieces of fruit cooked in syrup; shape is retained

condiments – highly flavoured sauces, chutney, seasonings and spices

crepe – a thin delicate pancake often served folded or rolled and filled with sweet or savoury mixtures

crouton – small cubes of fried bread

cube – to cut into small squares

deep fry – to submerge food in hot fat and cook until crisp

dice – small cubes of food

drizzle – to pour oil or other liquids in a thin stream

dry breadcrumbs – slices of bread baked till crisp and golden and then crushed to produce fine crumbs

dry fry – to cook food in a non-stick pan with only a light brushing or spray of cooking oil

entree – a light dish of meat, chicken, seafood or dressed vegetables served immediately before the main course

fat-reduced spreads – 60 per cent or more fat spreads are suitable as butter/margarine replacements. 50–59 per cent fat is a satisfactory replacement for butter or margarine. Less than 40 per cent fat is not a successful replacement for butter or margarine for baking or frying.

fillets – pieces of fish free from bones; undercuts of meat

flan – an open tart

fresh breadcrumbs – 1 to 2 day old bread made into crumbs by grating or processing

garnish – to decorate food

ghee – a pure butter fat which can be heated to high temperatures without burning because all the milk solids and salt have been removed

glaze – to brush with either egg and milk or sugar and water to give gloss and improve appearance

hors d'oeuvres – appetisers served at the beginning of a meal

kebab – Turkish name for dishes which include pieces of meat grilled on a skewer

knead – to shape flour mixture by hand or combine ingredients well and make dough smooth

legumes – plants bearing edible pods, e.g., peas, beans

marinade – flavoured and spiced mixture of oil and vinegar or wine for soaking raw meats and fish before cooking

meringue – a mixture of stiffly beaten egg white and sugar

minestrone – thick Italian vegetable soup

mocha – a mixture of coffee and chocolate used for flavouring

mornay – a cheese flavoured sauce used with seafood, eggs, vegetables

par-boil – to partly cook food in liquid

poaching – cooking in liquid just below boiling point

pulses – edible dried seeds of leguminous plants such as beans, peas and lentils

puree – to reduce to a pulp by rubbing through a sieve or processing

roux – a mixture of equal weights of flour and melted butter, cooked and used for thickening soups and sauces

rub in – lightly combine flour with shortening using the fingertips

sauté – to cook by tossing food gently in a little hot butter, in a shallow pan

scald – to pour boiling water over food or utensils

shallow fry – to cook food in a small amount of hot fat usually 1–2 mm

shortening – a fat

simmer – slow cooking at approximately 70°–80°C. A bubble will rise occasionally to the surface.

skim – to clean a liquid of matter floating on the surface

stew – to simmer foods in sufficient liquid to cover

stock – liquid resulting from simmering bones, meat or vegetables in water for several hours

syrup – a solution of sugar and water

tepid – slightly warm. Use two parts cold liquid to one part boiling liquid.

vol au vents – puff pastry shells filled with a variety of ingredients bound together with a thick white sauce

whip – to beat rapidly to increase volume by introducing air

wilted – to lose crispness and to become soft and limp

Herbs and spices

Herbs are the aromatic leaves of plants.

Spices are aromatic products which are the dried seeds, buds, fruit or flower parts, bark or roots of plants, usually of tropical origin.

Herbs and spices are used to flavour both sweet and savoury dishes.

Fresh herbs are easily grown in the garden or in pots. Use about four times as much as for dried herbs. Use less in the case of strong flavours such as sage and thyme.

Dried herbs and spices should be purchased in small quantities as over time volatile oils evaporate and the flavour and aroma dissipates.

HERBS

Basil, Sweet – The flavour is spicy and sweet. Use in tomato dishes, meat seasonings, soups, stews, fish, poultry and stuffings, vegetables, pasta sauces, salads and herb vinegars.

Bay – Leaves are one of the herbs in bouquet garni. Use in stock, soups, sauces, stews, casseroles and any slow-cooked dishes.

Chives – They have a mild onion flavour. Use with most foods but particularly with potatoes, eggs and cheese. Garlic chives are stronger and impart a flavour of garlic. May be used in sauces and salads.

Coriander – The flavour is lemony and the leaves are used in Asian, Indian, Middle-Eastern and Mexican dishes. Should be added in the last 10 minutes of cooking as the delicate flavour is driven off by prolonged cooking.

Dill – Dill has a distinct parsley-like aroma and a subtle hint of anise. May be used in cottage- and cream-cheese combinations, white sauce for serving with chicken and seafood, scrambled eggs and omelettes, fish dishes, salad dressings and herb vinegars.

Fennel – Fennel leaves have a slightly anise aroma. The fresh leaves are used in salads, white sauces, with seafoods and to garnish terrines or soups.

Fennel Seeds – These seeds have an anise flavour which is warm and spicy. Used in soups, breads, pasta, tomato dishes, pickles and salads.

Galangal – As a member of the ginger family it has a ginger aroma and a biting, hot flavour. Used in Thai soups, curries, Asian dishes and with seafoods.

Garlic – A member of the onion family and it has a sweet but sharp taste. Used in spice mixes and curry powders and it complements most savoury dishes, e.g., meats, vegetables, rice and pasta.

Lemon Grass – Lemon grass has a tangy lemon flavour. Used with red meats, white meats, vegetables, rice, Asian soups, curries, stir-fries, seafoods, marinades for fish, pork and chicken and it forms part of Thai seasonings.

Marjoram – One of the herbs in bouquet garni. Used to flavour stuffing, rissoles, sausages, omelettes, chicken and pork dishes.

Mint – Garden mint is used for mint sauce and for flavouring vinegar. Used in pork and lamb dishes, salads, peas, tomatoes, salad dressings, sorbets, drinks and as a garnish.

Oregano or Wild Marjoram – It is stronger in flavour than marjoram and is much used in Italian and Greek dishes such as pasta sauces, pizza, with roast beef and lamb and in omelettes, stuffing mixes and salads.

Parsley – Probably the most used of herbs. Use in all savoury dishes and sauces. Valuable as a garnish and in omelettes, scrambled eggs, souffles, mashed potatoes, tabouleh, soups, pasta dishes and sauces for fish and chicken.

Rosemary – A very strong and overpowering flavour so use lightly. Use with lamb, veal and chicken. It will also improve the flavour of vegetables.

Sage – Flavour is strong so should be used sparingly. Used with rich and fatty foods like pork and duck, in stuffings and with sausages, rissoles, pork, poultry and savoury scones.

Tarragon – Use to flavour vinegar, salad dressings and sauces. May be used in chicken, turkey, egg, seafood and veal dishes.

Thyme – Strong flavour which blends well with other herbs. One of the herbs of bouquet garni. Use in meat and poultry dishes, soups, stews, stuffings, terrines, patés and potato salads.

SPICES

Allspice – Use in cakes and biscuits. Will enhance the flavour of stews, pot roasts, soups and marinades.

Cardamom – Whole seeds are used in pickling. Ground cardamom is used in yeast breads and coffee cakes. Also used in lamb and beef dishes, sausages and hamburgers.

Cinnamon – Use in cakes, pastries, biscuits, milk drinks, custards, rice dishes, yeast buns and loaves, on toast, in compote of fruits and curry powders. Cinnamon is available in powder or bark form.

Chilli powder – A Mexican spice used with meat, beans and sauces and fillings for tacos and enchiladas.

Cloves – A hot pungent flavour which should be used sparingly. Use in curry powders and curries, chutneys, pickles, sauces, baked ham and apple desserts.

Coriander (seeds) – A lemon-scented spice for use in bread, cakes and biscuits, pickles, stuffing for poultry, sausages and meat loaves.

Cayenne – The most pungent of spices so is used in small quantities. Add to egg, cheese, fish and vegetable dishes.

Cumin – Has a pungent aroma and flavour and is used in oriental, Mexican and Middle Eastern dishes, curries and stews and in stir-fry pork, lamb, beef, seafood, rice and vegetable dishes.

Curry Powder – A blend of spices used in all curry dishes. Mild to hot varieties are available.

Ginger – Available in syrup, or ground, root or crystallised. Use in drinks, chutneys, pickles, vegetable dishes, curries, Asian stir-fries, with red meats and seafoods in sauces, marinades, cakes and biscuits.

Mace – Similar to nutmeg but with a more subtle flavour. Use in the same dishes.

Mustard – A pungent flavour which improves dips, spreads, sauces, salad dressings, pickles, spiced vinegars, meat seasoning, curries and egg and cheese dishes.

Nutmeg – Use for desserts, custards, milk drinks, fruit cakes and puddings and on white sauce-coated vegetables, with pumpkin, potato, carrots, spinach and in cheese sauce.

Paprika – A mild flavour and attractive colour. Use in casseroles and stews with chicken, veal and pork. Provides a garnish for vegetables, potato salad, mashed potatoes and eggs, and use in sauces, tandoori blends and curry mixes.

Peppercorns – When freshly ground they give the best pepper flavour. Use whole in pickles, stock or when boiling corned beef. Ground pepper is used in most savoury foods like eggs, fish, beef, chicken, vegetables, sauces, rice and pasta dishes.

Poppy Seeds – Mainly used as a topping on rolls and breads. Complements breads, biscuits, cakes, pasta and muffins.

Saffron – Saffron has a pungent flavour and is used in Indian, rice and couscous dishes, with seafood and chicken. It is popular as a colouring in fish soups, rice dishes, Spanish rice, mashed potatoes, buns and cakes.

Sesame Seeds – Primary ingredient of tahini and is used when lightly toasted as a topping on rolls and breads, giving a nutty flavour. Use in cakes, biscuits, stuffings, meat dishes, cheese spreads, scrambled eggs and salads.

Turmeric – A bright yellow colour, this spice is used in mustard pickles, meat and egg dishes. It is an ingredient of Asian and Indian curries, stir-fried chicken, seafoods, vegetables, sauces and rice dishes.

Appetisers are flavoursome, attractive-to-look-at morsels of food served with drinks at social functions. They are bite-sized portions intended to excite and stimulate the appetite and so make the meal, which is to follow, more enjoyable. It is important therefore to present the food attractively and to have a variety of shapes, flavours and colours.

To reduce the fat content of these appetisers the following substitutions can be made:

sour cream — light sour cream, plain low-fat yoghurt or $\frac{1}{2}$ sour cream and $\frac{1}{2}$ low-fat yoghurt

mayonnaise — low-fat mayonnaise or low-fat yoghurt

cream cheese — cottage cheese or low-fat ricotta or light cream cheese

cream — light cream, evaporated skim milk, lightly beaten soft tofu or low-fat yoghurt

grated cheese — reduced-fat grated cheese

coconut milk or coconut cream — evaporated skim milk and $\frac{1}{2}$ teaspoon coconut essence or low-fat yoghurt and 1 to 2 tablespoons desiccated coconut.

CANAPÉS

Canapés form the basis for many savouries or hors d'oeuvres and may be any of the following cut into small, neat shapes.

Toast	Pastry
Fried bread	Bread and butter
Baked bread	Mini pancakes
Plain or cheese biscuits	

Except in the case of fresh bread and pancakes the canapés should be crisp. Do not spread with toppings until shortly before serving.

Toppings

Use a base of soft cheeses, goat's cheese, cream cheese, mayonnaise or sour cream. To these add one or two flavourings such as:

Chopped celery	Gherkins or onion	Semidried tomatoes
Asparagus	Sweet corn	Pesto
Shaved ham	Sardines	Tapenade
Olives	Chopped walnuts	Salsa
Chutney	Tomato sauce	Oven roasted vegetables
Caviar	Anchovy paste	Capers.

Season well, using fresh herbs, pepper and a few drops of lemon juice.

In addition there are commercially produced spreads — ham, chicken, seafood, cheese, gherkin — which may be used alone or incorporated in other mixes. Relishes, such as Corn and Tomato Relish, make tasty toppings. (See page 293.)

Serving: Canapés may be arranged in groups or rows on trays covered with paper doilies to prevent them moving about. They should be attractively garnished.

Curried Salmon Spread

1 small can pink salmon
1 teaspoon curry powder (or less)
1 tablespoon white onion
chopped parsley
pepper
2 teaspoons mayonnaise

1. Remove bones and skin from salmon.
2. Mash well with curry powder, finely chopped onion, parsley and pepper and sufficient mayonnaise to bind all together.
3. Use as a spread for biscuits.

Mushroom Topping

oil
200 g mushrooms, finely chopped
2 shallots, finely sliced
½ capsicum, finely diced
1 clove garlic, crushed
2 tablespoons sesame seeds

1. Spray or brush pan with oil, heat, and add mushrooms, shallots, capsicum and garlic and cook until lightly browned. Stir in sesame seeds.
2. Use as a topping for mini pancakes or bread rounds.

Mock Chicken Spread

1 onion
oil
1 tomato
1 egg
2 tablespoons grated cheese
pepper
savoury biscuits

1. Peel and chop onion finely.
2. Brush or spray pan with oil, heat and add onion and cook until soft but not brown.
3. Skin tomato and chop up. Add to onion and cook until soft.
4. Add beaten egg and grated cheese and cook gently until mixture thickens but do not allow to boil.
5. Add pepper to taste.
6. Allow to cool then spread on biscuits or use as a dip.
7. Decorate with pieces of red onions, olives or oven roasted capsicum.

Tapenade

150 g black olives, pitted

50 g anchovy fillets, drained

50 g capers, washed and diced

50 g canned tuna

1 teaspoon fresh thyme leaves

1 clove garlic, crushed

1 tablespoon brandy (optional)

freshly ground pepper

2 tablespoons olive oil

1. Place all ingredients except olive oil in a food processor and process until combined but still chunky.
2. Drizzle in olive oil, with the motor running.
3. Use as a dip, or spread on crusty bread rounds.

Pesto

1 cup basil leaves, washed and removed from stems

125 g parmesan cheese

125 g pine nuts

4 cloves garlic, chopped

pinch salt

olive oil

1. Place all ingredients in a food processor with a little olive oil and process until the mixture is the consistency of thick cream. Add a little more olive oil if required.
2. Use immediately or place in a clean jar and cover with a thin layer of oil. May be stored in the refrigerator for up to 2 weeks. Pour away oil before using.

Chicken Liver Paté

oil

500 g chicken livers, chopped

1 onion, finely chopped

2 rashers bacon, trimmed and diced

garlic

1 tablespoon sherry or brandy

rosemary

75 g butter

1. Spray or brush pan with oil, heat and add chicken livers, onion, bacon and garlic. When cooked add sherry and rosemary.
2. Lower heat, add the butter and stir until melted. Cool slightly.
3. Place in a blender and blend until smooth.
4. Pour into paté bowls and serve with biscuits.

Note: Extra melted butter may be poured over paté if it is to be kept.

Cheese Straws

1 cup finely grated cheese
1 cup plain flour
1 tablespoon soft
  breadcrumbs
pinch cayenne pepper
60 g butter
1 egg

1. Place all dry ingredients into a bowl.
2. Rub butter in lightly.
3. Mix into a paste with the beaten egg.
4. Turn onto a floured board and knead until smooth.
5. Roll out thinly and cut into straws approximately 7 cm long and 6 mm wide.
6. Cut out rings about 5 cm in diameter, allowing one ring to each seven straws.
7. Place on a flat baking tray.
8. Bake in a slow oven for 10 to 15 minutes or until a golden yellow.

Variation

Cheese Biscuits

Roll pastry out thinly and cut out with a small round or fluted cutter. Bake in a slow oven until golden yellow.

Savoury Pinwheels

1 cup plain flour
pinch cayenne pepper
pinch mustard
60 g butter or margarine
½ cup finely grated tasty
  cheese
2 tablespoons cold water
  (approx.)
¾ cup chutney
a little milk
½ cup peanuts, chopped

1. Sift flour, cayenne pepper and mustard.
2. Rub in the butter then add the cheese.
3. Mix into a fairly stiff dough with water.
4. Turn onto a floured board, knead lightly then roll out into a rectangle about 16 cm wide and 6 mm thick.
5. Spread with chutney and roll up.
6. Wrap in plastic wrap and chill until firm.
7. Cut into pinwheels about 6 mm thick.
8. Place on a greased tray, brush with milk and sprinkle with nuts.
9. Bake in a moderate oven for about 15 minutes or until brown.

Salami and Cheese Rounds

1 bread stick
100 g salami, finely chopped
1 tablespoon chopped
  chives
1½ cups grated tasty
  cheese

1. Slice bread stick into 1.5 cm wide rounds.
2. Combine salami and chives and press a small amount onto each round.
3. Sprinkle with cheese and press cheese on firmly.
4. Grill rounds until cheese is melted.

HOT SAVOURIES

A variety of savouries may be made using the following as cases for hot fillings:

Short pastry boats and tartlets

Cheese pastry boats and tartlets

Bread cases

Choux pastry cases or profiteroles

Puff pastry vol au vent cases

Filo pastry cases

Boats and Tartlets

1 cup plain flour

¼ teaspoon baking powder

60 g shortening

2 tablespoons cold water (approx.)

egg and milk for glazing

1. Make short pastry and cut shapes with boat-shaped or round cutter.
2. Line the tins and prick well.
3. Brush over with egg and milk glaze.
4. Bake in a moderate oven until browned.

Cheese Boats and Tartlets

Use the cheese straws recipe (page 4). Roll pastry thinly and cut out as above. Line savoury tins, prick well and bake until golden yellow.

Bread Cases

thinly sliced white or wholemeal bread

melted butter or margarine

1. Remove crusts from the bread and roll with a rolling pin to make thinner.
2. Cut rounds or squares to fit patty tins.
3. Brush each piece on both sides with melted butter and fit into patty tins.
4. Bake in a moderate oven until golden brown.

Variation

Brush four 8–10 cm squares of filo pastry with melted butter and fit in patty tin. Bake in a moderate oven until browned.

Choux Pastry Cases

Make up a quantity of choux pastry as per recipe in Pastry section (page 221).
Make the puffs very small, approximately 1 teaspoon of mixture per puff.

Puff Pastry Vol au Vents

Make puff pastry as per recipe in the Pastry section (page 212) or use convenience product.
Alternatively, use ready-made vol au vent cases of the smallest size.

HOT FILLINGS

Asparagus Filling

2 tablespoons butter
3 tablespoons flour
1 cup milk
1 small can asparagus cuts
pepper

1. Melt butter in a small saucepan, stir in flour, mix well and remove from heat.
2. Gradually add milk and mix well.
3. Replace on heat and bring to boil stirring constantly until thickened.
4. Add drained asparagus and pepper to taste.
5. Fill cases and bake in a moderate oven for 5 minutes.

Sweet Corn Filling

1 tablespoon butter
1½ tablespoons flour
½ cup milk
1 small can cream style sweet corn (130 g)
1 bacon rasher, trimmed, diced and sautéed
pepper

1. Melt butter in a small saucepan, stir in flour, mix well and remove from heat.
2. Gradually add milk and mix well.
3. Replace on heat and bring to boil stirring constantly until thickened.
4. Add sweet corn and bacon.
5. Fill cases and bake in a moderate oven for 5 minutes.

Prawn Filling

1 cup thick white sauce
½ teaspoon curry powder
250 g shelled prawns, chopped
¼ teaspoon mustard
pepper

1. Make white sauce (as in steps 1, 2 and 3 of Asparagus Filling above) and add curry powder.
2. Add prawns and season with pepper and mustard.
3. Fill cases and bake in a moderate oven for 5 minutes.

Olive and Tomato Filling

oil
1 onion, chopped
1 clove garlic, crushed
1 small zucchini, chopped
⅓ cup semi-dried tomatoes, chopped
⅓ cup sliced black olives
2 tablespoons fresh basil, chopped
2 tablespoons parmesan

1. Brush or spray pan with oil, heat, add onion, garlic and zucchini. Cook, stirring until onion is soft.
2. Remove from heat. Stir in tomatoes, olives and basil.
3. Place in cases, sprinkle with parmesan and bake in a moderate oven for 5 minutes.

Ham and Vegetable Filling

100 g ham, diced

1 cup grated vegetables (carrots, zucchini, onion, sweet potato)

½ cup cottage cheese

2 small/medium eggs, lightly beaten

1 tablespoon wholeseed mustard

½ teaspoon oregano

freshly ground pepper

12 pre-cooked tartlet shells

½ cup grated cheese

1. Place ham, vegetables, cottage cheese, eggs, mustard, oregano and pepper in a bowl and mix well.
2. Spoon mixture into tartlet shells and sprinkle with grated cheese.
3. Bake in a moderate oven (180°C) for 15 minutes until filling is set.

Spring Rolls

240 g pork, minced

½ cup bean sprouts, chopped

1 cup cabbage, finely shredded

½ cup shallots, finely sliced

2 teaspoons soy sauce

12 spring roll wrappers

1 tablespoon oil

1. Place pork, bean sprouts, cabbage, shallots and soy sauce in a bowl and combine well.
2. Divide meat mixture into 12 portions and place each portion on one corner of each spring roll wrapper.
3. Roll each wrapper firmly around the filling, folding in the edges.
4. Brush the edge of each wrapper with water to secure it in place.
5. Heat the oil in a pan and fry spring rolls until golden, turning frequently.

DIPS

Dips are among the most popular appetisers served. They are quickly and easily prepared, are tasty and require only biscuits, crackers, toast triangles, oven-baked bread shapes or vegetables as an accompaniment. In addition there are commercially produced dips in a variety of flavours.

Biscuits

Most people select from a large variety of commercially produced biscuits but home-cooked biscuits may also be used.

Care should be taken in the choice of biscuits. Plain cracker biscuits are acceptable with all dips. In the case of flavoured biscuits, flavour compatibility should be considered.

Pita Crisps

2 small pocket breads
60 g butter, melted
1 clove crushed garlic
2 teaspoons cumin
2 teaspoons ground coriander
¼ teaspoon chilli powder

1. Split pitas to make 4 rounds and place smooth side down on the board.
2. Mix butter and garlic together and brush over each round.
3. Mix spices and sprinkle over pita rounds.
4. Cut rounds into strips and then into diamond shapes.
5. Place on a greased tray, buttered side up and bake in a hot oven (200°C) for 10 minutes or until golden and crisp.
6. Serve as a snack or accompaniment to dips.

Oven Baked Croutons

1 bread stick
60 g butter
1 tablespoon oil

1. Slice bread stick thinly.
2. Soften butter and combine with oil and brush over bread.
3. Place on baking paper on an oven tray and bake in a hot oven (200°C) until crisp. This will take about 5 minutes. Cool.

Vegetables

A selection of vegetables cut into suitable shapes.

Serving

A popular serving dish for dips is one with a central bowl for the dip mixture with space around it for a selection of biscuits and/or vegetables.

Garnish

A simple garnish may be arranged centrally on the dip or attached to the edge of the dip bowl, e.g., a prawn, indicating the flavour of the dip. Though not always easily achieved some indication of the flavour is desirable.

Hummus

1 400 g can chickpeas, drained

2 cloves garlic, crushed

2 tablespoons tahini (smooth peanut paste can be used)

4 tablespoons olive oil

2 tablespoons lemon juice

½ teaspoon cayenne pepper

1 tablespoon sesame seeds

1. Rinse chickpeas well and place in blender. Add garlic and tahini and puree until fairly smooth.
2. With the blender still running, slowly add the oil and lemon juice.
3. Stir in cayenne pepper and add a little cold water if the mixture is too thick.
4. Heat a small non-stick pan and cook sesame seeds 2 to 3 minutes until golden, shaking the pan throughout the process. Allow to cool and sprinkle over puree when serving.
5. Serve with fresh Lebanese bread.

Guacamole (Mexico)

1 very ripe avocado

1 tablespoon lemon juice

1 large tomato, diced

1 medium onion, chopped

1 small red chilli, diced

pepper

1. Cut avocado flesh into small pieces and sprinkle with lemon juice.
2. Add the other ingredients finely chopped and mix.
3. Place in a blender and blend until smooth.

Note: These small chillies are very hot and should be added with caution.

Avocado Dip

1 large avocado

1 125 g pkt cream cheese

1 tablespoon mayonnaise

1 tablespoon lemon juice

1 teaspoon grated onion

pepper

Place all ingredients in an electric blender and blend until smooth.

Avocado and Prawn Dip

1 avocado
2 tablespoons white wine
   or vinegar
2 tablespoons cream
½ teaspoon curry powder
120 g shelled prawns

1. Peel avocado and remove stone.
2. Place in an electric blender with the other ingredients and blend until smooth.

Tropicana Dip

1 250 g pkt cream cheese
1 450 g can crushed
   pineapple
½ pkt mushroom soup

1. Place cream cheese in a basin and beat until smooth.
2. Gradually add ¼ cup pineapple juice while continuing to beat.
3. Add soup mix and well-drained pineapple and stir well.
4. Chill for at least 1 hour.

Mexican Dip

1 310 g can red kidney
   beans
¾ cup natural yoghurt or
   sour light cream
1 small clove garlic,
   crushed
1 pkt French onion soup
¼ teaspoon chilli powder

1. Drain beans and combine with yoghurt in a blender and process until smooth.
2. Stir in remaining ingredients, cover and refrigerate at least 1 hour.

Satay Dip

½ cup crunchy peanut
   butter
½ cup light coconut cream
2 tablespoons sweet chilli
   sauce
2 tablespoons lemon juice
1 teaspoon cumin
1 small onion, finely
   chopped
½ small Lebanese
   cucumber, finely
   chopped

1. Combine peanut butter, coconut cream, chilli sauce, water, lemon juice, cumin and onion in a saucepan.
2. Gently heat until mixture is hot, stirring all the time.
3. Stir in the cucumber and serve warm.

Salsa

1 medium tomato, diced

1 small red onion, diced

1 130 g can corn kernels, drained

2 tablespoons chopped fresh coriander leaves

1 clove garlic, crushed

1 tablespoon sweet chilli sauce

¼ cup mild taco sauce

Combine all ingredients in a bowl. Garnish with coriander and serve with corn chips.

Salmon Dip — Low fat

2 cups ricotta cheese

1 220 g can salmon or tuna, drained and flaked

2 tablespoons chopped parsley

2 shallots, finely chopped

1 stalk celery, finely chopped

2 drops tabasco sauce

freshly ground black pepper

1. Combine ricotta cheese, salmon, parsley, shallots, celery and tabasco sauce.
2. Season to taste with pepper.
3. Chill 2 to 3 hours before serving.

Cocktail Meat Balls

500 g steak mince *or* 375 g steak mince

125 g pork and veal mince

1 cup fresh breadcrumbs

2 teaspoons mixed herbs

¼ cup tomato sauce

¼ cup barbecue or chilli sauce

1 egg

pepper

oil for frying

1 small onion, finely chopped

1. Place minced meat in a bowl. Add breadcrumbs, herbs, sauces, egg and pepper.
2. Brush or spray pan with oil, heat, add onions and cook until golden in colour. Add to mixture and mix well.
3. Shape into small balls (about 24) using wet hands.
4. Heat oil in a frying pan and fry meat balls a few at a time. Shake pan frequently so meat balls maintain their shape.
5. Drain on absorbent paper.
6. Serve hot or cold with cocktail sticks inserted.
7. To serve, arrange around small bowls of various sauces e.g. tomato sauce or sweet chilli sauce.

(Serves 6–8)

Spicy Chicken Meat Balls — Low fat

250 g chicken mince

1 egg, lightly beaten

1/4 teaspoon ground coriander or 1 teaspoon fresh, finely chopped coriander

1/4 teaspoon paprika

1/4 cup fresh breadcrumbs

1 small onion, finely chopped

1. Combine mince, egg, coriander, paprika, breadcrumbs and onion.
2. Shape into small balls (about 15).
3. Place on greased oven trays and bake in a hot oven (200°C) for 15 minutes or until golden brown.
4. Serve hot with cocktail sticks.
5. To serve, arrange around a small bowl of Thai sweet chilli sauce.

Greek Triangles

oil

1 bunch spinach, finely chopped

pepper

4 shallots, chopped

1 1/2 tablespoons margarine

2 tablespoons flour

pinch nutmeg

3/4 cup milk

125 g fetta cheese, crumbled

500 g filo pastry

Spinach Filling

1. Spray or brush pan with oil, heat and add spinach, pepper and shallots. Sauté until spinach is tender.
2. Melt margarine in a pan, stir in flour and nutmeg and cook, stirring, for 1 minute. Remove from heat.
3. Add milk gradually. Return to heat and stir until sauce boils and thickens.
4. Remove from heat and stir in spinach mixture and fetta cheese. Allow to cool.

Triangles

5. Take out one pastry sheet at a time, as pastry dries out very quickly or cover unused sheets with a wet tea towel until required.
6. Cut each sheet into 8 cm wide strips and spray or brush each strip with oil. One strip makes a triangle.
7. Put a teaspoonful of filling on the end of each strip. Take corner of pastry and fold over to form a triangle.
8. Lift first triangle up and over to form a second triangle. Continue folding over and over to the end of pastry strip. Trim surplus if necessary. Repeat the process until all spinach mixture is used.
9. Place triangles on a greased baking tray.
10. Bake in a hot oven (200°C) for 10 to 15 minutes or until golden brown.
11. Serve hot.

Prunes and Bacon

4 bacon rashers, thinly cut
16 prunes, stoned

1. Remove rind from bacon rashers and cut into four pieces to give lengths of 6 to 7 cm.
2. Roll each prune in a strip of bacon and thread onto skewers.
3. Place under a heated griller and cook carefully until bacon is crisp but not hard. Keep turning skewers during cooking.
4. Remove skewers and insert cocktail sticks.
5. Serve immediately garnished with parsley.

Note: If desired prunes may be filled with cream cheese before being rolled in bacon. Use canned pineapple pieces as an alternative to prunes.

Stuffed Eggs

6 hard boiled eggs
2 tablespoons mayonnaise
pepper
2 teaspoons finely chopped parsley
red capsicum

1. Cut eggs in halves and remove yolks.
2. Mash the yolks well then add mayonnaise, pepper to taste and parsley.
3. Pipe into egg-white cups.
4. Decorate each with parsley and a small piece of red capsicum.
5. Serve on a bed of lettuce.

Variations of basic stuffed eggs

Small quantities of any one of the following may be added to the basic mixture: sardines, salmon, curry, fish pastes. Process in a blender to make the mixture smooth for piping.

Cheese and Celery

1 125 g pkt cream cheese
1 teaspoon lemon juice
½–1 tablespoon chilli sauce
½ cup peanut paste
2 tablespoons milk
celery stalks

1. Beat cream cheese until soft and light.
2. Add the other ingredients and beat well.
3. Wash celery well and cut into short lengths.
4. Fill with the mixture. This may be done more easily with an icing bag and tube.
5. Chill well and serve with other savouries.

Smoked Salmon Mini Muffins

⅔ cup self-raising flour

⅓ cup plain flour

2 eggs, lightly beaten

⅓ cup milk

⅓ cup cream

1 tablespoon fresh, finely chopped parsley

½ cup cream cheese, softened

1 tablespoon fresh, chopped chives

freshly ground pepper

3 slices (75 g) smoked salmon, diced for garnishing

1. Sift flours into a bowl and add eggs, milk, cream and parsley and mix until just combined.
2. Spoon into greased 24-hole mini-muffin pan.
3. Bake in a moderate oven (180°C) for 12 to 15 minutes.
4. When cool, cut a V shape in the top of the muffins and top with a little cream cheese, smoked salmon, chives and pepper.

Chicken Sticks

1.5 kg chicken wings or use the skinned wing pieces

Marinade

¼ cup soy sauce

1 clove garlic, crushed

1 teaspoon grated green ginger

pepper

1 teaspoon sugar

1 tablespoon honey

2 tablespoons dry sherry

1. Wash and dry wings. Cut off wing tips at joints. (Use tips for making soup.)
2. Holding small end of bone, trim around bone with a sharp knife to cut meat free from bone. Cut, scrape and push meat down to large end.
3. Using fingers, pull skin and meat down over end of bone to make small drumsticks.
4. In a large bowl combine soy sauce, garlic, ginger, pepper, sugar, honey and sherry. Pour over chicken sticks and refrigerate overnight. Stir occasionally.
5. Pour chicken sticks and the marinade into a baking dish and spread evenly.
6. Bake in a moderate oven for 35 to 40 minutes or until cooked. Baste and stir occasionally.
7. Remove from oven, spoon any remaining marinade over the chicken sticks and serve immediately with drinks.

Crudités

A selection of at least 4
  vegetables, e.g., carrot,
  cauliflower, celery,
  cucumber, parsnip,
  radish, shallot, zucchini

Dipping Sauce

plain yoghurt or sour
  cream
one or more of the
  following:
sauces (tomato, soy,
  Worcestershire)
chutney
onion, finely chopped
nuts, chopped
fresh herbs, finely chopped

1. To the yoghurt or sour cream add selected flavouring cautiously until flavour is acceptable.
2. Place dipping sauce in a small bowl.
3. Select young crisp vegetables (taking colour into consideration).
4. Prepare vegetables and cut into thin strips about 7 cm in length.
5. Carrots and zucchini may be cut into diagonal slices about 0.5 cm in thickness.
6. Divide cauliflower into flowerets.
7. Unless very large, leave radishes whole with a tiny length of stalk.
8. Drop vegetable pieces into iced water and stand for 30 minutes to become crisp.
9. Dry vegetables on paper towels and serve with dip.
10. Garnish with fresh herbs.

Cheese Ball

1 250 g pkt cream cheese
2 cups matured cheddar
  cheese
1 cup chopped ham
1 tablespoon chopped
  gherkins
1 tablespoon finely
  chopped chives
¼ cup chopped olives
2 cloves garlic, crushed
60 g butter
mayonnaise to mix
½ cup walnuts, finely
  chopped
parsley, finely chopped

1. Beat cream cheese until softened.
2. Add all the ingredients except nuts and parsley and mix well. Add sufficient mayonnaise to bind the ingredients together.
3. Form into a ball and refrigerate until well chilled.
4. Before serving coat the ball in a mixture of finely chopped nuts and parsley.
5. Stand the ball on a serving plate and garnish with salad vegetables.
6. Small plain biscuits should accompany the cheese ball.

Chicken Vol au Vents

oil

**2 bacon rashers, trimmed
  and diced**

1 onion, diced

1½ cups cooked chicken

1 tablespoon lemon juice

**6 vol au vent cases
  (10 cm radius)**

**½ cup cheddar cheese,
  grated**

Sauce

40 g margarine

2½ tablespoons flour

1½ cups milk

pepper

1. Spray pan with oil, heat and add bacon and onion and cook until transparent.
2. Turn onto absorbent paper to drain.
3. Prepare chicken by removing all bones and cutting into bite-sized pieces.
4. Make white sauce then add chicken and bacon mixture and mix well.
5. Add a little lemon juice or vinegar to sharpen the taste. Add more seasoning if necessary.
6. Spoon into warmed cases. Sprinkle with grated cheese.
7. Brown under hot griller, taking care not to burn the pastry.
8. Serve immediately, garnished with parsley and thin strips of red capsicum.

Note: Cases may be made by fitting layers of filo pastry brushed with oil into small ramekin dishes, or muffin pans. Use unoiled filo or brush with skim milk to lower fat content and brush the pastry edges only with oil. Trim pastry level with tops of dishes and bake.

(*Serves 6*)

Variation

Mushroom Filling

Omit chicken and lemon juice and add 120 g sautéed, sliced mushrooms. Sprinkle tops with a little paprika. Decorate as required.

(*Serves 6*)

Fruit Cocktail

¾ **cup rockmelon balls**
¾ **cup watermelon balls**
¾ **cup honeydew melon balls**
¾ **cup pineapple pieces**
¾ **cup juice from pineapple and rockmelon**
1 **tablespoon sugar**
2 **teaspoons sherry (optional)**

1. Prepare the fruits and chill.
2. Dissolve sugar in the juices and flavour with sherry.
3. Arrange a mixture of fruits in suitable glass dishes.
4. Spoon some of the juice over each.
5. Garnish each with a twisted slice of lime and a small sprig of mint.

(Serves 4)

Minted Pineapple

2–2½ **cups pineapple pieces**
sugar if needed
finely chopped mint
garnish, e.g. strawberries, cherries, kiwi fruit slices or mint leaves

1. Choose a sweet pineapple and cut into bite-sized pieces.
2. Sprinkle with sugar if necessary.
3. Add chopped mint and fork through pineapple.
4. Spoon into suitable glass dishes.
5. Garnish with any of the listed garnishes to give colour contrast.
6. Chill well before serving.

(Serves 4)

Avocado with Seafood

½ **cup crab meat**
½ **cup small prawns, shelled**
½ **cup chopped celery**
1 **tablespoon chopped shallots**
3 **avocados**
lemon juice

Sauce

2 **tablespoons mayonnaise**
2 **tablespoons whipped cream**
1 **teaspoon Worcestershire sauce**
pepper
2 **teaspoons chopped parsley**
2 **teaspoons tomato sauce**
few drops Tabasco sauce

1. Make the sauce by mixing all the ingredients together. Chill well.
2. Divide crab and prawns into small pieces. Add chopped celery and shallots.
3. Cut avocados in half and remove seeds. Scoop out a little of the flesh and mix with the seafood.
4. Brush the surface of the avocado with lemon juice.
5. Spoon filling into avocado halves. Chill well.
6. Just before serving, spoon the sauce over filling and garnish with parsley and a small knot of red capsicum.
7. Serve in avocado dishes or on lettuce leaves on small plates.

(Serves 6)

Prawn Cocktail

300 g shelled prawns (small)

4 small lettuce leaves

1 lemon

parsley

Sauce

2 tablespoons tomato sauce

2 teaspoons Worcestershire sauce

2 teaspoons white vinegar

a few drops Tabasco sauce

½ teaspoon mustard

2 tablespoons cream, lightly whipped

1. Prepare the prawns. Arrange lettuce leaves in suitable dishes.
2. Fill with prawns and top with sauce.
3. Garnish side of glass with a slice of lemon. Top with a small sprig of parsley.
4. Serve with triangles of buttered brown bread.

(Serves 4)

Seafood Cocktail

150 g seafood mixture, e.g. fish, crab, prawns, oysters

4 lettuce or witlof leaves

1 lemon

parsley

Sauce

2 tablespoons tomato sauce

3 tablespoons mayonnaise

1 tablespoon lemon juice

1 teaspoon Worcestershire sauce

2 tablespoons thick cream

2 pinches nutmeg

1 pinch cayenne

1. Mix all the ingredients for the sauce together and stir well.
2. Arrange lettuce or witlof leaves in suitable dishes. Fill with prepared seafood.
3. Spoon sauce over and garnish with a thin slice of lemon and a sprig of parsley. Serve chilled with brown bread triangles.

(Serves 4)

Oysters Kilpatrick

12 oysters in the shell

2 bacon rashers, trimmed and diced

2 teaspoons Worcestershire sauce

2 tablespoons tomato sauce

2–3 drops Tabasco sauce

1. Place oysters on tray and remove any grit from the surface of the oyster flesh.
2. Sauté bacon over a medium heat until browned.
3. Add sauces to bacon and stir to combine. Remove from heat.
4. Spoon bacon mixture onto each oyster and grill for 5 to 7 minutes. Serve immediately garnished with lemon wedges and fresh fennel.

(Serves 2)

Salmon Mousse

1 440 g can red salmon

2 eggs

1 tablespoon tomato puree

1 tablespoon white vinegar

1 teaspoon dill

3 teaspoons gelatine

½ cup whipped cream

parsley

lettuce leaves

1. Remove skin and bones from the salmon.
2. Place salmon, egg yolks, tomato puree, vinegar and dill in a blender and blend until smooth.
3. Dissolve gelatine in a little hot water and add to the mixture.
4. Fold in first the whipped cream then the beaten egg whites.
5. Pour into individual moulds and refrigerate until set.
6. Turn onto small lettuce leaves standing on small plates or dishes.
7. Decorate with fresh herbs.

(Serves 6)

Avocado Mushrooms

12 medium size mushrooms

¾ cup finely chopped bacon (fat removed)

1 large avocado

1 tablespoon lemon juice

¼ teaspoon Tabasco sauce

1 clove garlic, crushed

⅓ cup shelled unsalted pistachios

½ cup grated cheese

fresh herbs for garnish

1. Wipe mushrooms and remove stalks.
2. Brush or spray non-stick pan with oil and cook bacon until crisp.
3. Combine avocado, lemon juice, bacon, Tabasco sauce, garlic and pistachios in a food processor.
4. Spoon mixture into mushroom cups and sprinkle with cheese.
5. Bake in moderate oven for 12 minutes.
6. Serve immediately garnished with fresh herbs.

(Serves 4)

Spicy Prawns

2 tablespoons olive oil

3 cloves garlic, crushed

1 teaspoon ground cumin

½ teaspoon fresh ginger, finely grated

500 g green prawns, shelled

1 tablespoon chopped parsley

1 tablespoon chopped coriander

1. Heat oil in pan and cook garlic for 1 minute.
2. Add cumin and ginger and stir over heat for another minute.
3. Add prawns and turn frequently until the prawns turn pink.
4. Serve sprinkled with parsley and coriander and accompanied with a mix of salad greens.

Variation

Other fresh seafood, e.g. cubed whiting, scallops and calamari, may be substituted for prawns.

(Serves 4)

Skewered Seafood

500 g green shelled prawns (leave tail on)

500 g scallops

Marinade

¼ cup olive oil

¼ cup dry sherry

1 teaspoon grated fresh ginger

2 cloves garlic, crushed

freshly ground pepper

4 shallots, finely chopped

8 wooden skewers, pre-soaked

1. De-vein prawns and leave coral intact on scallops.
2. Mix all marinade ingredients together in a bowl.
3. Place prawns and scallops in a bowl, cover with marinade and leave at least one hour.
4. Drain and reserve marinade.
5. Thread prawns and scallops alternately onto pre-soaked skewers, leaving a space between each.
6. Grill until lightly browned, brushing frequently with marinade.
7. Serve garnished with salad greens.

Variation

Cubed fresh fish could be used instead of scallops and prawns.

(Serves 6)

Chicken and Ham Crepes

1 420 g can cream of chicken soup
¾ cup chopped ham
1 cup chopped cooked chicken
½ cup finely chopped shallots
freshly ground pepper
8 crepes, 15 centimetres in diameter (see page 172)
flaked, toasted almonds

1. Reserve ⅓ cup soup.
2. Combine remaining soup with ham, chicken, shallots and pepper.
3. Divide mixture between crepes, roll up and place in a greased baking dish.
4. Dilute reserved soup with 2 tablespoons of milk and pour over crepes.
5. Bake in a moderate oven for 10 to 15 minutes until warmed throughout.
6. Serve sprinkled with flaked and toasted almonds and accompanied by a mix of salad greens.

(Serves 4)

Thai Chicken Skewers

750 g chicken breasts cut into 2 cm cubes
½ cup sweet chilli sauce
1 tablespoon soy sauce
1 lime, juice and rind grated
1 tablespoon fish sauce
1 tablespoon fresh mint, chopped
8 wooden skewers, pre-soaked

1. Place chicken, chilli sauce, soy sauce, lime juice and rind, fish sauce and mint into a bowl. Mix well and marinate for 10 minutes.
2. Thread chicken onto pre-soaked skewers and grill for a few minutes on each side until chicken is cooked.
3. Serve with rice and garnish with fresh herbs.

(Serves 4)

Chicken Sesame

2 chicken fillets
2 tablespoons sesame seeds
2 tablespoons oil
2 cups snow pea shoots
1 large zucchini, sliced in sticks
4 tablespoons plum sauce

1. Cut chicken into long strips and then into 6 to 8 cm lengths.
2. Coat with sesame seeds and press on firmly.
3. Heat oil in pan and fry chicken until golden brown.
4. Arrange a layer of snow pea shoots over each serving plate, top with zucchini sticks and chicken.
5. Drizzle plum sauce over chicken and serve.

(Serves 4)

Nicoise Salad

6 tablespoons olive oil
2 tablespoons vinegar
1 tablespoon Dijon mustard
1 clove garlic, crushed
pepper
100 g green beans
12 new potatoes, washed and skins left on
1 small lettuce, cut into bite-sized pieces
200 g tuna, drained
12 olives, stoned (optional)
4 tomatoes, chopped
4 spring onions, finely chopped
2 hard-boiled eggs, chopped
2 tablespoons pine nuts, toasted

1. Mix oil, vinegar, mustard, garlic and pepper in a large bowl.
2. Cook beans and potatoes in separate pans of boiling water (or microwave if preferred) until just tender.
3. Drain beans and potatoes, cool and cut beans into 6 cm lengths and halve potatoes and add to oil mixture with lettuce, flaked tuna, olives, tomatoes, spring onions and eggs.
4. Toss all ingredients together and serve on individual plates sprinkled with pine nuts.

(Serves 4)

Avocado, Prawn and Mango Salad

1 mango, sliced
1 avocado, sliced
200 g cooked small prawns
2 tablespoons French dressing
½ cup light sour cream
1 teaspoon chopped dill
4 chopped macadamia nuts

1. On each plate, arrange mango and avocado slices alternately in a fanned semicircle.
2. Arrange prawns around fruit.
3. Mix French dressing, sour cream, dill and nuts and pour over the fruit and prawns.

(Serves 4)

Beef Stock

1 kg shin of beef
1 kg beef or veal bones
2½ litres water
1 carrot
1 turnip or parsnip
1 brown onion
1 bunch fresh herbs
1 dozen peppercorns
1 clove garlic
½ dozen cloves

1. Trim and wash bones, remove fat and slash meat well.
2. Place bones and water into a large saucepan.
3. Allow to soak for 30 minutes.
4. Bring slowly to simmering point.
5. Prepare the vegetables and cut up roughly.
6. Add vegetables, herbs, peppercorns, garlic and cloves.
7. Simmer gently for 4½ hours.
8. Remove bones and strain.
9. Allow to cool then remove fat.
10. Store in refrigerator or freeze for future use.

Second Stock

cooked bones from cold joints e.g. ham, chicken
4 cups water to each 500 g bones
pepper
vegetables and seasonings as in beef stock

1. Break up the bones.
2. Place in a saucepan with water.
3. Allow to boil for 1 hour.
4. Add prepared vegetables.
5. Allow to simmer for 3 to 4 hours.
6. Strain and use as required.

Fish Stock

500 g and bones of white fish
1 litre water
1 onion
5 white peppercorns
sprigs of parsley, thyme, marjoram
1 bay leaf

1. Wash and chop fish and trimmings and place in a saucepan.
2. Add water, sliced onion, peppercorns and herbs.
3. Stand for 30 minutes if possible.
4. Simmer gently for about 1 hour.
5. Strain and use as required.

Vegetable Stock

2 onions

2 carrots

6 celery stalks, including leaves

1 small turnip

5–6 sprigs of fresh herbs (parsley, thyme, chives) or 1 teaspoon mixed herbs

6–8 peppercorns

6 cups water

1. Roughly chop onions, carrots, celery and turnip.
2. Place vegetables in a large saucepan with herbs, peppercorns and water.
3. Cover and simmer gently for 1 hour.
4. Cool and strain the stock and discard the vegetables.
5. Add sufficient water to make the volume of stock up to 6 cups.

Chicken Stock

2 kg chicken pieces or whole chicken carcass

2½–3 litres water

2 white onions

2 carrots

2 stalks celery with tops

1 clove garlic

4 sprigs parsley

black pepper

1. Place chicken pieces or carcass in a large saucepan.
2. Add water and bring to boiling point.
3. Cover and simmer for 1 hour.
4. Add prepared vegetables and pepper. Cook for a further 1 to 1½ hours.
5. Strain stock and allow fat to rise. Remove fat and use as required or store in refrigerator or freezer.

Chicken Soup

3 chicken pieces (inexpensive pieces, e.g. backs or thighs)

1 large onion, finely chopped

1 carrot, chopped

2 sticks celery, finely sliced

pepper to taste

1½ litres (6 cups) water

2 tablespoons chopped parsley

1. Remove skin from chicken pieces.
2. Place chicken pieces in saucepan and add onion, carrot, celery, pepper and water.
3. Bring to boil, skimming well.
4. Reduce heat and simmer covered for 1 hour.
5. Remove chicken pieces from saucepan, remove all meat from bones, chop meat and return meat to saucepan.
6. Stir in parsley, reheat if necessary and serve.

Note: If preferred, after chicken pieces are removed, soup can be pureed. Then return chopped meat to soup with parsley, reheat and serve.

Scotch Broth (Scotland)

750 g shin beef
beef bones
2 litres water
4 tablespoons barley
pepper
1 large onion
1 carrot
1 turnip
1 stick celery
small piece cabbage
2 or 3 pieces pumpkin
1 tablespoon chopped
   parsley

1. Trim any fat off the meat and cut into small cubes.
2. Place in a saucepan with water.
3. Prepare vegetables and chop finely.
4. Add vegetables and barley.
5. Season with pepper.
6. Bring to boiling point and allow to simmer for 3 hours.
7. Add more water if necessary but make sure the finished soup is thick with vegetables and barley.
8. Just before serving add the finely chopped parsley.

(Serves 8–10)

Minestrone Soup (Italy)

1 onion
1 teaspoon oil
1 carrot
1 potato
1 turnip
1 large leek
5 cups beef stock
2 tomatoes
2 tablespoons pasta,
   e.g. macaroni
60 g cabbage
400 g red kidney beans,
   cooked or canned
pepper
grated parmesan cheese
chopped parsley

1. Chop onion, potato, carrot and turnip.
2. Cut leek into thin slices and shred cabbage thinly.
3. In a large saucepan, sauté onion in oil, add carrot, potato, turnip and leek.
4. Add stock, cover and simmer for 30 minutes.
5. Add tomatoes, macaroni, cabbage and kidney beans and simmer for a further 20 minutes.
6. Add pepper to taste.
7. Serve sprinkled with grated parmesan cheese and chopped parsley.

(Serves 6)

Vichyssoise (France)

500 g potatoes
2 white onions
2 leeks (white and pale green part)
oil
4 cups chicken stock
white pepper
½ cup light cream

1. Peel potatoes and dice. Peel and chop onions and leeks, discarding almost all of the green tops.
2. Spray saucepan with oil, heat and add potatoes, onions and leeks and cook gently for 5 minutes.
3. Add the stock and seasoning, cover and simmer for about 30 minutes or until vegetables are soft.
4. When cool, puree in an electric blender until soup is smooth or rub through a fine sieve.
5. Check seasoning and chill for several hours.
6. Serve in chilled bowls. Swirl a little cream through the soup to give a marbled effect.
7. Top with finely chopped chives.

(Serves 6)

Pea and Ham Soup

1 cup split peas
500 g ham or bacon bones
1 litre water
1 large onion, chopped
2 stalks celery, chopped
1 large carrot, chopped
1 small parsnip, chopped
coarsely ground black pepper
1 teaspoon mixed fresh herbs

1. Soak peas overnight in cold water. Drain.
2. Place all ingredients in a large saucepan.
3. Bring to boil. Reduce heat and simmer until peas are soft — about 1 to 2 hours. While simmering, skim off any scum that rises to the surface.
4. After simmering, remove the bones from saucepan, strip meat from bones and chop.
5. Puree the remaining soup in a blender.
6. Add chopped meat, reheat and serve.

(Serves 6)

Asparagus Soup

1 large can asparagus
1 litre vegetable stock
1 onion
400 mL milk
3 tablespoons cornflour

1. Turn asparagus into a saucepan.
2. Reserve tips of asparagus for garnishing.
3. Add stock and chopped onion to asparagus and simmer for about 30 minutes.
4. Add milk and blended cornflour and allow to boil for 2 or 3 minutes.
5. Rub through a sieve or process in a blender.
6. Serve hot garnished with asparagus tips.

(Serves 6–8)

Lentil Soup — Low fat

½ teaspoon oil
1 clove garlic, crushed
1 onion, diced
1 teaspoon coriander
1 teaspoon cumin
½ teaspoon turmeric
pinch chilli powder
1 cup water
80 g red lentils, rinsed
3 cups chicken or vegetable stock
1 small carrot, diced
½ stalk celery, sliced
½ cup pumpkin, diced

1. Heat oil in large saucepan and sauté garlic, onion and spices until onion is tender.
2. Add water, lentils and stock.
3. Cover and simmer for 12 minutes.
4. Add vegetables and simmer approximately 15 to 20 minutes until tender.
5. Serve with crusty bread.

(Serves 6)

Pumpkin Soup

1 kg rich-coloured pumpkin
1 onion
4 cups chicken or beef stock
1 tablespoon sugar
pepper
½–¾ cup cream
parsley

1. Peel pumpkin and cut into pieces. Peel and chop onion.
2. Place both in a large saucepan. Add the stock, sugar, pepper and cook until soft.
3. Cool then place in a blender, about one-third at a time, and blend until smooth.
4. Lastly add the cream and mix well.
5. Check flavour and add more seasoning if needed.
6. Heat but do not boil. Serve immediately.
7. Garnish with a little chopped parsley or nutmeg or a swirl of cream.

(Serves 6)

Pumpkin Soup — Low fat

¼ teaspoon oil
1 diced onion
4 chopped shallots
3 cups peeled and cubed pumpkin
2 medium peeled and cubed potatoes
4 cups chicken stock
pinch nutmeg
pepper
finely chopped parsley

1. Heat oil in a large saucepan.
2. Sauté the onions and shallots until soft.
3. Add the pumpkin, potato, chicken stock and nutmeg.
4. Cover with a lid and simmer until soft (approximately 15 minutes).
5. Cool slightly and puree in a blender until smooth.
6. Season with pepper to taste.
7. Serve sprinkled with parsley.

(Serves 6)

✳ Pumpkin Soup

1 kg rich-coloured pumpkin
1 onion
3 cups chicken or beef stock
2 teaspoons sugar
pepper
½–⅓ cup cream
parsley

1. Peel pumpkin and cut into pieces. Peel and chop onion.
2. Place both into a 4 litre microwave-safe dish. Cook on HIGH for 12 to 14 minutes. Add the stock, sugar, pepper and cook on HIGH for 3 to 4 minutes until soft.
3. Cool then place in a blender, about one-third at a time, and blend until smooth.
4. Lastly add the cream and mix well. If too thick add more stock.
5. Check flavour and add more seasoning if needed.
6. Heat on HIGH for 5 to 6 minutes but do not boil.
7. Garnish with a little chopped parsley or nutmeg.

(Serves 6)

Gingered Carrot Soup — Low fat

6 medium carrots, sliced

2 medium potatoes, cubed

4 cups chicken stock

**¼ teaspoon ground ginger
or 1 teaspoon finely
grated fresh ginger**

**½ cup low-fat natural
yoghurt**

**freshly ground black
pepper**

1. Place carrots, potatoes, stock and ginger in a large saucepan.
2. Cover and simmer 15 to 20 minutes until tender.
3. Cool slightly and puree in a blender until smooth.
4. Stir in yoghurt and season to taste with pepper.
5. Reheat if necessary but do not boil.

(Serves 6)

* Gingered Carrot Soup

Prepare vegetables as above.
1. Cover and cook vegetables on HIGH for 15 to 20 minutes or until tender.
2. Puree and complete as instructed above.

Vegetable Soup — Asian Style

oil

1 clove garlic, crushed

**1 teaspoon fresh, finely
chopped ginger**

1 onion, sliced finely

¼ capsicum, thinly sliced

**100 g cabbage or bok choy,
thinly sliced**

150 g mushrooms, sliced

3 cups chicken stock

1 teaspoon soy sauce

**100 g chicken thigh meat,
sliced**

1. Spray or brush pan with oil, heat and add garlic, ginger and onion and sauté for 1 minute.
2. Add capsicum, cabbage and mushrooms, stir-fry for 1 to 2 minutes.
3. Add stock and soy sauce and bring to the boil.
4. Add chicken, reduce heat, cover and simmer until chicken is cooked and cabbage is tender.
5. Serve garnished with sliced shallots.

Variation

Add instant or pre-cooked noodles to make soup suitable as a main course.

(Serves 4)

Thai Noodle Soup

2 litres chicken stock

250 g chicken or lean pork, cooked and thinly sliced

1 tablespoon sugar

2 tablespoons fish sauce

150 g rice or egg noodles

4 cloves garlic, crushed and lightly fried

50 g bean sprouts

3 lettuce leaves, shredded

coriander

1. Place stock in saucepan, bring to boil and add meat, sugar and fish sauce.
2. Add noodles, stir to combine, reduce heat and simmer for 5 minutes or until noodles are just tender.
3. Add garlic, sprouts and lettuce, stir in and then remove from heat.
4. Serve garnished with chopped coriander.

(Serves 8)

Tomato and Basil Soup

1 kg tomatoes or 2 × 400 g cans whole peeled tomatoes, chopped (undrained)

1 onion, diced

3 sticks celery, sliced

4 bay leaves

2 cups vegetable stock

2 tablespoons chopped fresh basil

pepper

1. If using fresh tomatoes, blanch and remove skins and chop roughly.
2. Place tomatoes, onion, celery, bay leaves, stock, basil and pepper into a large saucepan.
3. Simmer for 20 to 25 minutes or until onion is tender.
4. Remove bay leaves, cool slightly and puree.
5. Serve hot or chilled.

(Serves 6)

Gazpacho (Spain)

2 large ripe tomatoes

1 large white onion

1 clove garlic

1 cucumber

1 large green or red capsicum

1 cup fine fresh breadcrumbs

1 tablespoon white vinegar

2 tablespoons olive oil

water

pepper

1. Skin and seed tomatoes and chop up.
2. Peel and chop onion, garlic and cucumber.
3. Core, seed and chop capsicum.
4. Puree all ingredients, except oil, in an electric blender.
5. Add olive oil and enough water to make soup fairly fluid. Season well.
6. Pour into a bowl or tureen and stand in a bowl of ice cubes in the refrigerator for at least 3 hours.
7. Serve with accompaniments. These are small bowls of finely chopped tomatoes, cucumbers, onions and green or red capsicums.

(Serves 4)

Fish in Batter

fillets of fish
batter
frying oil

1. Make sure there are no bones remaining in fish.
2. Heat oil in a pan until very hot.
3. Test with a square of bread or a piece of potato.
4. Dip each piece of fish in batter and drop gently into oil.
5. Cook until a light golden brown.
6. Drain on absorbent paper.
7. Serve garnished with parsley, lemon wedges and tartare sauce.

Fish in Crumbs

fillets of fish
plain flour
pepper
beaten egg and milk
dry breadcrumbs (light colour)
frying oil

1. Remove any bones in fillets.
2. Roll fillets in seasoned flour.
3. Dip in beaten egg and milk.
4. Toss in breadcrumbs and shake off surplus. If time refrigerate for 30 minutes to set crumbs.
5. Shallow fry until golden brown.
6. Drain on absorbent paper.
7. Serve garnished with parsley and lemon wedges and tartare sauce.

Variation

Instead of plain breadcrumbs use the following mix for coating the fish.
For four fillets:

1 cup finely crushed cornflakes
$\frac{1}{3}$ cup finely chopped almonds or macadamia nuts
$\frac{1}{4}$ cup parmesan cheese
$\frac{1}{4}$ cup chopped parsley
1 tablespoon chopped chives
pepper
$\frac{1}{2}$ teaspoon paprika

Baked Fish

**1 large fish — mullet,
snapper (about 500 g)**
1 cup water

Stuffing

½ cup soft breadcrumbs
**2 tablespoons chopped
parsley**
**1 tablespoon chopped
onion**
1 egg yolk
2 teaspoons milk
pepper

Sauce (Optional)

1 tablespoon margarine
1 tablespoon cornflour
**2 teaspoons anchovy paste
or sauce**
liquor from cooked fish
½ cup water or milk
1 teaspoon lemon juice
½ teaspoon sugar

1. Wash and dry fish. Remove eyes.
2. Place breadcrumbs in a bowl and add chopped parsley,
   chopped onion, egg yolk, milk and pepper.
3. Mix well together. Insert stuffing and skewer edges
   together.
4. Place fish in a well-greased baking dish and pour water
   around it. Cover with greased alfoil.
5. Bake in a slow oven for 30 to 40 minutes.
6. When flesh is milk white and will flake easily, remove from
   oven and if desired pull out fins and tail. Head may be
   left on or removed.
7. Serve accompanied by sauce.

Sauce

8. Place margarine in a small saucepan.
9. Add strained liquor from fish, and cornflour blended with
   water or milk.
10. Place over heat and allow to thicken.
11. Flavour with anchovy sauce, lemon juice and sugar.

(Serves 3–4)

Steamed Fish

fillets of whiting
lemon juice
milk

1. Wash and dry fillets. Sprinkle with lemon juice.
2. Roll fillets and place on greased alfoil side by side in the
   top of a steamer. Brush with a little milk.
3. Cover with lid.
4. Stand over a saucepan of boiling water and steam for
   15 minutes or until flesh is milk white.
5. Carefully lift onto a serving plate.
6. Coat with parsley or egg sauce.
7. Serve garnished with lemon wedges and tartare sauce.

Fish Cakes

2 tablespoons margarine
2 tablespoons plain flour
strained salmon liquor
1 tablespoon milk
2 cups flaked salmon or
  tuna
1 teaspoon lemon juice
pepper
1 cup soft breadcrumbs
flour
1 egg
1 cup dry breadcrumbs
oil for frying

1. Melt margarine in a saucepan. Add flour and blend.
2. Stir in salmon liquor and milk and allow to thicken.
3. Add flaked salmon, lemon juice, pepper and soft breadcrumbs and mix well.
4. Divide into uniform pieces and make into round, flat cakes.
5. Roll in flour, beaten egg and breadcrumbs.
6. Shallow fry until golden brown.
7. Drain on absorbent paper. Serve garnished with parsley and lemon wedges.

(Serves 4)

Thai Fish Cakes

500 g boneless white fish
4 shallots, chopped
1 egg
2 tablespoons fresh basil,
  chopped
2 tablespoons fish sauce
2 tablespoons Thai curry
  fish paste
oil for frying

1. Place fish, shallots, egg, basil, fish sauce and Thai curry fish paste in a food processor and blend until smooth.
2. Leave to stand in the refrigerator for 1 hour.
3. Form into fish cakes and shallow-fry until brown.
4. Serve with rice, lime wedges and chilli sauce.

(Serves 4)

Savoury Salmon

1 440 g can salmon
2/3 cup long grain rice
1/2 cup matured cheese,
  grated
1 440 g can cream of
  asparagus soup
2–3 tablespoons chopped
  onion
1 cup crushed breakfast
  cereal
50 g grated cheese
pepper

1. Boil rice until barely cooked. Drain and allow to dry a little.
2. Remove bones and skin from the salmon.
3. Combine salmon, rice, cheese, soup and onion which has been fried until transparent. Add pepper to taste. If mixture is too thick add a little milk.
4. Turn into a greased, ovenproof dish.
5. Mix cereal with cheese and sprinkle over salmon mixture.
6. Bake, uncovered, in a moderate oven, for about 20 minutes to crisp the topping and heat the mixture. Garnish with parsley.

(Serves 6)

Salmon Kennaway

3 cups cooked rice
1 440 g can salmon
6 eggs, hard boiled
½ cup grated cheese

Sauce

60 g margarine
2 tablespoons flour
pinch cayenne
2 teaspoons curry powder
2 cups milk
pepper

1. Place rice in the base of a greased, ovenproof dish.
2. Remove skin and bones from salmon and flake. Spread over the bed of rice.
3. Cut hard boiled eggs into slices and arrange on top of salmon.
4. Melt margarine in a saucepan then add flour, cayenne and curry powder. Mix well and cook for a few minutes.
5. Gradually add the milk and stir constantly until thick. Allow to cook for 2 minutes. Add seasoning to taste.
6. Pour over salmon mixture and sprinkle with grated cheese.
7. Bake in a moderate oven until cheese has browned.

Note: Tuna may be used instead of salmon.

(Serves 6)

Salmon Mornay

1 quantity mornay sauce (see recipe on page 150)
1 onion, diced
½ teaspoon dry mustard
1 teaspoon lemon juice
1 440 g can salmon
2 tablespoons grated cheese
2 tablespoons soft breadcrumbs

1. Spray saucepan with cooking spray, heat and fry onion then add to mornay sauce.
2. Season with lemon juice and mustard.
3. Fold in flaked salmon, free from bones and skin.
4. Turn into a greased, ovenproof dish. Sprinkle with cheese and breadcrumbs.
5. Bake in a moderate oven until sauce bubbles and cheese melts.
6. Serve with boiled rice.

Note: Tuna may also be used.

(Serves 4–6)

Cajun Fish

1½ cups stale bread, crumbed

1 tablespoon Cajun spice mix

2 teaspoons ground coriander

1 to 2 tablespoons flour

1 egg

4 white fish fillets

oil for frying

lemon

1. Combine breadcrumbs, spice mix and coriander in bowl.
2. Spread flour on plate.
3. Beat egg in bowl.
4. Dry fish fillets with paper towel and roll in flour.
5. Dip in beaten egg and drain away excess.
6. Toss in crumb mixture, coat evenly and press on firmly.
7. Heat oil in non-stick pan and shallow fry, turning when needed until both sides are golden brown and fish is cooked through.
8. Serve with salad and garnish with lemon wedges.

Curried Salmon

1 440 g can salmon

400 mL milk

2 tablespoons margarine

2 tablespoons flour

2 teaspoons curry powder

2 teaspoons lemon juice

pepper

2 tomatoes, skinned and chopped

1 cup hot, cooked rice

1. Drain liquor from salmon.
2. Measure and make up to 450 mL with milk.
3. Melt margarine, add flour and curry powder.
4. Gradually add liquid, stirring constantly. Allow to boil for 2 minutes.
5. Add pepper, lemon juice, salmon and tomatoes.
6. Return to stove and heat thoroughly.
7. Serve in a ring of rice.
8. Garnish with slices of lemon and parsley.

(Serves 4–6)

Fish Amandine

500 g fish filets

flour

pepper

1 tablespoon oil

1 small onion, chopped

1 clove garlic, crushed

100 g mushrooms

1 cup blanched almonds, slivered

1 tablespoon lemon juice

½ cup dry white wine

1 tablespoon chopped parsley

1. Dry fish fillets on paper towels.
2. Dust each fillet with seasoned flour.
3. Heat oil in a pan and brown fish on both sides.
4. Arrange on a serving dish.
5. Sauté onion, garlic, mushrooms and almonds and add lemon juice, parsley and wine and simmer to reduce to desired consistency.
6. Pour over the fish.
7. Serve with vegetables.

(Serves 4)

Curried Prawns

1 onion
1 apple
1 tablespoon margarine
2 teaspoons curry powder
2 tablespoons flour
1 cup fish stock or water
2 teaspoons lemon juice
1–2 teaspoons sugar
2 tablespoons sultanas
1 tablespoon chutney
250 g shelled prawns

1. Peel and chop onion and apple finely.
2. Heat margarine in a pan and fry onion, apple and curry powder until onion is soft and lightly coloured.
3. Add flour and mix well.
4. Gradually add stock and milk, stirring constantly until mixture boils and thickens.
5. Add lemon juice, sugar, sultanas and chutney and cook for a few minutes.
6. Adjust flavour according to taste, adding more curry, lemon or sugar as required.
7. Add prepared prawns and heat through.
8. Serve with plain boiled rice and fresh herbs.

(Serves 4)

Prawn Cutlets (China)

1 kg green king prawns
cornflour for rolling
2 eggs, beaten
1 tablespoon soy sauce
dry breadcrumbs
oil for deep frying

1. Shell prawns, leaving tails intact. Remove the black vein.
2. Wash prawns well under cold running water, drain and pat dry.
3. With a sharp, pointed knife cut a deep slit down the back of each prawn taking care not to cut through completely.
4. Coat with cornflour. Shake off excess.
5. Add soy sauce to beaten eggs.
6. Dip prawns into egg mixture then coat well with breadcrumbs. Press each prawn down onto table to flatten. Place on a plate and stand in refrigerator for 2 hours.
7. Deep fry prawns in hot oil, a few at a time, until golden brown and crisp.
8. Drain on absorbent paper. Serve immediately.

(Serves 4–6)

Tuna, Cheese and Tomato Ricebake

1 tablespoon butter or oil

1 cup uncooked rice (long grain)

2 medium onions, finely chopped

1 large can tuna, undrained

1 can whole peeled tomatoes (or 4 freshly skinned tomatoes)

1 green capsicum, finely chopped

water

250 g cheddar cheese, grated

1. Using a large frying pan or saucepan, heat oil.
2. Brown the rice, do not allow to burn.
3. Add onions to rice, cook until onions are clear.
4. Add the can of undrained tuna, tomatoes roughly chopped and capsicum. Allow to simmer, stirring frequently.
5. As mixture becomes dry, add water and continue with this process until the rice grains become soft.
6. In a greased casserole dish, place a layer of rice mixture then cheese. Continue until all is used, ending with a layer of cheese.
7. Bake in a moderate oven for 50 minutes or until cheese topping is brown. Serve with vegetables or a salad.

(Serves 6)

Pacific Pie

1 large can tuna or salmon

1 can condensed cream of chicken soup

1 cup frozen peas, cooked

3 medium tomatoes

1 large packet plain potato crisps

2 tablespoons finely grated cheese

1. Plunge tomatoes into boiling water. Leave five minutes. Take out and peel off skins and slice.
2. Drain and flake tuna. Put a layer of fish into ovenproof casserole, with half the soup, half the peas, half the tomatoes and half the crisps. Repeat the layers, finishing with remaining crisps and grated cheese.
3. Bake in oven 175°C for 30 minutes then brown under grill.
4. Serve with rice or jacket potatoes.

(Serves 4–6)

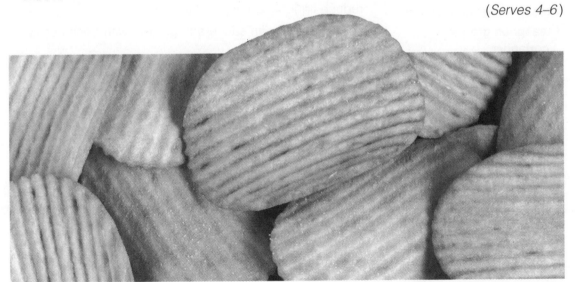

Fish au Gratin

1 tablespoon margarine

1½ tablespoons flour

1 cup milk

1 cup cold flaked fish *or*
  1 medium can tuna or
  salmon

pepper

few drops lemon juice

½ cup soft breadcrumbs

2 tablespoons dry
  breadcrumbs

2 tablespoons grated
  cheese

1. Melt margarine in a saucepan. Add flour and mix well.
2. Gradually add milk then stir over heat until mixture boils.
   Boil for 1 minute.
3. Add flaked fish, free from skin and bones.
4. Season with pepper and lemon juice.
5. Grease a pie dish or scallop shells.
6. Place half of fish mixture in pie dish, cover lightly with soft
   breadcrumbs.
7. Cover with remaining mixture then sprinkle with dry
   breadcrumbs and grated cheese.
8. Heat for 15 to 20 minutes in a moderate oven.
9. Garnish with parsley.

(Serves 2–3)

Fish Kebabs

500 g boneless fish fillets,
  cubed

2 cloves garlic, crushed

¼ cup lime juice

3 tablespoons sesame
  seeds

4 tablespoons olive oil

1 cup cherry tomatoes

1 onion, finely chopped

1 teaspoon ground cumin

1 teaspoon ground
  coriander

¼ cup sherry

3 tablespoons sesame
  paste (tahini)

1 tablespoon honey

2 tablespoons peanut
  butter

1 tablespoon lime juice
  (extra)

¼ cup water

1. Roll fish cubes in combined garlic, lime juice, sesame
   seeds and oil and marinate for 30 minutes.
2. Thread fish and tomatoes alternately onto pre-soaked
   skewers and grill for approximately 3 minutes on each
   side, basting regularly with the marinade.
3. Spray a saucepan with cooking spray, heat and add
   onion, cumin, coriander, sherry, tahini, honey, peanut
   butter, extra lime juice and water. Simmer for 5 minutes to
   reduce liquid and thicken the sauce.
4. Serve kebabs with sauce and garnish with fresh herbs.

(Serves 4)

Thai Fish Curry

oil

1 medium onion, finely
   chopped

1 tablespoon green curry
   paste

1 cup coconut cream

1 cup fish stock

1 tablespoon brown sugar

1 tablespoon fish sauce

4 fillets white fish, cubed

lemon juice to taste

1. Spray pan with cooking spray, heat and cook onion until softened.
2. Add curry paste and continue to cook for 1 to 2 minutes.
3. Add coconut cream and stock and simmer for 10 minutes.
4. Add sugar, fish sauce and fish and simmer gently for 5 to 10 minutes until fish is cooked.
5. Add lemon juice to taste and serve with rice.

(Serves 4)

Salmon Fettuccine

500 g fettuccine

oil

1 onion, finely chopped

1 clove garlic, crushed

freshly ground pepper

1–2 tablespoons chopped
   fresh basil

¼ cup white wine

½ cup tomato puree

¼ cup cream

10 small slices Atlantic
   salmon, cut into 1 cm
   wide strips

50 g parmesan

1. Cook pasta in a large pan of boiling water for 12 minutes. Drain.
2. Brush or spray pan with oil, heat, and add onion, garlic, pepper and basil and sauté until onion is transparent.
3. Add wine, tomato puree and cream and stir until mixed thoroughly.
4. Add pasta and salmon and heat through.
5. Serve garnished with shaved parmesan cheese.

(Serves 4)

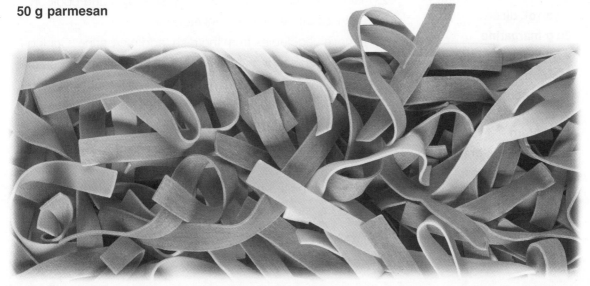

Chicken Supreme

oil
1 red capsicum, chopped
120 g mushrooms, sliced
1 carrot, diced
1 onion, chopped
30 g margarine
2 tablespoons flour
1½ cups chicken stock
¼ teaspoon turmeric
**¼ teaspoon prepared
   mustard**
2 tablespoons cream
⅓ cup frozen peas
**1 kg cooked chicken,
   chopped**

1. Brush or spray pan with oil, heat and add the vegetables except peas and cook until tender.
2. Remove vegetables from the pan, add margarine. When melted stir in the flour and cook for 1 minute. Gradually add the chicken stock and bring to the boil, stirring constantly.
3. Add turmeric, mustard and cream.
4. Add cooked vegetables, peas and chicken meat, cover and simmer for 5 minutes or until heated through.
5. Serve with boiled rice.

(*Serves 4–5*)

✳ Chicken Supreme

1½ kg chicken
1 red capsicum, chopped
1 onion, chopped
120 g mushrooms, sliced
1 carrot, diced
30 g margarine
2 tablespoons flour
1½ cups chicken stock
¼ teaspoon turmeric
**¼ teaspoon prepared
   mustard**
2 tablespoons cream
⅓ cup frozen peas

1. Remove skin and bones and cut chicken meat into small pieces. Place in microwave-safe dish and cook on MEDIUM for 10 to 12 minutes.
2. Place vegetables in a microwave-safe dish and cook on HIGH for 3 to 4 minutes until tender.
3. Remove vegetables from the dish, add margarine. Cook on HIGH for 30 seconds until melted, stir in flour and cook on HIGH for 30 to 60 seconds. Gradually add the chicken stock, stirring well, and cook on HIGH for 2 to 3 minutes until boiling.
4. Add turmeric, mustard and cream.
5. Add vegetables, including peas, and chicken meat, cover and cook on HIGH for 4 to 5 minutes or until heated through.
6. Serve with boiled rice.

(*Serves 4–5*)

Roast Chicken

2 kg chicken
oil

Stuffing
2 cups soft breadcrumbs
1 egg and a little milk
2 teaspoons herbs
pepper
1 onion, finely chopped

1. Mix together in a bowl, breadcrumbs, herbs, pepper and onion.
2. Moisten with egg and milk.
3. Make sure prepared chicken is thoroughly dry inside and out.
4. Place stuffing inside chicken.
5. Secure openings with skewers.
6. Heat a small amount of oil in a baking dish.
7. Place chicken, breast up, on a rack. Baste well.
8. Allow to cook for approximately 1½ hours in a slow to moderate oven or until tender — basting at least once during cooking time.
9. Drain on absorbent paper then serve on a hot dish.
10. Pour fat off, retaining browning.
11. Add water to dissolve browning then thicken a little.
12. Serve in a gravy boat.

Note: Chicken may be protected with a sheet of alfoil while baking.

(Serves 6)

* Roast Chicken

2 kg chicken

Stuffing
2 cups soft breadcrumbs
2 teaspoons herbs
pepper
1 onion, finely chopped
1 egg and a little milk
1 tablespoon butter

1. Mix together in a bowl breadcrumbs, herbs, pepper and onion.
2. Moisten with egg and milk.
3. Make sure prepared chicken is thoroughly dry inside and out.
4. Place stuffing inside chicken.
5. Secure openings with toothpicks or wooden skewers.
6. Place chicken in a microwave-safe dish and brush with melted butter.
7. Cook on MEDIUM for 50 to 60 minutes. Turn halfway through cooking. Drain chicken and stand covered for 10 minutes while making gravy.
8. Thicken retained juices and serve in a gravy boat.

(Serves 6)

Curried Chicken

1.5 kg cooked chicken
2 tablespoons margarine
1 onion, chopped
1 clove garlic, crushed
2 tablespoons flour
1–2 tablespoons curry powder (mild)
¼ teaspoon ginger
¼ teaspoon turmeric
pinch cayenne
1 teaspoon sugar
1 tablespoon chutney
1½ cups chicken stock
2 teaspoons lemon juice
3 tablespoons cream (optional)

1. Remove flesh from the chicken and cut into bite-sized pieces.
2. Melt margarine and add onion and garlic and fry until soft.
3. Add flour, curry powder, ginger, turmeric and cayenne.
4. Cook over low heat for 2 minutes.
5. Add sugar, chutney and stock and stir until the sauce boils and thickens slightly.
6. Add chicken pieces and simmer for 2 to 3 minutes to heat through.
7. Stir in lemon juice and lastly add cream. Reheat before serving but do not boil.
8. Serve with boiled rice.

(Serves 6–8)

* Curried Chicken

1 kg cooked chicken, chopped
2 tablespoons margarine
1 onion, chopped
1 clove garlic, crushed
2 tablespoons flour
1–2 tablespoons curry powder
¼ teaspoon ginger
¼ teaspoon turmeric
pinch cayenne
1 teaspoon sugar
1 tablespoon chutney
1½ cups chicken stock
2 teaspoons lemon juice
3 tablespoons cream (optional)

1. Place margarine into a microwave-safe dish and cook on HIGH for 30 seconds. Add onion and garlic and cook on HIGH for 3 to 4 minutes or until soft.
2. Add flour, curry powder, ginger, turmeric and cayenne.
3. Cook on HIGH for 30 to 60 seconds.
4. Add sugar, chutney and stock and stir until the sauce boils and thickens slightly, cooking on HIGH for 2 to 4 minutes.
5. Add chicken, stir in lemon juice and cream. Reheat before serving. (Do not boil.)
6. Serve with boiled rice.

(Serves 6–8)

Chicken Curry (Sri Lanka)

oil

2 large onions, finely chopped

2 to 3 cloves garlic, crushed

2 teaspoons finely grated ginger

½ teaspoon turmeric

¼ teaspoon chilli powder

½ teaspoon ground cumin

1 teaspoon paprika

2 tablespoons vinegar

1.5 kg chicken pieces

3 tomatoes, peeled and chopped or a 400 g can diced tomatoes

1 stalk lemon grass or 2 strips lemon rind

1 cup thick coconut milk

1. Brush or spray a large pan with oil, heat, add onions, garlic and ginger and fry gently until soft.
2. Add turmeric, chilli, cumin, paprika and vinegar and stir well.
3. Add chicken and stir over medium heat until chicken is thoroughly coated with spices.
4. Add tomatoes and lemon grass and cook uncovered, over a low heat for 30 to 40 minutes or until chicken is cooked, stirring occasionally.
5. Add coconut milk and add a squeeze of lemon juice if desired.
6. Serve with rice and curry accompaniments.

(Serves 4)

Chicken and Vegetable Casserole

oil

1 kg chicken breast or chicken thighs, cut into bite-size pieces

1 onion, diced

2 bacon rashers, chopped

3 medium mushrooms, sliced

1 stick celery, sliced

1 carrot, sliced

1 420 g can chicken and vegetable soup, cream of chicken soup or chicken and corn soup

2 medium potatoes, cooked and cut into bite-sized pieces

freshly ground pepper

1 tablespoon fresh chopped parsley

100 mL water

1. Brush or spray a large pan with oil, heat and fry chicken until browned. Remove from pan, drain and place into greased casserole dish.
2. Add vegetables (except potato) and bacon to pan and cook until onion is transparent.
3. Add soup to pan with vegetable mixture and combine well.
4. Add potatoes, parsley, pepper and water, mix well and pour over chicken in the casserole dish.
5. Cover and bake in a moderate oven for 20 to 30 minutes.
6. Serve with rice or noodles.

(Serves 4)

Chicken Macaroni Bake

250 g macaroni or spiral pasta

1 tablespoon margarine

1 onion, diced

2 rashers bacon, diced (optional)

2 tablespoons plain flour

2½ cups milk

2 tablespoons tomato paste

2 cups cooked chicken, boned, skinned and cut into bite-sized pieces

½ cup grated cheese

1 zucchini, quartered and sliced

1 tomato, chopped

Topping

¼ cup dry breadcrumbs

¼ cup grated cheese

1. Cook pasta in boiling water until tender. Drain.
2. Melt margarine in a large saucepan and sauté onion and bacon.
3. Add flour and cook for 2 minutes.
4. Remove from heat and add milk gradually.
5. Stir over heat until thickened. Remove from heat.
6. Add tomato paste and mix well.
7. Add pasta, chicken, cheese, zucchini and tomato and mix well.
8. Pour into a large, greased, oven-proof dish or individual ramekin dishes.
9. Combine breadcrumbs and cheese (topping) and sprinkle over top of the dish.
10. Bake in a moderate oven for 20 to 25 minutes or until golden brown.

Note: For a quicker result, use 1 packet of white sauce to replace butter, flour and milk. Make up sufficient packet mix to make 2½ cups of sauce and continue with recipe from step 6.

(Serves 6)

Chicken Mornay

1 quantity Mornay Sauce (see page 150)

lemon juice

2–2½ cups chicken, cooked

2 tablespoons grated cheese

2 tablespoons soft breadcrumbs

1. Add diced chicken to mornay sauce. A little lemon juice may improve the flavour.
2. Pour into an ovenproof dish and sprinkle with cheese and crumbs.
3. Bake in a moderate oven until sauce bubbles and cheese melts.
4. Serve with boiled rice.

(Serves 4–5)

Chicken Maryland (U.S.A.)

4 chicken pieces, skinned
flour for coating
pepper
1 egg, beaten with a little
  milk
dry breadcrumbs
butter
cooking oil

Garnish
4 bananas
lemon juice
flour
4 bacon rashers
fresh herbs

1. Coat the chicken pieces in flour seasoned with pepper then dip in egg mixture.
2. Coat with breadcrumbs, making sure the chicken is well coated. Allow to stand for 30 minutes in refrigerator.
3. Heat equal amounts of butter and oil in a frying pan. Fry chicken pieces gently until browned on all sides.
4. Transfer to an ovenproof dish and bake in a moderate oven for about 45 minutes or until tender.
5. While the chicken is cooking peel the bananas, sprinkle with lemon juice and roll in flour.
6. Fry in the pan until golden brown. Keep warm.
7. Make bacon rolls by stretching the rashers with a knife, cutting and rolling and threading on a skewer. Grill until crisp, turning occasionally.
8. To serve, place chicken pieces on a platter and garnish with fried bananas and bacon rolls. Decorate with sprigs of fresh herbs. Serve immediately.
9. Sweetcorn fritters may also be served.

(Serves 4)

Apricot Chicken

1½ kg chicken pieces
1 pkt French onion soup
1 can apricot nectar
  (400 mL)

1. Skin chicken pieces, and arrange in a shallow casserole dish.
2. Blend soup with the apricot nectar and pour over the chicken.
3. Bake in a moderate oven for 1 hour or until tender.

(Serves 4–6)

❋ Apricot Chicken

1 kg chicken pieces
1 pkt French onion soup
1 can apricot nectar
  (400 mL)

1. Skin chicken pieces and arrange in a shallow microwave-safe dish.
2. Blend soup with the apricot nectar and pour over the chicken until it is barely covered.
3. Cook on MEDIUM for 20 to 25 minutes or until tender. Rearrange pieces during cooking.

(Serves 4–6)

Chicken and Almonds (China)

¾ cup blanched almonds

1 onion, chopped

1 kg cooked chicken, chopped

100 g mushrooms, sliced

1 tablespoon fresh ginger, chopped

3 stalks celery, chopped

1 red capsicum, chopped

1½ cups chicken stock

2 teaspoons sugar

2 tablespoons soy sauce

2 tablespoons cornflour

1. Brush or spray pan with oil, heat and cook almonds until light brown.
2. Drain on paper.
3. Add more oil if necessary and fry onion lightly.
4. Add chicken, mushrooms, ginger, celery and capsicum, chicken stock, sugar and soy sauce.
5. Heat thoroughly.
6. Blend cornflour with a little cold water and thicken mixture.
7. Cook for 3 minutes.
8. Add almonds just before serving and serve with hot fluffy rice.

(Serves 5–6)

Nasi Goreng (Indonesia)

1 large onion

1 clove garlic, crushed

1½–1¾ cups shredded cabbage

1 cup rice (long grain)

½ cup chopped celery

600 mL chicken stock

1 teaspoon mixed spice

750 g chicken, cooked and chopped

220 g prawns, shelled and chopped

3 tablespoons soy sauce

¼ cup sultanas

Accompaniments

prawn or potato crisps

chutney

omelette, cut into strips

1. Slice onion thinly, cut rings in half and separate.
2. Brush or spray frypan with oil, heat and add garlic and onions.
3. Fry until well cooked. Remove from pan.
4. Sauté cabbage for 1 minute and remove.
5. Fry rice and celery for 1 to 2 minutes.
6. Reduce heat to moderate, add stock and spice and simmer gently for 15 minutes.
7. Add chicken and prawns to rice with soy sauce, sultanas, onions, garlic and cabbage.
8. Cook until rice is tender.
9. Serve hot with accompaniments.

(Serves 4–6)

Chicken Roulade in Filo Pastry

**2 chicken breasts or boned
chicken which can be
pounded till thin and flat**

packet of filo pastry

1 tablespoon oil

**1 tablespoon sesame
seeds**

Stuffing

2 spinach leaves

1 onion, finely chopped

**1 bacon rasher, trimmed
and diced**

**1 teaspoon finely chopped
parsley**

**1 teaspoon finely chopped
oregano**

1 clove garlic, crushed

**1 tablespoon pine nuts,
chopped**

½ cup soft breadcrumbs

1 egg yolk

1. Pound chicken till thin and flat and cut each breast in half.
2. Par cook spinach in microwave for approximately
   1 minute.
3. Brush or spray pan with oil, heat, sauté onion and bacon
   and place in bowl with herbs, garlic, pine nuts,
   breadcrumbs and egg yolk.
4. Lay chicken flat, outside surface down, and layer spinach
   flat on top of each piece of chicken.
5. Spread with stuffing mix and roll up.
6. Using 3 sheets of filo, roll chicken in filo pastry and place
   on a greased baking tray. If desired, each layer can be
   lightly brushed with oil or sprayed with cooking spray.
7. Brush parcels with oil and sprinkle with sesame seeds.
8. Bake in a moderate oven for 30 to 40 minutes.
9. Garnish with fresh herbs and serve whole or in slices
   1.5 cm thick.

(Serves 4)

Chicken Parcels

1 carrot, grated

1 apple, grated

**2 cups chopped cooked
chicken**

½ cup sultanas

¼ teaspoon cinnamon

½ cup cottage cheese

8 sheets filo pastry

2 tablespoons oil

1. Grate carrot and apple and squeeze out as much juice as
   possible.
2. Place in a bowl with chicken, sultanas, cinnamon and
   cheese. Mix together.
3. Layer two sheets of pastry together, brushing each with oil.
4. Fold in half and place one-quarter of the chicken mixture
   in centre of pastry. Fold up to form a parcel.
5. Make three more parcels and place all on a lightly greased tray.
6. Bake in a moderate oven for about 15 minutes or until well
   browned and heated through.

(Serves 4)

Chicken Satay Sticks

500 g chicken breast fillet or chicken tenderloins

1 tablespoon oil

3 tablespoons crunchy peanut butter

1½ tablespoons soy sauce

¼ teaspoon ground cumin

wooden skewers

1. Soak skewers in water to avoid burning during cooking process.
2. If using chicken fillets, slice into strips and thread chicken onto drained skewers.
3. Combine oil, peanut butter, soya sauce and cumin and mix well.
4. Brush each chicken skewer with peanut butter mixture and refrigerate for at least 30 minutes.
5. Grill satays for a few minutes on each side or until chicken is cooked.
6. Serve with salad and rice.

(Serves 4)

Chicken Carbonara — Low fat

250 g flat egg noodles

500 g cooked chicken breast or thighs, skinned and cut into bite-sized strips

6 slices ham, cut into thin strips

6 shallots, chopped

1 capsicum, sliced

1 zucchini, halved and sliced (optional)

2 large eggs

300 mL low-fat evaporated milk

¼ cup grated parmesan cheese

1. Cook noodles in boiling water until tender.
2. Drain and keep hot in a colander over simmering water.
3. Brush or spray a large saucepan with oil, heat.
4. Add chicken, ham, shallots, capsicum and zucchini and sauté for 2 to 3 minutes.
5. Add noodles and gently toss through.
6. Beat eggs, evaporated milk and cheese together.
7. Toss through noodles over a gentle heat until egg is softly scrambled.
8. Serve with crusty bread.

(Serves 4)

Spicy Chicken Burritos

500 g chicken breasts or tenderloins

1 packet taco seasoning mix (salt reduced)

1 tablespoon oil

6–8 flour tortillas

taco sauce (mild, medium or hot)

shredded lettuce

1 tomato, diced

1 cucumber, diced

1 avocado, chopped

tasty grated cheese

1. Slice chicken breasts into long strips approximately 2 to 3 cm wide and 8 cm long.
2. Place seasoning mix on a plate and toss chicken pieces in seasoning until covered. Shake to remove excess.
3. Brush or spray a non-stick pan with oil, heat, and cook chicken in batches until cooked through. Drain.
4. Heat tortillas in oven or microwave.
5. Place chicken onto each tortilla towards one edge.
6. Top with taco sauce, lettuce, tomato, cheese, avocado and cucumber.
7. Fold in bottom section of tortilla and roll up firmly.

(Serves 6–8)

Tandoori Chicken

1 large onion, diced

2 cloves garlic, crushed

½ teaspoon fresh, finely chopped ginger

½ teaspoon ground coriander

½ teaspoon ground cumin

1 teaspoon turmeric

¼ teaspoon chilli powder

100 g low-fat plain yoghurt

2 teaspoons white vinegar

3 teaspoons Worcestershire sauce

1 tablespoon lemon juice

½ teaspoon garam masala

1 tablespoon tandoori curry paste

1 kg chicken breasts or chicken thighs, cut in serving size pieces

1. Combine all ingredients except chicken in a food processor and process until smooth.
2. Place chicken in a non-metal bowl, pour over marinade and allow to stand overnight in refrigerator.
3. Place chicken on a greased rack in baking tray and bake in a moderate oven (180°C) for 30 to 35 minutes or until chicken is tender.
4. Serve garnished with fresh coriander.

(Serves 6)

Chicken Stroganoff

1 tablespoon oil

2 onions, thinly sliced

2 cloves garlic, crushed

500 g chicken breast or thighs, sliced

250 g mushrooms, sliced

2 large tomatoes, skinned and chopped

2 teaspoons paprika

1 cup light sour cream

¼ cup tomato paste

freshly ground pepper

2 tablespoons chopped fresh parsley

1. Brush or spray pan with oil, heat and add onion and garlic and cook for 2 to 3 minutes until onion is soft.
2. Add chicken and cook until tender.
3. Add mushrooms, tomato and paprika and cook until mushrooms are tender.
4. Combine sour cream, tomato paste and pepper in a bowl and stir into chicken mixture in pan until just heated through.
5. Sprinkle with parsley and serve with pasta.

(*Serves 4–6*)

Sweet and Sour Chicken

1½ tablespoons dry sherry

1½ tablespoons soy sauce

1 teaspoon freshly grated ginger

oil

500 g chicken breasts or thighs, diced

1 onion, cut into wedges

½ green capsicum, chopped

½ red capsicum, chopped

½ cup celery, sliced

3 shallots, chopped

2 teaspoons cornflour

¾ cup pineapple juice from drained pineapple pieces

2 tablespoons white vinegar

2 tablespoons tomato paste

2 teaspoons brown sugar

1 225 g can pineapple pieces in natural juices, drained

1. Combine sherry, soy sauce, ginger and marinate chicken for 15 to 20 minutes.
2. Brush or spray a non-stick pan with oil, heat, and cook chicken in batches until cooked through. Remove and place chicken on a plate.
3. Brush or spray again with oil if necessary, heat and add onion, capsicum and celery and cook for 2 to 3 minutes. Add shallots and cook for a further minute.
4. Blend cornflour with pineapple juice and add vinegar, tomato paste and brown sugar. Add to pan off the heat, stirring continuously.
5. Return to heat and continue to stir and cook until sauce boils and thickens.
6. Return chicken to pan, add pineapple and heat through.
7. Serve with rice and garnish with finely chopped shallots.

(*Serves 4–6*)

Filo Chicken

1 tablespoon oil

2 chicken breasts cut into bite-sized pieces

1 onion, chopped

1 clove garlic, crushed

1 capsicum, chopped

200 g mushrooms, sliced

2 tablespoons flour

1½ cups chicken stock

¼ teaspoon prepared mustard

¼ teaspoon turmeric

2 tablespoons cream

8 layers filo pastry

extra oil for brushing over pastry

1. Heat oil in large saucepan and sauté chicken. Remove from pan.
2. Add onion and garlic to pan and cook for 1 to 2 minutes.
3. Add capsicum and mushroom and cook for 1 minute.
4. Remove from heat. Sprinkle flour over mixture and mix well.
5. Add stock gradually, stirring until blended.
6. Return to heat and bring to the boil stirring all the time.
7. Add mustard and turmeric. Season to taste. Remove from heat. Add cream and stir gently.
8. Allow to cool.
9. Take two layers of filo pastry and cut in half.
10. Brush each layer with olive oil and place four layers on top of one another.
11. Place one-quarter of the chicken mixture in centre of pastry and fold sides over to wrap up as a parcel. Brush top with olive oil.
12. Repeat to make four parcels in all.
13. Place on greased oven tray.
14. Bake in oven on 190°C for 25 to 30 minutes.
15. Serve with salad.

(Serves 4)

Chicken Noodle Stir-fry

500 g Hokkien noodles

oil

500 g chicken breasts or thighs, cut into strips

1 clove garlic, crushed

1 tablespoon fresh ginger, finely grated

1 onion, sliced

1 red capsicum, sliced

2 cups sliced vegetables e.g. broccoli, carrot, snow peas, celery, zucchini

¼ cup hoisin sauce

¼ cup plum sauce

1 teaspoon sweet chilli sauce

2 tablespoons water

1. Place noodles in a large bowl and cover with boiling water. Separate noodles with a fork. Drain.
2. Brush or spray pan with oil, heat, and cook chicken in batches until browned and remove to plate.
3. Sauté garlic, ginger and vegetables for approximately 2 to 3 minutes.
4. Add sauces, water and noodles and stir through well.
5. Heat until sauce boils and thickens slightly.
6. Serve garnished with fresh herbs.

(Serves 4)

Roast Beef

sirloin, rib roast, or rib fillet
flour
pepper
oil

1. Place sufficient oil to make a thin layer in baking dish.
2. Heat in the oven or on top of stove.
3. Weigh meat and calculate cooking time. Allow at least 20 minutes for each half kilogram and 30 minutes over. If joint is very large allow 30 minutes for each half kilogram.
4. Roll meat in flour which has been seasoned with pepper.
5. Place in hot oil and baste.
6. Cook in a hot oven for 10 minutes to seal the outside.
7. Reduce heat and cook gently at 150° to 160°C.
8. Baste meat every 20 minutes and turn over when half the cooking time has elapsed.
9. To complete browning, cook without the lid for the last 45 minutes.
10. Add prepared vegetables at this stage. Turn once during cooking. If there is too much fat in the dish pour some off so vegetables will become crisp.
11. Drain meat and vegetables on absorbent paper then serve on hot dishes.
12. Pour fat off carefully and retain browning.
13. Add about 2 cups of water and heat until browning has dissolved.
14. Add sufficient blended flour to make a fairly thin gravy. Boil for 2 or 3 minutes.
15. Add pepper to taste.
16. Pour into a gravy boat.
17. Serve roast with gravy, baked vegetables, Yorkshire pudding and horseradish sauce.

Roast Beef — Low fat

sirloin or rib roast
oil
pepper
½–¾ cup water

1. Weigh meat and calculate cooking time as in previous recipe.
2. Brush meat with oil, sprinkle with pepper and place in a greased baking dish on a greased rack.
3. Add ½ to ¾ cup water or beef stock to the baking dish.
4. Bake in a hot oven (200°C) for 10 minutes, then reduce the heat to moderate (180°C).
5. Turn meat when half the cooking time has elapsed.
6. Remove meat, slice and serve.

(Serves 4–6)

Roast Veal

veal

1. Cook as for beef but allow 25 minutes per half kilogram and 30 minutes over.
2. Serve with gravy and baked vegetables.

Roast Lamb

leg or shoulder of lamb
flour
sprigs of rosemary

1. Grease a baking dish and place a rack in the dish.
2. Weigh meat and calculate cooking time. Allow at least 20 minutes for each half kilogram and 20 minutes over. Allow extra time if joint is large.
3. Place floured lamb in baking dish with fat side up. Insert sprigs of rosemary.
4. Cook in a hot oven for 10 minutes then reduce heat to moderate and cook more slowly for the required time. A lid may be used for part of the time.
5. As juices collect in base of pan, baste every 20 minutes.
6. When ready to add vegetables transfer lamb to another dish and return to oven.
7. Remove rack and add vegetables. Baste and bake for approximately 45 minutes, turning them once.
8. Drain vegetables on absorbent paper then serve in a hot dish.
9. Make gravy as for roast beef and pour into a gravy boat.
10. Serve lamb with baked vegetables, gravy and mint sauce or mint jelly.

✳ Roast Lamb

1 tablespoon soy sauce
1 tablespoon honey
1 tablespoon dry sherry
leg or shoulder of lamb

1. Combine soy sauce, honey and sherry and brush over lamb.
2. Place lamb fat side up on a rack set in a 3-litre, microwave-safe dish.
3. Cook on MEDIUM for:
   Medium — 10 to 12 minutes per 500 g
   Well done — 12 to 14 minutes per 500 g.
4. Turn halfway through cooking.
5. Allow to stand covered for 10 minutes before carving.

Stuffed Shoulder of Lamb

shoulder of lamb
pepper
oil

Stuffing
2 cups soft breadcrumbs
2 teaspoons fresh herbs —
   e.g. rosemary
1 onion
pepper
1 egg and a little milk

1. Weigh the boned shoulder then flatten it out on a board with fat side down. Trim off excess fat.
2. Mix breadcrumbs, herbs, finely chopped onion and pepper together in a bowl.
3. Moisten with egg and a little milk.
4. Place stuffing on top of shoulder and roll up.
5. Place in cooking net or tie securely with white string or make firm with skewers.
6. Place on a greased rack in a greased baking dish and brush with oil.
7. Bake in a hot oven for the first 10 minutes then cook slowly allowing 20 minutes for each half kilogram and 30 minutes over.
8. Brush with oil if necessary during the cooking time.
9. When cooked remove from baking dish.
10. Serve with baked vegetables, gravy and mint sauce.

Note: Alternatively, bake in an oven bag. The lamb will be more moist and tender.

(Serves 6)

Stuffed Veal

veal
stuffing

1. Use shoulder or loin of veal or topside with a pocket cut in it. Allow 25 to 30 minutes for each half kilogram. Add extra butter and a little chopped celery to the stuffing.
2. Serve with gravy and baked vegetables.

Roast Pork

leg or loin of pork
oil
salt
pepper
flour for thickening

1. Weigh joint and calculate cooking time. Allow 30 minutes for each half kilogram and 30 minutes over.
2. Score the rind and brush well with any cooking oil. Sprinkle with salt.
3. Place on a greased rack in a greased baking dish, rind side up and do not turn it over during cooking.
4. Place in a hot oven for about 20 minutes or until crackling has bubbled, reduce heat to moderate and cook slowly for the required time.
5. When ready to add vegetables transfer pork to another dish and return to oven.
6. Cook vegetables for the last 45 minutes.
7. Drain pork and vegetables on absorbent paper then serve on hot dishes.
8. Pour fat off carefully, retaining browning.
9. Add about 2 cups water and heat until browning has dissolved.
10. Add blended flour to make a fairly thick gravy. Boil for 2 or 3 minutes.
11. Add pepper to taste.
12. Serve in gravy boat.
13. Serve joint with gravy, baked vegetables and apple sauce.

Roast Loin of Pork with Stuffing

2 kg loin of pork, boned
salt
oil
1 cup water
2 chicken stock cubes

Stuffing

4 bacon rashers
1 onion
2 cups soft white
  breadcrumbs
pepper
2 eggs
2 tablespoons chopped
  parsley
1 teaspoon dried sage

Stuffing

1. Brush or spray pan with oil, heat and cook chopped bacon and onion until golden brown.
2. Add crumbs, seasoning, beaten eggs, parsley and sage and mix well.
3. Carefully remove rind from the pork and place on a baking tray. Rub well with salt.
4. Bake in a hot oven for 45 minutes. Drain off fat as it accumulates. Place rind under a hot griller until very crisp. When cool break into pieces.
5. While rind is baking, place pork, fat side down, on a board and spread stuffing along centre.
6. Roll up and secure with string tied at 2 to 3 cm intervals.
7. Rub pork with oil.
8. Place in baking dish with water and dissolved stock cubes.
9. Bake in a moderate oven for 1½ hours or until meat is cooked.
10. Remove from baking dish and stand for 15 minutes before removing string. Place on a serving dish and keep warm.
11. Make gravy with the pan juices.
12. Serve pork thinly sliced with gravy and pieces of crackling.

(*Serves 8–10*)

Apricot Pot Roast of Beef

½ **cup dried apricots**

1–1½ **kg topside steak in one piece**

2–3 **tablespoons oil**

1 **large onion, sliced**

2 **tablespoons water**

2 **teaspoons grated lemon rind**

1 **cup diced celery**

¼ **teaspoon pepper**

1 **tablespoon sugar**

1 **beef cube**

1. Select a saucepan large enough to cook meat and vegetables if required.
2. Soak apricots in a little cold water.
3. Heat oil and brown meat thoroughly on all sides. Pour off most of the fat.
4. Add onion, water, lemon rind, celery and pepper.
5. Cover and cook for 1 hour over low to moderate heat. Turn meat occasionally.
6. Add soaked apricots, a little more water and the sugar.
7. Cook for a further 1 hour or until tender.
8. Remove meat and apricots to a serving dish.
9. To make gravy add crumbled stock cube and water to make sufficient quantity. Blend a little flour or cornflour with a small amount of water, add to mixture and continue heating until thickened.
10. Pour into a jug and serve hot with meat and apricots.

Note: Cooking time will depend on the age of the meat so care should be taken that the meat is not overcooked.

(Serves 6–8)

Grilled or Barbecued Steak or Chops

steak or chops as required

Marinade

(sufficient for 750 g)

2 **tablespoons vinegar**

1 **tablespoon soy sauce**

1 **tablespoon oil**

1 **tablespoon plum jam**

1 **tablespoon brown sugar**

1 **onion, grated**

¾ **cup pineapple or orange juice**

pepper

1. Nick outside seam of fat and connective tissue in steak. Trim chops and remove outside skin and excess fat.
2. Mix ingredients for marinade.
3. Place meat in a shallow dish and pour marinade over. Allow to stand in refrigerator for at least 1 hour, turning meat occasionally.
4. Grill or barbecue meat until done to individual satisfaction. Any left-over marinade may be spooned over the meat as it cooks.
5. Serve immediately with hot vegetables or salad.

Note: This marinade may be used with sausages prior to grilling or barbecuing.

Rolled Shoulder of Lamb Pot Roast

250 g sausage meat

1 onion, finely chopped

2 tablespoons chopped parsley

1 shoulder of lamb, boned

2 bacon rashers

2 tablespoons oil

¼ cup water

1 stalk celery

1 onion

1 carrot

1–2 tomatoes

pinch ground ginger

¼ teaspoon pepper

1. Combine sausage meat, chopped onion and parsley and spread over boned shoulder.
2. Arrange bacon pieces on top then roll meat firmly and enclose in elastic cooking net or secure with string and small skewers.
3. Using a large heavy-based saucepan brown meat on all sides in the heated oil.
4. Pour off most of the oil then add water, coarsely chopped celery, onion, carrot and skinned tomatoes.
5. Add seasonings, cover and cook over low heat for 1 to 1½ hours or until cooked. Do not overcook.
6. Lift meat onto a plate and stand for 15 minutes before removing the net or string.
7. Meanwhile place vegetable mixture in blender and process until a thick sauce results.
8. Add sufficient water or stock to make sauce of good pouring consistency.
9. Adjust seasonings to taste.
10. Serve with baked and green vegetables.

(Serves 6)

Spicy Lamb Chops

8 lamb loin chops

1 teaspoon curry powder

¾ teaspoon ground coriander

½ cup pawpaw and mango chutney

1 tablespoon oil

1 tablespoon water

1. Trim fat from chops.
2. Place remaining ingredients in a food processor and blend until smooth.
3. Combine chops and spicy mixture in a bowl and allow to marinate in the refrigerator for at least 30 minutes.
4. Grill chops until tender and serve garnished with fresh coriander.

(Serves 4)

Crumbed Cutlets

lamb cutlets

flour

beaten egg and milk

dry breadcrumbs

pepper

oil for frying

1. Trim cutlets and roll in flour.
2. Dip in a mixture of egg and milk seasoned with pepper.
3. Toss in breadcrumbs. Allow to stand on a plate in refrigerator to become firm.
4. Heat a small amount of oil in frying pan.
5. Fry cutlets gently for about 4 minutes each side.
6. Drain on absorbent paper.
7. Serve hot with vegetables.

Variation

Coating

As an alternative, cutlets may be dipped in evaporated milk then rolled in crumbs.

Alternative method of cooking:

Prepared cutlets may be placed on greased aluminium foil and baked in a moderate oven for 20 to 30 minutes or until well done.

Lamb Kebabs

500 g lamb fillets (or allow 2 fillets per person)

150 g mushrooms

2 capsicums — 1 red
            — 1 green

1 onion

1 zucchini

10 cherry tomatoes

Satay

1 tablespoon hot chilli paste

2 tablespoons soy sauce

1 tablespoon peanut butter

1/4 teaspoon lemon juice

1 teaspoon honey

8–10 wooden skewers, pre-soaked

1. Cut lamb into bite-sized pieces.
2. Slice mushrooms, capsicums, onions, zucchini and cherry tomatoes into similar size pieces.
3. Thread alternately onto kebab sticks.
4. Blend satay ingredients together and brush over kebabs.
5. Grill 10 minutes, turn, brush with satay and grill a further 10 minutes.
6. Serve with brown rice.

(Serves 4–5)

Lamb Noisettes (France)

8 lamb loin chops
oil

Sauce
1 large onion, finely chopped
1 clove garlic, crushed
440 g tomatoes, skinned and chopped
1 tablespoon tomato puree
½ cup dry white wine
black pepper
1 tablespoon parsley

1. Using a sharp, pointed knife carefully remove bones from chops. Remove outside skin.
2. Roll each chop and secure with cocktail sticks.
3. Spray pan with oil, heat, and fry noisettes until cooked. Drain on absorbent paper.
4. Fry onion and garlic until soft.
5. Add the tomatoes, tomato puree and wine and bring to boiling point.
6. Allow to cook uncovered for 10 to 15 minutes, stirring occasionally. Season to taste.
7. Serve chops and pour the sauce over them. Sprinkle with parsley and serve with small, whole, boiled potatoes and green vegetables.

(Serves 4)

Lamb in Plum Sauce

oil
600 g lean lamb strips cut from the leg (five 1.5 cm strips)
1 onion, cut in 8 wedges
½ cup red capsicum, cut into thin strips
½ cup plum sauce
1 teaspoon cumin
50 g snow peas
1 cup bean sprouts (optional)
1 pkt quick-cooking noodles (85 g)
pepper

1. Brush or spray pan or wok with oil and heat. Add onion and capsicum and stir-fry for 1 to 2 minutes. Remove to a plate.
2. Add lamb strips and stir-fry for 3 to 5 minutes or until brown all over. Do not allow lamb to boil in its juices.
3. Put water on to boil for the noodles.
4. Add plum sauce to lamb, stir in cumin, then add vegetables. Stir to combine well. Bring to the boil, reduce heat and simmer for 4 to 5 minutes or until cooked. Add pepper to taste.
5. Cook noodles according to directions. Top with lamb and vegetable mixture.

(Serves 4)

Mongolian Lamb

1½ **cups rice**

oil

750 g lean lamb strips

4 medium onions,
quartered

2 cloves garlic, crushed

3 shallots, chopped

2 red chillies, finely
chopped

2 teaspoons cornflour

2 tablespoons light soy
sauce

1 tablespoon oyster sauce

½ **cup chicken stock**

1. Cook rice and keep hot.
2. Brush or spray pan with oil and heat.
3. Stir-fry lamb, in two batches, for 2 to 3 minutes. Remove lamb and set aside.
4. Stir-fry the onions, garlic, shallots and chillies for 2 minutes.
5. Blend cornflour with soy sauce, oyster sauce and stock. Return lamb to pan. Stir in cornflour mixture and cook for 2 to 3 minutes or until slightly thickened.
6. Serve hot with rice.

(Serves 4–6)

Lamb Rosemary

4–6 lamb leg steaks or
chops

freshly ground black
pepper

oil

1 clove garlic, crushed

1 tablespoon fresh
rosemary leaves

⅓ **cup red or white wine**

2 teaspoons cornflour

½ **teaspoon sugar**

½ **cup chicken stock**

2 tablespoons cream
(optional)

1. Trim lamb and season with pepper.
2. Brush or spray pan with oil, heat and cook lamb for 3 to 4 minutes on each side (meat should still be pink in the middle).
3. Remove from heat and keep warm.
4. Add garlic and rosemary to pan and cook for a few seconds, add wine and stir well.
5. Mix cornflour and sugar into stock and add slowly to pan, stirring until sauce thickens.
6. Add cream if desired, pour sauce over lamb and serve with noodles tossed with chives.

(Serves 4)

Souvlakia (Greece)

1 kg boneless lamb loin or boned lamb leg, trimmed and cut into 3 cm cubes

1 green capsicum, cut in 2 cm squares

1 red capsicum, cut in 2 cm squares

½ cup olive oil

⅓ cup lemon juice

1 tablespoon wine vinegar

2 cloves garlic, crushed

1 tablespoon fresh, chopped oregano leaves

freshly ground pepper

wooden skewers, pre-soaked

1. Thread meat and capsicum alternately onto pre-soaked skewers and place in a non-metal dish.
2. Combine oil, lemon juice, vinegar, garlic, oregano and pepper and pour over skewered food.
3. Cover with plastic wrap and refrigerate for 1 to 2 hours or overnight, turning occasionally.
4. Drain and reserve marinade and place skewers on bbq or a lightly greased grill tray. Cook on a medium heat for approximately 10 minutes, or until cooked. Brush frequently with the marinade and turn several times during the cooking.
5. Serve with warm pocket bread and Greek salad.

(Serves 4)

Navarin of Lamb (France)

oil

1 large onion, chopped

1 clove garlic

6 lamb chump chops

flour for coating

black pepper

1 420 g can tomatoes, chopped

1 tablespoon tomato puree

fresh sprigs of herbs — rosemary or parsley

1 teaspoon sugar

2 large carrots

1–2 white turnips

extra parsley

1. Brush or spray pan with oil and heat. Add onion and garlic and cook until transparent. Remove to a greased casserole dish.
2. Trim fat from chops and coat with flour.
3. Place in hot pan and brown quickly on each side. Arrange in casserole.
4. Add tomato puree, canned tomatoes and juice and flavourings to casserole dish.
5. Peel and slice carrots and turnips and place on and around chops.
6. Cover and cook in a slow to moderate oven for 1½ to 2 hours or until tender.
7. Taste for seasoning, remove herbs and sprinkle with chopped parsley.
8. Serve with potatoes and green vegetables.

(Serves 6)

Lamb Mediterranean Style

oil

8 lamb cutlets, trimmed

1 onion, thinly sliced

1 clove garlic, crushed

freshly ground pepper

1 capsicum, thinly sliced

1 400 g can diced tomatoes

3 tablespoons chopped fresh basil

2 tablespoons chopped black olives (optional)

1. Brush or spray pan with oil, heat and cook cutlets on each side until brown.
2. Add onion, garlic, pepper and capsicum and cook for 1 to 2 minutes.
3. Add tomatoes and basil and stir to combine.
4. Cover and simmer 15 to 20 minutes until lamb is tender.
5. Stir in olives and serve with pasta and garnish with fresh basil.

(Serves 4)

Biriani (Pakistan)

1 cup long grain rice

500 g boned shoulder lamb, cubed

¼ cup plain yoghurt

2 medium onions, finely chopped

1–2 cloves garlic, crushed

12 mm piece green ginger

¼ teaspoon ground coriander

¼ teaspoon ground cardamom

4–5 tablespoons ghee or oil

¼ cup sultanas

¼ cup blanched almonds, slivered

½ teaspoon turmeric

25 mm strip cinnamon bark

½ cup water

3 tablespoons cream

½ cup frozen peas

1. Boil rice in plenty of boiling water for 10 minutes. Drain and keep hot.
2. Place lamb in a bowl with yoghurt, half the onion, garlic, ginger, coriander and cardamom.
3. Heat half the ghee, fry sultanas and almonds for a few minutes until sultanas are puffed up and almonds golden. Remove and drain.
4. Put meat into pan and brown well.
5. Reduce heat, add remainder of onion, turmeric, cinnamon and a little water.
6. Cover and simmer for 30 minutes or until meat is tender.
7. Drain meat and onions, reserving liquid.
8. Melt remaining ghee, coat sides and base of casserole.
9. Place a layer of rice over the base and sprinkle with a third of the sultanas and almonds. Top with meat.
10. Continue with layers, ending with a layer of rice sprinkled with sultanas and almonds.
11. Add cream and peas into reserved liquid and pour over.
12. Cover and bake in a moderate oven for 30 to 45 minutes or until all liquid has been absorbed and rice is dry and fluffy.
13. Serve hot.

(Serves 4–6)

Casserole Steak

500 g topside, blade or
   skirt steak
¼ cup flour
2 teaspoons gravy powder
1 onion, sliced
1 carrot, sliced
1 stick celery, sliced
1 parsnip, sliced
1 white turnip, chopped
1–1½ cups water or beef
   stock
2 pinches pepper
1 tablespoon
   Worcestershire sauce
1 tablespoon vinegar
a little oil

1. Cut meat into serving size pieces.
2. Roll in flour then fry in a little hot oil in a frying pan until well browned.
3. Arrange meat and vegetables in layers in a casserole dish, finishing with vegetables.
4. Blend 1 tablespoon flour and gravy powder with a little cold water, add sauce, vinegar and pepper.
5. Pour mixture over meat and vegetables and add sufficient water to barely cover. Dissolve browning in pan and add.
6. Cover with a tight-fitting lid and cook in a slow to moderate oven for about 2 hours.
7. Serve with mashed potatoes and a green vegetable.

(Serves 4)

Irish Stew

500 g lamb neck or
   shoulder chops, trimmed
1 large onion
500 g potatoes, peeled and
   cubed into 2 cm pieces
1 large carrot, peeled and
   sliced
1 parsnip, peeled and
   sliced
freshly ground pepper
2 cups beef or chicken
   stock
1 teaspoon Worcestershire
   sauce
parsley

1. Layer lamb and vegetables in a greased, flameproof casserole dish and season with pepper.
2. Pour stock and sauce over lamb and vegetables, place over heat and bring to the boil. Skim off fat and scum if necessary.
3. Cover with a tight-fitting lid and bake in a moderately slow oven (160°C) or simmer on the stove top for approximately 3 hours or until well cooked.
4. Before serving, thicken with a little flour blended with water if necessary and serve sprinkled with fresh parsley accompanied by green vegetables.

(Serves 4)

Beef Sukiyaki (Japan)

500 g fillet or rump steak
1 doz. French beans, sliced
2 medium carrots, cut into thin strips
2 onions, finely sliced
½ bunch shallots, chopped
100 g mushrooms, sliced (optional)
6 flowerets cauliflower
2 cups finely shredded spinach, Chinese cabbage or cabbage
2 tablespoons oil
1 teaspoon fresh root ginger, finely chopped
2 teaspoons sugar
2 tablespoons soy sauce
1 cup beef stock
boiled rice

1. Cut meat into paper-thin strips.
2. Drop the cauliflower and carrots into boiling water and cook for 7 minutes. Drain thoroughly.
3. Arrange all the ingredients on a platter.
4. Heat oil in the pan with the ginger. When hot add a layer of shallot pieces and onion slices then pile meat in the centre.
5. Surround with piles of all other vegetables.
6. Gently turn the pieces all the time until vegetables are hot. Do not stir.
7. When meat has changed colour sprinkle with sugar and pour in the soy sauce.
8. Increase heat a little. Add the stock.
9. Continue as before turning and gently moving the ingredients for another 3 minutes.
10. Meat and vegetables must be only lightly cooked.
11. Cook for about 15 minutes in all.
12. Serve with boiled rice.

(Serves 4)

Steak Diane

oil
4 pieces lean beef steak
4 tablespoons red wine
1 dessertspoon Worcestershire sauce
4 tablespoons tomato sauce
1 tablespoon chopped parsley
4 tablespoons cream

1. Brush or spray pan with oil, heat and seal steaks on both sides. Cook steaks to suit taste. Remove from pan and keep warm.
2. Combine red wine and both sauces and add to pan. Bring to boil, turn heat off and stir in parsley and cream.
3. Place meat on serving plates and pour sauce over.

(Serves 4)

Beef and Vegetable Fajitas

oil

500 g lean beef, sliced thinly

1 red capsicum

1 onion, finely sliced

1 zucchini, thinly sliced

6 large mushrooms, sliced

3 tablespoons taco sauce

10 flour tortillas

1. Brush or spray pan with oil, heat and cook beef until well browned.
2. Add capsicum, onion, zucchini and mushrooms and cook until vegetables are tender.
3. Stir in taco sauce and heat through.
4. Heat tortillas as instructions on packet indicate and top each tortilla with beef and vegetable mixture. Roll up and serve.

(*Serves 5*)

Beef Stir-fry

500 g lean beef strips

3 spring onions

1 clove garlic, crushed

1 teaspoon freshly grated ginger

3 tablespoons barbecue sauce

⅓ cup oyster sauce

oil

3 cups finely sliced vegetables (celery, broccoli, carrots, baby corn, beans, snow peas, bok choy, yellow baby squash)

shallots

1. Place beef, spring onions, garlic, ginger, barbecue sauce and oyster sauce in a bowl and mix well.
2. Brush or spray pan with oil and heat. Cook meat mixture in batches until beef is cooked. Remove meat mixture and place in a bowl.
3. Add vegetables to pan and stir-fry for 2 to 3 minutes.
4. Return meat mixture to pan, mix well and continue to cook until the sauce boils. Add some water if sauce is too thick.
5. Serve with rice or noodles, garnished with finely chopped shallots.

(*Serves 4*)

Steak and Onions

500 g grilling steak
2 tablespoons soy sauce
clove of garlic, crushed
2 teaspoons sugar
oil
4 onions, sliced
water or stock
1–2 tablespoons flour

1. Divide steak into four equal-sized pieces.
2. Mix soy sauce, garlic and sugar. Pour over steak and stand for 1 hour. Turn meat occasionally.
3. Brush or spray pan with oil, heat and fry onions until golden brown. Remove to a plate.
4. Fry steak until cooked. Remove to a plate.
5. Pour off oil and add water or stock.
6. Thicken with flour blended with a little water and boil for 2 to 3 minutes.
7. Return steak and onions to pan and allow to heat through. Check seasoning.
8. Serve with vegetables.

(Serves 4)

Pork and Vegetable Satay

500 g diced pork
1 onion, quartered
1 red capsicum, cut into 3 cm squares
fresh herbs to garnish
12 wooden skewers, pre-soaked

Marinade

1 clove garlic, finely chopped
1 tablespoon grated fresh ginger
¼ teaspoon chilli powder
1 teaspoon ground cumin
1 teaspoon ground coriander
1 tablespoon lemon juice
1 tablespoon soy sauce
1 tablespoon honey
2 tablespoons crunchy peanut paste
¾ cup water

1. Trim pork pieces. Break up onion quarters into pieces.
2. Thread pork, onion and capsicum onto skewers and place in a large shallow dish.

Marinade

3. Combine ingredients in a bowl, adding more water if necessary. Pour over skewers. Cover and stand for several hours or overnight in refrigerator.
4. Drain skewers and reserve marinade.
5. Cook skewers under a hot grill for about 6 minutes each side or until cooked.
6. Pour marinade into saucepan and bring slowly to boiling point.
7. Serve hot with skewers.
8. Garnish with fresh herbs.

(Serves 4–5)

Butterfly Pork Steaks

oil

4 butterfly steaks, pork medallions or pork loin or leg chops

Sauce

1 onion, chopped

1 stick celery, chopped

1 bacon rasher, chopped

1 tablespoon tomato sauce

1 small clove garlic, crushed

pepper

1½ cups chicken stock

cornflour for thickening

1. Brush or spray pan with oil and heat. Cook steaks or chops until done. Drain on absorbent paper and keep hot.
2. Sauté onion, celery and bacon for 2 to 3 minutes.
3. Add tomato sauce, garlic, pepper and stock.
4. Simmer for 10 minutes or until vegetables are soft.
5. Thicken with a little cornflour blended with water.
6. Strain sauce and serve with steak.

Note: Sauce may be put in a blender and reduced to a smooth mixture. Reheat before serving.

Variations

Sauce 2

Cook steak as above then drain.

Add: ½ cup orange juice

      1 cup water

      pepper

      a little grated orange rind

      1 teaspoon sugar

Bring to the boil, stirring well to dissolve pan brownings. Thicken with a little blended cornflour. Taste and add more orange juice if liked. Serve spooned over steak.

Sauce 3

Cook steak as above then drain.

Add: 1½ cups chicken stock

      pepper

      ⅓ cup plum jam

      1 tablespoon vinegar

Bring to the boil, stirring well to dissolve pan brownings. Thicken with a little blended cornflour. Check taste then serve spooned over steak.

(Serves 4)

Sweet and Sour Pork (China)

500 g lean pork, cubed

2 onions, sliced

4–5 shallots, chopped diagonally

1 red capsicum, cut into thin strips

100 g mushrooms, sliced

1 medium cucumber, halved and sliced

1 cup pineapple pieces (drained)

cornflour for coating

oil for frying

¾ cup pineapple juice

2–3 teaspoons cornflour

2 teaspoons tomato sauce

pepper

Marinade

1½ tablespoons sugar

1 tablespoon soy sauce

3 tablespoons vinegar

1. Mix together sugar, soy sauce and vinegar.
2. Place pork in sauce mixture.
3. Stir well to coat pieces of pork with marinade.
4. Allow to stand for 1 hour. Stir occasionally.
5. Brush or spray pan with oil and fry onions until clear.
6. Add capsicum and shallots and cook for a further 4 minutes.
7. Add mushrooms, cook until soft.
8. Stir in pineapple pieces and cucumber. Remove from pan and keep hot.
9. Drain meat from the marinade.
10. Toss in cornflour.
11. Fry in a little heated oil until cooked through. Drain on absorbent paper.
12. Add meat to vegetables and keep hot.
13. Blend cornflour with pineapple juice and add tomato sauce and remaining marinade.
14. Bring to boiling point, stirring continuously. Season to taste.
15. Pour sauce over meat and vegetables and stir to coat evenly.
16. Serve hot with boiled rice.

(Serves 4–5)

Hoisin Pork Stir-fry

500 g lean pork, thinly sliced

1 small red chilli, finely chopped (optional)

1 teaspoon grated fresh ginger

1 clove garlic, crushed

1 teaspoon sesame oil

2 tablespoons hoisin sauce

oil

4 shallots, sliced

250 g green beans, cut in 5 cm lengths

200 g broccoli, chopped

2 teaspoons fish sauce

1 teaspoon chicken stock powder

1 teaspoon cornflour

½ cup water

fresh coriander

1. Place pork, chilli, ginger, garlic, sesame oil and hoisin sauce in a bowl and mix well.
2. Brush or spray pan with oil, heat and stir-fry pork mixture in batches until pork is cooked. Remove from pan.
3. Add shallots, beans and broccoli and cook for 1 to 2 minutes.
4. Add fish sauce, stock powder and pork mixture to pan. Mix well.
5. Blend cornflour with water, add to pan and stir until sauce boils and thickens.
6. Serve with noodles or rice and garnish with fresh coriander.

(Serves 4)

Curry and Rice

500 g topside or blade steak, cubed

2 tablespoons oil

1 small carrot or 1 tomato

1 apple, diced

1 onion, diced

1 tablespoon curry powder

2 tablespoons sultanas

2 teaspoons sugar

pepper

2 teaspoons lemon juice

water

2 tablespoons flour

1. Brush or spray pan with oil, heat and add diced carrot, apple, onion and curry powder.
2. Fry without browning for about 5 minutes.
3. Add sultanas, sugar, pepper and lemon juice and about 1¼ cups water.
4. Add meat and simmer gently for 1½ hours or until meat is tender.
5. Thicken with blended flour and add more curry powder if necessary.
6. Serve with brown or white rice.

(Serves 4)

Beef Stew with Dumplings

**750 g bladebone steak,
  cubed**

3 tablespoons flour

pepper

1 tablespoon oil

2 onions, sliced

2½ cups water

2 carrots, sliced

blended flour

1. Roll pieces of steak in seasoned flour.
2. Heat oil in a frying pan.
3. Brown steak well on all sides.
4. Drain on absorbent paper then place in a saucepan.
5. Fry onions for 1 to 2 minutes in pan.
6. Lift onions out and place with meat.
7. Pour off any oil remaining in pan.
8. Add water and allow to boil.
9. Pour over meat. Cover with a close-fitting lid.
10. Simmer gently for 1 hour.
11. Add carrots to stew.
12. Cook for a further 1½ hours, adding more water if necessary.
13. Stir in sufficient blended flour to thicken gravy a little.
14. Place dumplings on top of stew, cover with lid and cook for 20 minutes.
15. Serve immediately.

Dumplings

2 cups self-raising flour

2 tablespoons margarine

**¾ cup cold water
  (approximately)**

Dumplings

16. Sift flour into a bowl.
17. Rub in margarine with the fingers.
18. Mix into a moist dough with water.
19. Divide into 12 parts.
20. Using floured hands roll dough into balls.

(Serves 5–6)

Beef in Black Bean Sauce

2 teaspoons soy sauce

¼ cup dry sherry

600 g lean beef strips

½ cup water

oil

½ cup shallots

½ red capsicum, sliced

½ cup bean sprouts

**60 g transparent noodles
  e.g. cellophane noodles**

**2 tablespoons black bean
  sauce**

cornflour

1. Mix soy sauce and sherry.
2. Marinate beef strips in this mixture for 10 minutes.
3. Put a large saucepan of water on to boil.
4. Brush or spray pan with oil, heat and sauté shallots, capsicum and bean spouts for 2 minutes. Remove to a plate.
5. Add beef in batches and cook until browned, turning frequently. This will take 3 to 4 minutes.
6. Return vegetables, add black bean sauce and remainder of marinade and heat through. Season to taste.
7. Add noodles to water and cook according to packet instructions, then drain.
8. Blend cornflour with a little water and add to pan. Heat and stir until thickened.
9. Serve beef accompanied by noodles.

(Serves 4–5)

Beef Stroganoff (Russia)

1 tablespoon oil

**750 g beef steak, e.g. rib
  fillet or rump, sliced thinly**

freshly ground pepper

1 large onion, sliced finely

300 g mushrooms, sliced

**1 tomato, skinned and
  chopped**

1 tablespoon tomato paste

2 teaspoons paprika

**2 teaspoons French
  mustard**

¼ cup white wine

¼ cup chicken stock

1 cup light sour cream

**1 tablespoon chopped
  fresh parsley**

1. Heat oil in large pan and cook meat quickly, in small batches, until well browned. Remove from pan and drain.
2. Add onions to pan and cook for 2 to 3 minutes until soft.
3. Add mushrooms and tomato and cook until mushrooms are tender.
4. Add tomato paste, paprika, mustard, wine and stock to the pan and bring to the boil. Reduce heat and simmer uncovered for 5 minutes, stirring occasionally.
5. Return meat to pan, add sour cream and stir until combined and just heated through.
6. Sprinkle with parsley and serve with pasta.

(Serves 4–6)

Rissoles

1 onion

1 tablespoon fresh herbs
(sage, marjoram, thyme)
or 1 teaspoon mixed
dried herbs

2 slices brown bread

500 g lean minced beef

pepper

1 egg

1 tablespoon tomato or soy
sauce

¼ cup flour

1 tablespoon oil

1. Place onion, herbs and bread in a processor and process until finely chopped.
2. Add to mince with pepper, egg and sauce and mix well together.
3. Form into even-sized balls, then flatten and roll in flour.
4. Heat oil and fry rissoles until meat is cooked.
5. Drain on absorbent paper.
6. Serve hot with vegetables.

(Serves 4–5)

Spaghetti Bolognese (Italy)

400 g spaghetti

oil

1 onion, diced

1 carrot, diced

1 stick celery, diced

1–2 cloves garlic, crushed

400 g lean minced beef

½ cup tomato paste

1 420 g can chopped
tomatoes

1 cup beef stock

½ teaspoon dried basil

½ teaspoon dried oregano

pepper

½ cup grated cheese

1. Place spaghetti in boiling water and cook for about 12 minutes or until tender.
2. Brush or spray pan with oil, heat and fry vegetables until lightly browned.
3. Add mince and stir well until colour has changed.
4. Add tomato paste, chopped tomatoes, stock, herbs and pepper and simmer uncovered for 40 minutes until sauce is a thick consistency.
5. Combine spaghetti and sauce.
6. Turn into serving dish and sprinkle with cheese.

(Serves 4–6)

Teriyaki Meat Balls

500 g minced lean beef
3 shallots, chopped
1 clove garlic, crushed
1 teaspoon grated fresh ginger
¼ cup soy sauce
1 tablespoon sugar
1 cup rice
1 tablespoon oil
2 medium carrots, thinly sliced
150 g snow peas
⅓ cup water
1 teaspoon cornflour

1. Put a pan of water on to boil. In a bowl mix shallots, garlic, ginger, soy sauce and sugar.
2. Place minced beef in another bowl and add half of the soy sauce mixture. Mix well to combine, then shape into 20 meat balls.
3. Add rice to boiling water and cook until tender.
4. Put another pan of water on to boil. Prepare carrots and top and tail snow peas.
5. Heat oil in a large frying pan and fry meat balls, turning frequently, until they are browned and cooked through, about 10 minutes.
6. Meanwhile, add carrots to boiling water, cook for 5 minutes, then add snow peas and cook for a further 3 minutes.
7. Blend cornflour with water and mix with remaining soy sauce mixture. Add to meat balls and stir until sauce thickens and bubbles. Simmer for 1 to 2 minutes then serve meat balls and sauce with the drained rice and vegetables.

(Serves 4–5)

Porcupines

500 g lean minced beef
1 small onion, grated
2 tablespoons flour
½ cup rice, uncooked
pepper
1 egg, lightly beaten
1 440 g can tomato soup

1. Place mince, grated onion, flour, rice and pepper in a bowl.
2. Add beaten egg and mix well together.
3. With floured hands form into balls.
4. Place soup in a large saucepan, add ½ can of water and heat to boiling point.
5. Place meat balls in the saucepan, making only one layer.
6. Simmer gently for 40 to 45 minutes.
7. Serve hot with vegetables.

Note: Porcupines may be cooked in a casserole dish in the oven.

(Serves 4–6)

Meat Balls Napoli (Italy)

300 g green fettucini noodles

Meat Balls

400 g minced steak

250 g pork mince

1 onion, grated

1 cup soft breadcrumbs

1 egg, beaten

¼ cup milk

¼ cup finely chopped green capsicum

2 tablespoons chopped parsley

1 clove garlic

pepper

cooking oil

Sauce

1 clove garlic

¼ cup white vinegar

1 420 g can tomatoes

1 110 g can tomato paste

2 teaspoons sugar

1½ cups water

2 chicken stock cubes

2 tablespoons chopped fresh parsley

1 teaspoon chopped fresh basil

pepper

1. Combine all the ingredients for the meat balls and mix well. Shape into about 30 balls.
2. Heat oil in a pan and fry meat balls until brown all over. Drain on absorbent paper and drain fat from pan.
3. For the sauce, add crushed garlic to pan and cook for a few seconds.
4. Add vinegar, chopped tomatoes with liquid, tomato paste, sugar, water, stock cubes, herbs and seasonings.
5. Heat until boiling then cover and simmer for about 20 to 25 minutes.
6. Add the meat balls and coat with sauce.
7. Cook noodles in boiling water until tender. Do not overcook.
8. Drain and arrange on a flat dish making a nest shape. Place meat balls and sauce on noodles without spilling sauce on noodle ring. Serve hot.

(Serves 4–6)

Moussaka (Greece)

1 large eggplant, cut into
  1 cm slices

1 tablespoon salt

oil

Meat Sauce

1 large onion, finely
  chopped

2 cloves garlic, crushed

500 g lean minced lamb or
  beef

2 teaspoons flour

1 teaspoon cinnamon

1 cup beef stock

freshly ground pepper

1 tablespoon freshly
  chopped parsley

1 420 g can chopped
  tomatoes, drained

1 tablespoon parmesan
  cheese

Topping Sauce

30 g margarine

2 tablespoons flour

1 cup milk

2 egg yolks, beaten

1. Sprinkle eggplant with salt and stand in a colander for 15 to 30 minutes. Rinse under cold water and pat dry with paper towels.

Meat Sauce

2. Spray or brush non-stick pan with oil, heat and cook eggplant on both sides until golden brown.
3. Respray or brush pan with oil if required, heat and add onion and garlic, cook until onion is transparent.
4. Sprinkle meat with flour and add to pan and cook for 1 to 2 minutes.
5. Add cinnamon, stock, pepper, parsley and tomatoes and simmer uncovered for 15 to 20 minutes, then remove from heat.

Topping Sauce

6. Melt margarine in a saucepan and stir in flour and cook gently for 1 to 2 minutes, stirring constantly. Remove from heat.
7. Add milk gradually, stirring constantly, replace on heat and stir until sauce boils and thickens.
8. Remove from heat and gradually add egg yolks, stirring constantly.
9. Place ⅓ of eggplant on the base of a greased, ovenproof dish and spread with half of the meat sauce. Add a second layer of eggplant, the remaining meat sauce and finish with a layer of eggplant.
10. Pour topping sauce over the eggplant and top with parmesan cheese.
11. Bake in a moderate oven for 35 to 40 minutes or until golden.
12. Serve with salad greens and crusty bread.

(Serves 4–6)

Kofta Curry (India)

1 large onion, finely
    chopped
1 clove garlic, crushed
1 green capsicum, diced
½ cup shredded cabbage
pinch ground ginger
pinch ground cloves
1 tablespoon curry powder
750 g lean minced beef
1 teaspoon lemon juice
seasoned flour
oil for frying

Curry Sauce
oil
2 onions, diced
1 clove garlic, crushed
½ teaspoon ground ginger
½ teaspoon turmeric
1 tablespoon curry powder
pinch cayenne
pinch cinnamon
2 large tomatoes, skinned
    and chopped
1 small potato, cubed
1 cup pineapple pieces
1½ cups coconut milk
boiled rice

Meat Balls

1. Mix together cabbage, ginger, cloves, curry powder and meat.
2. Add lemon juice.
3. Add vegetables and mix well.
4. Roll into balls, dust with seasoned flour.
5. Fry balls in hot oil until brown.
6. Drain, then put aside.

Curry Sauce

7. Brush or spray pan with oil, add onion and garlic, sauté until light brown.
8. Add ginger, turmeric, curry powder, cayenne and cinnamon.
9. Stir well. Cook for 3 minutes.
10. Add tomatoes, potato and pineapple.
11. Cook gently for 5 minutes, stirring all the time.
12. Add coconut milk and check flavour.
13. Add meat balls to curry sauce.
14. Cover and simmer gently for 15 to 20 minutes.
15. Do not stir but shake pan occasionally to prevent sticking.
16. Serve with boiled rice.

Note: To skin tomatoes place in a deep bowl, pour boiling water over and stand for 2 to 3 minutes. Lift out and when cool peel off skin.

(Serves 6–8)

Herbed Meat Balls

Meat Balls

750 g lean minced beef
1 teaspoon dried basil
1 cup rolled oats
1 clove garlic, crushed
½ cup tomato sauce
½ cup water
flour
oil

Sauce

1 440 g can tomato soup or juice
½ cup green capsicum, sliced
1½ cups water
½ teaspoon basil
4 onions, sliced
pinch chilli powder

1. Combine steak, basil, oats, garlic, sauce and water.
2. Blend thoroughly and shape into balls using a dessertspoon. Toss in flour.
3. Brown the meat balls in a little hot oil. Shake pan frequently to prevent sticking.
4. Drain and place in a large saucepan.
5. Combine all ingredients for the sauce and pour over meat balls.
6. Simmer for about 30 minutes.
7. Serve with spaghetti or rice.

(Serves 6–8)

Shepherd's Pie

500 g lean minced beef
1 onion, chopped
1 small carrot, grated
½ cup water
pepper
1 beef stock cube
1 teaspoon Worcestershire sauce
1 tablespoon tomato sauce
2 tablespoons flour
1 or 2 tomatoes, sliced (optional)
4 large potatoes, cut in 2 cm squares
1 teaspoon butter (optional)
2–3 tablespoons milk
parsley

1. Spray or brush a large saucepan with oil, heat and sauté onion and carrot for 2 minutes.
2. Add meat and continue to cook for 2 to 3 minutes.
3. Add water, pepper, beef cube and sauces.
4. Cook over gentle heat until well cooked. Add extra water if necessary. Remove from heat.
5. Return to heat and stir until sauce thickens and bubbles. Blend flour with a little water and add to saucepan stirring well.
6. Pour into pie dish and cover with tomato.
7. Cook potatoes in boiling water for 15 minutes or until tender.
8. Drain, mash well and add butter and milk.
9. Spread potatoes over top of meat and mark with a fork.
10. Bake in a moderate oven until a golden colour.
11. Serve hot garnished with parsley.

Variation

Lamb mince may be substituted for beef mince.

(Serves 6)

Mexican Beef (Mexico)

oil

1 large onion, cut into chunky pieces

1 clove garlic, crushed

600 g lean minced beef

1 tomato, chopped

½ small capsicum, chopped

1 small potato, cut into 1 cm cubes

½ cup chopped green beans, cut into 2 cm lengths

1 teaspoon Mexican chilli powder

1 tablespoon red wine *or* 1 teaspoon vinegar

1 teaspoon Worcestershire sauce

1 teaspoon soy sauce

¾ cup beef stock or water

1 tablespoon cornflour

pepper

1. Spray or brush pan with oil, heat and brown the onion and garlic.
2. Add the mince and cook until brown, stirring frequently.
3. Add all the vegetables, chilli powder, wine, sauces and stock.
4. Heat through then thicken with blended cornflour.
5. Add pepper to taste.
6. Simmer for 15 minutes.
7. Serve with fried rice.

Fried Rice

1½ cups rice

8 cups water

oil

1 onion, chopped

1 egg, beaten

2 teaspoons soy sauce

1 teaspoon curry powder

1. Boil water, add rice and boil without a lid for 12 minutes. Remove from heat and drain. Brush or spray pan with oil, heat and add onion and cook for 2 minutes.
2. Add rice, soy sauce and curry powder. Cook for 1 to 2 minutes, turning rice constantly so it does not burn.
3. Add beaten egg, stirring while egg cooks and is distributed through the rice.
4. Serve hot with Mexican beef.

Note: Fried rice can also be served with curries.

(Serves 5)

Tacos (Mexico)

1 pkt 10 taco shells
3 cups selected filling
shredded lettuce
chopped tomatoes
grated cheese

1. Warm the taco shells in the oven for 2 to 3 minutes or microwave for 1 minute.
2. Spoon 2 tablespoons of hot filling into the shells.
3. Top with lettuce, tomato and cheese.
4. Serve at once.

Filling 1: Beef and Beans

oil
¾ cup finely chopped onion
1 clove garlic, crushed
200 g steak mince
1 tomato, skinned and diced
1 tablespoon taco seasoning mix
1 tablespoon chopped parsley
¼ cup beef stock
¼ teaspoon dried basil
pinch cinnamon (optional)
1 375 g can red kidney beans
pepper

1. Brush or spray pan with oil, heat and cook onion and garlic until tender.
2. Add the meat and brown well. Add the tomato, taco seasoning, parsley, stock, basil and cinnamon.
3. Simmer until mixture is almost dry. Add the beans and heat through.
4. Add pepper to taste. Makes about 3 cups.

Filling 2: Chicken

2 cups chopped cooked chicken
1 cup grated cheese
¼ cup chopped onion
1–2 tablespoons chopped parsley
1 clove garlic, crushed
¼ teaspoon dried basil
¼ teaspoon dried oregano
pepper
¼–½ cup cream

1. Combine ingredients adding sufficient cream to bind.
2. Heat gently until hot, stirring occasionally. Makes about 3 cups.

Filling 3: Vegetable

2 tablespoons butter or margarine
2 tablespoons flour
1½ cups milk
½ cup grated carrot
½ cup sliced mushrooms
¼ cup chopped shallots
1 cup shredded spinach
½ cup grated cheese
2 hard boiled eggs
pepper

1. Melt butter, add the flour and mix well. Remove from heat and gradually stir in the milk. Cook over moderate heat stirring constantly until thickened.
2. Add the vegetables and cook for 10 minutes over low heat.
3. Add the cheese and melt over gentle heat.
4. Add chopped eggs and pepper to taste. Makes about 3 cups.

(Serves 10)

Enchiladas (Mexico)

1 quantity basic pancake mixture (12 pancakes)
6 slices ham
1–2 small chillies, seeded and finely chopped

Cheese Sauce

1 tablespoon margarine
1 tablespoon flour
¾ cup milk
¾ cup grated cheese
¼ teaspoon dry mustard
pepper

1. Make the pancakes and stack with baking paper between them. Keep warm.
2. Melt the butter in a small saucepan, add the flour and mix well. Cook for 1 minute and remove from heat.
3. Gradually add the milk, return to heat and stir until mixture thickens and boils. Remove from heat.
4. Add grated cheese, mustard mixed with a little water, and pepper to taste. Mix well.
5. On each pancake place a half slice of ham. Sprinkle with a little chilli.
6. Roll up and place side by side in a greased serving dish.
7. Spoon cheese sauce over the centre and garnish with a little chopped chives or parsley.

Variation

Use any of the fillings given for tacos and top with taco or tomato sauce.

(Serves 4–6)

Lasagne (Italy)

1 250 g pkt instant lasagne

Meat Sauce
oil
1 onion, chopped
2 cloves garlic, crushed
1 medium carrot, grated
1 stalk celery, chopped
500 g lean minced beef
1–2 cans chopped
  tomatoes
1 110 g can tomato paste
pepper
½ teaspoon oregano

Cheese Sauce
60 g butter or margarine
⅓ cup plain flour
2 cups milk
pepper
¼ teaspoon nutmeg
½ cup grated cheddar
  cheese
1 tablespoon parmesan
  cheese

Meat Sauce

1. Brush or spray pan with oil, heat and cook onion, garlic, carrot and celery until tender.
2. Add meat and stir over heat until browned.
3. Add tomatoes, tomato paste, pepper and oregano and bring to the boil.
4. Simmer uncovered until sauce has thickened and ingredients are well cooked (approximately 30 minutes).
5. Sauce should be fairly thin as moisture is required to soften the lasagne.

Cheese Sauce

6. Melt butter in a saucepan, add flour and mix until smooth.
7. Cook for 1 minute then gradually stir in milk and stir over heat until sauce thickens and boils for 1 minute.
8. Add pepper, nutmeg and grated cheddar cheese. Stir until melted.
9. *To assemble:* Grease a large flat ovenproof dish. Fill with alternate layers of meat sauce, lasagne sheets and cheese sauce, having 2 or 3 layers of each. Finish with pasta, cover with cheese sauce and top with parmesan cheese. Bake uncovered in a moderate oven for 30 minutes or until brown.

Note: 120 g mushrooms may be added to the meat sauce if desired.

(Serves 6–8)

Cannelloni (Italy)

1 pkt instant cannelloni

Filling

500 g lean minced beef

½ cup soft breadcrumbs

1 medium onion, chopped

2 tablespoons parmesan
cheese

1 tablespoon chopped
parsley

pepper

½ teaspoon nutmeg

1 egg

Sauce

1.4 kg tomatoes, chopped

3 tablespoons tomato
puree

3 carrots, diced

1 onion, diced

3 stalks celery, sliced

2 cloves garlic, crushed

2 tablespoons parsley,
chopped

freshly ground pepper

1–2 tablespoons parmesan
cheese

Filling

1. Place all ingredients in a bowl and bind together with the
   beaten egg.
2. Fill cannelloni tubes with the stuffing and arrange in a
   greased dish, side by side.

Sauce

3. Combine tomatoes, tomato puree, carrots, onion, celery,
   garlic, parsley and pepper in a saucepan. Bring to boil.
4. Simmer mixture for approximately 45 minutes until
   vegetables are cooked and sauce is a thick consistency.
   (If a smoother sauce is desired this mixture can be
   pureed.)
5. Pour over the cannelloni and sprinkle with cheese.
6. Bake in a moderate oven (180°C) for 45 minutes.
7. Serve with salad greens and crusty bread.

Variation

Alternative Filling

1 440 g can salmon

3 or 4 shallots, chopped

½ cup long grain rice,
cooked

pepper

½ cup grated tasty cheese

1 egg, beaten

1–2 tomatoes, chopped and
drained

1. Remove skin and bones from salmon and flake.
2. Add shallots, rice, pepper, half the cheese, beaten egg
   and tomatoes.
3. Fill cannelloni tubes and proceed as above. Mix well.

(*Serves 5*)

Beef Macaroni

250 g macaroni

oil

2 onions, chopped

1 small green capsicum,
  chopped

120 g bacon pieces,
  chopped

500 g lean beef mince

1 440 g can tomato soup

1½ cups water

1 beef stock cube

pepper

1. Boil water in a large saucepan then add macaroni gradually.
2. Boil rapidly without the lid for 12 minutes or until tender, then drain.
3. Spray or brush pan with oil, heat and sauté bacon pieces for 2 to 3 minutes.
4. Add onions and capsicum and cook for a further 2 minutes.
5. Add mince and stir constantly until well browned.
6. Add soup, water and crumbled stock cube. Season with pepper.
7. Cover pan and simmer for 20 minutes.
8. Add macaroni and heat through.

(Serves 6)

Stir-Fried Beef with Pasta and Vegetables

250 g spiral pasta

oil

1 onion, finely chopped

2 cloves garlic, crushed

1 carrot, peeled and diced

1 zucchini, quartered and
  sliced

1 small red capsicum,
  diced

500 g lean minced beef

1 440 g can diced
  tomatoes

2 tablespoons tomato
  paste

½ teaspoon dried oregano

ground pepper

2 tablespoons chopped
  fresh parsley

shaved, fresh parmesan
  cheese

fresh herbs

1. Add pasta to a large pan of boiling water and boil uncovered for 12 minutes or until tender. Drain.
2. Brush or spray pan with oil and heat. Add onion, garlic, carrot, zucchini and capsicum and cook until tender.
3. Add mince and cook until well browned.
4. Add undrained tomatoes, tomato paste, oregano and pepper, bring to the boil and then simmer for 5 to 10 minutes to thicken.
5. Stir in pasta and parsley and reheat.
6. Serve garnished with shaved parmesan, fresh herbs and crusty bread.

(Serves 4)

Meat Loaf

1 kg lean minced beef
½ cup fine dry
   breadcrumbs
1 cup finely chopped onion
2 tablespoons chopped
   parsley
1 egg
1 tablespoon
   Worcestershire sauce
½ 440 g can tomato soup
1 or 2 tomatoes, skinned
   and sliced
½ cup grated cheese

1. Combine all ingredients, except tomatoes and cheese. Mix thoroughly.
2. Grease a shallow baking pan. Shape mixture into a loaf shape taking care to do this firmly so it will retain its shape. Place in baking pan.
3. Bake in a moderate oven for 1 hour.
4. Remove and top with sliced tomato and grated cheese.
5. Bake for a further 15 minutes.
6. Serve hot or cold.

Note: 1. If serving hot make a brown gravy using a packet of sauce mix.
2. Can be made by cooking individual serves in greased muffin tins. Reduce cooking time to 15 to 20 minutes.

(Serves 8)

Chilli Con Carne (Mexico)

oil
1 onion, diced
2 cloves garlic, crushed
1 green capsicum, diced
500 g lean minced beef
1 410 g can peeled and
   chopped tomatoes
¼ cup tomato paste
1 410 g can red kidney
   beans, drained
½ teaspoon dried oregano
1 teaspoon cumin
1 teaspoon paprika
chilli powder to taste

1. Brush or spray pan with oil, heat and sauté onion and garlic for 1 minute.
2. Add capsicum and mince and cook until mince is browned.
3. Add tomatoes, tomato paste, beans, oregano, cumin, paprika and chilli.
4. Cover and simmer for 20 to 30 minutes, stirring occasionally.
5. Serve with crusty bread or rice and tossed salad.

(Serves 4–6)

Crispy Mexican Casserole

oil

**1 small onion, finely
chopped**

500 g lean minced beef

1 200 g can diced tomatoes

**1 200 g can red kidney
beans**

¼ teaspoon cumin

1 teaspoon paprika

2 tablespoons taco sauce

**4 medium potatoes, cooked
and sliced**

½ cup grated cheese

1 50 g packet corn chips

1. Brush or spray pan with oil, heat and cook onion until
   transparent.
2. Add mince and cook for 5 minutes.
3. Add tomatoes, kidney beans, cumin, paprika and taco
   sauce and mix well.
4. Simmer until a thick consistency.
5. Layer ⅓ of the potatoes on the base of a greased
   oven-proof dish, spoon ½ of the mince on top. Top with
   next ⅓ of the potatoes and add the remainder of the
   mince.
6. Top with the remaining potatoes, cover with corn chips,
   sprinkle with cheese and bake in a moderate oven until
   cheese is golden brown.

(Serves 4–6)

Beef Nachos

oil

**1 small onion, finely
chopped**

500 g lean minced beef

**1 200 g can red kidney
beans**

**2 teaspoons paprika or
taco seasoning mix**

1 tablespoon tomato paste

1 200 g packet corn chips

**1 avocado, mashed with a
little lemon juice**

100 g light sour cream

**1 tablespoon fresh chives,
chopped**

1. Brush or spray pan with oil, heat and cook onion until
   transparent.
2. Add mince and cook until colour changes.
3. Add beans, paprika and tomato paste and stir until well
   combined.
4. To serve, arrange corn chips around the edge of an
   ovenproof serving plate and heat in moderate oven for
   5 minutes or in microwave on HIGH for 1 minute.
5. Spoon mince mixture into the centre and top with
   avocado, sour cream and chives.

(Serves 6)

Beef Burrito Bake

oil

1 onion, diced

500 g lean minced beef

2 cloves garlic, crushed

½ cup celery, diced

½ cup carrot, diced

½ cup zucchini, diced

3 teaspoons taco seasoning mix

½ cup tomato paste

1 220 g can diced tomatoes

¼ to ½ cup water

8 flour tortillas

1 200 g jar taco sauce

½ cup grated cheese

1. Brush or spray pan with oil, heat, cook onion until transparent.
2. Add mince and brown.
3. Add garlic, celery, carrot and zucchini, stir and continue to cook for 2 to 3 minutes.
4. Add taco seasoning, tomato paste, tomatoes and water and stir to combine. This mixture should be of a thick spreading consistency. Remove from heat.
5. Divide the mince mixture between the 8 tortillas.
6. Roll into parcel shapes and place seamside down in large greased baking dish.
7. Pour taco sauce over the parcels.
8. Sprinkle with cheese and bake in a moderate oven for 20 minutes.
9. Serve with a crispy green salad.

(Serves 4–6)

Macaroni Pie

1¼ cups macaroni

6–8 sheets filo pastry

oil

1 onion, finely chopped

500 g lean minced beef

1 carrot, grated

1 zucchini, chopped

1 teaspoon beef stock powder

1 200 g can diced tomatoes

1 tablespoon chopped fresh parsley

¼ cup dry breadcrumbs

¼ cup grated cheese

Sauce

2 tablespoons margarine

2 tablespoons flour

1 cup milk

1. Bring a large saucepan of water to the boil, add macaroni and cook uncovered for 12 minutes or until tender. Drain.
2. Line a greased, 23 cm ovenproof dish with the filo-pastry sheets.
3. Brush or spray a large saucepan with oil, heat and add onion, mince, carrot and zucchini and cook until meat is browned.
4. Add stock powder and tomatoes and cook until consistency is thick. Remove from heat.
5. In another saucepan, melt margarine, add flour and cook for 1 minute.
6. Remove from heat and add milk slowly, stirring constantly.
7. Return to heat and cook, stirring constantly until sauce boils and thickens.
8. Remove from heat and stir in parsley and macaroni.
9. Place mince mixture into pie shell and spread evenly.
10. Spread macaroni mixture over the mince mixture, sprinkle with breadcrumbs and cheese.
11. Bake in a moderate oven for 15 to 20 minutes until golden brown.

Note: For a quicker result, use 1 packet of white sauce to replace margarine, flour and milk. Make up sufficient packet mix to make 1 cup of sauce.

(Serves 4–6)

Boiled Corned Beef

rolled brisket or silverside
cold water
a bunch of herbs
few peppercorns
bay leaf

1. Wash beef, weigh and place in a large saucepan or boiler.
2. Cover with cold water. Add herbs.
3. Bring slowly to boiling point, remove any scum, reduce heat and simmer.
4. Allow at least 30 minutes for each ½ kilogram and 30 minutes extra.
5. Serve hot with parsley or onion sauce.
6. If required cold allow to stand in the water until cold.
7. Carrots and turnips may be cooked in the water with the meat. Add these about 1 hour before serving.

Veal Scallopini (Italy)

4 veal steaks
1 tablespoon oil
1 small onion, chopped
1 clove garlic, crushed
125 g mushrooms, sliced
¼ cup dry sherry
2 teaspoons flour
½ cup beef stock
freshly ground pepper

1. Pound steaks out thinly.
2. Heat oil in pan, add veal and cook quickly for 3 to 4 minutes, turning once. Remove from pan.
3. Add onion, garlic and mushrooms and cook for 1 to 2 minutes.
4. Add sherry and bring to boil and simmer uncovered for about 30 seconds. Remove from heat.
5. Blend flour with a little of the beef stock and add to pan gradually with the remainder of the stock. Mix well.
6. Return to heat and stir sauce until it boils and thickens.
7. Return steaks to pan, season with pepper and reheat.
8. Serve with pasta and crusty bread.

(Serves 4)

Veal Cordon Bleu (France)

8 medium veal steaks
4 slices ham
4 thin slices Swiss cheese
flour for rolling
1 egg
2 tablespoons milk
pepper
1 cup dry breadcrumbs
oil for frying

1. Flatten veal steaks between two sheets of plastic wrap by beating with the side of a meat mallet.
2. Pair steaks so that each piece is of a similar size.
3. Place a slice of ham and cheese between each pair, keeping ham and cheese enclosed. Beat edges to seal.
4. Coat veal well with seasoned flour, dip in beaten egg and milk then coat with breadcrumbs.
5. Cover with plastic wrap and allow to stand in refrigerator for 30 minutes before frying.
6. Shallow fry in hot oil over moderate heat until a light golden brown.
7. Turn and brown the other side.
8. Drain on absorbent paper and serve garnished with lemon and parsley.

(Serves 4)

Saltimbocca (Italy)

500 g veal steak, cut thinly
125 g ham, cut thinly
(prosciutto if possible)
½ teaspoon dried sage or
8 sage leaves
¼ cup white wine
¼ cup beef stock or water
black pepper

1. Cut veal into eight pieces. Place between two sheets of plastic wrap and flatten with the side of a meat mallet.
2. Season with pepper and cover each with a slice of ham and a pinch of sage or a little chopped fresh sage.
3. Roll up and pin with toothpicks.
4. Spray or brush pan with oil, heat and fry veal rolls gently on all sides until cooked, about 10 minutes.
5. Remove rolls from pan and place on a plate. Keep warm.
6. Add wine and stock to the pan and stir to dissolve pan juices. Add pepper to taste. Bring to the boil and simmer to reduce the sauce.
7. Return rolls to the pan and cook for a few minutes longer.
8. Serve with mashed potatoes and peas.

(Serves 4)

Veal Parmigiana (Italy)

50 g dry breadcrumbs

3 tablespoons parmesan cheese

ground pepper

4 thin veal steaks

flour

1 egg, beaten

2 tablespoons oil

1 quantity tomato sauce (recipe below)

50 g mozzarella cheese, thinly sliced

1. Mix breadcrumbs, parmesan cheese and pepper.
2. Toss veal in flour, dip in beaten egg, then breadcrumb mixture.
3. Refrigerate for 15 to 20 minutes.
4. Heat oil in pan and cook steaks until tender and golden brown on both sides.
5. Place steaks in a greased ovenproof dish, pour over tomato sauce and top with mozzarella cheese.
6. Bake in a moderate oven, uncovered for 10 to 15 minutes or until cheese melts and browns.
7. Serve immediately with crusty bread and salad.

Tomato Sauce

1 onion, finely chopped

1 clove garlic, crushed

1 stick celery, finely chopped

1 red capsicum, finely chopped

500 g ripe tomatoes, chopped roughly *or* 1 × 420 g can chopped tomatoes and juice

2 teaspoons fresh chopped basil

1 tablespoon fresh chopped parsley

1 teaspoon sugar

1 tablespoon tomato paste

1 cup water

1 chicken stock cube

freshly ground pepper

1. Brush or spray pan with oil, heat and sauté onion until transparent.
2. Add garlic, celery and capsicum and cook until tender.
3. Add remaining ingredients, cover, reduce heat and simmer gently for 45 minutes.
4. Remove lid, increase heat and boil until sauce is reduced to a thick, spreading consistency.

Variation

This sauce can be used as a topping for any pasta or in lasagna and cannelloni dishes.

(Serves 4)

Osso Buco (Italy)

1 kg knuckle of veal or veal shins cut into pieces

flour for rolling

oil

2 onions, sliced

2 carrots, sliced

1 stick celery, diced

2–3 tomatoes, skinned and chopped

sprigs of herbs

pepper

1 clove garlic, crushed

strips of peel and juice of ½ lemon

1 cup dry white wine

1 tablespoon tomato puree

1 cup water

1 tablespoon parsley

1. Roll meat pieces in flour.
2. Brush or spray pan with oil, heat and fry onions until softened.
3. Add meat, carrots, celery, tomatoes, herbs, seasoning and garlic.
4. Toss with the onions for 3 to 4 minutes over moderate heat.
5. Stir in lemon juice and peel, wine, tomato puree and water.
6. Cover with a close-fitting lid and simmer for 1½ hours or until tender. Add more water if necessary.
7. Lift meat onto a serving dish.
8. Remove herbs and rind and purée sauce in a food processor.
9. Pour sauce over meat and sprinkle with chopped parsley.
10. Serve with boiled rice.

Note: Cooking may be done in a covered casserole in the oven.

(Serves 6)

Wiener Schnitzel (Austria)

4 slices lean veal steak

½ cup flour

2 pinches pepper

1 egg

1¼ cups dry breadcrumbs

a little oil

2 lemons

1. Trim steaks and then place between several layers of plastic wrap. Pound with a mallet or rolling pin. Continue pounding until steaks are about 3 mm thick. This breaks up the fibres and makes the meat tender.
2. If time permits place steaks on a flat dish and sprinkle with lemon juice. Cover and allow to stand in the refrigerator for 1 hour, turning frequently.
3. Roll steaks in seasoned flour, dip in beaten egg then toss in breadcrumbs. Refrigerate 20 to 30 minutes to set crumbs.
4. Heat oil in frying pan, add meat and cook for 1½ minutes on each side.
5. Drain on absorbent paper.
6. Serve at once with lemon slices, green salad and boiled potatoes.

(Serves 4)

Boiled Rice (Long Grain White)

1 cup rice
8 cups water

1. Boil water in a large saucepan.
2. Add rice and boil rapidly without the lid for 12 minutes.
3. Drain in a colander and wash with hot running water.
4. Return to saucepan to reheat if necessary.
5. Serve with curry.

Boiled Rice (Long Grain Brown)

Cook as above but boil rapidly for 30 to 40 minutes.

✴ Rice

1 cup rice
1½ cups boiling water

Place rice in a large, shallow dish and add water. Cook uncovered on HIGH for 12 to 14 minutes, stirring occasionally. Allow to stand for 5 minutes.

Absorption Method

1 cup rice
2 cups cold water

1. Place ingredients in a saucepan with a tight-fitting lid.
2. Bring to boiling point, stirring occasionally.
3. Cover and simmer for approximately 20 to 25 minutes for white rice and 40 to 45 minutes for brown rice or until liquid has been absorbed and rice is tender.

Note: Rice may be cooked for a longer or shorter time according to the softness required.

Quick Risotto

oil

1 onion, diced

1 clove garlic, crushed

2 cups rice, arborio or
short-grain rice

1 cup vegetables (e.g.
diced capsicum, sliced
zucchini, sliced celery,
peas)

4 cups chicken stock

ground pepper

1–2 tablespoons parmesan
cheese, grated

1. Brush or spray pan with oil, heat and sauté onion and
garlic until onion is transparent.
2. Add rice and vegetables and stir to mix.
3. Add stock and stir well.
4. Bring to boil and simmer gently for 15 to 20 minutes or
until rice is tender, stirring occasionally.
5. Season with pepper and parmesan cheese and combine
well.
6. Serve garnished with fresh coriander or as an
accompaniment to chicken or fish.

(Serves 6)

Traditional Risotto (Italy)

1 to 2 tablespoons butter or
oil

2 rashers bacon, chopped

1 onion, finely chopped

1½ cups arborio or
short-grain rice

900 mL–1 litre beef stock

freshly ground pepper

freshly grated parmesan
cheese

1. Heat butter in a large saucepan and add bacon and onion
and sauté until soft and lightly golden.
2. Add rice and cook stirring constantly for 1 to 2 minutes.
3. Stir in 150 mL stock.
4. Continue to cook, adding stock as needed and stirring
from time to time until rice is cooked — approximately
20 to 25 minutes. When rice is done, all stock in the pan
should have been absorbed by the rice.
5. Season with pepper and serve with parmesan cheese.

Variation

Chicken stock can be used instead of beef stock. White wine can be substituted for some
of the stock. Diced cooked chicken or prawns can be added when rice is cooked.

(Serves 4–6)

Vegetable Rice Pie

Base

½ **teaspoon saffron or**
   turmeric

1 cup rice, short-grain

1 egg

Filling

1 small eggplant

oil

1 clove garlic, crushed

1 onion, chopped

2 medium sized zucchinis,
   sliced

5 large mushrooms, sliced

1 small red capsicum,
   diced

15 g margarine

2 tablespoons flour

1 cup milk

½ **teaspoon oregano**

pepper

125 g feta cheese,
   crumbled

3 eggs

50 g mozzarella cheese,
   grated

paprika

Base

1. Put saffron in large saucepan of boiling water.
2. Add rice, mix well and cook for 12 minutes or until rice is tender.
3. Drain well.
4. Add lightly beaten egg and mix well.
5. Press mixture over base and sides of a greased, 23 cm pie plate.

Filling

6. Cut eggplant into 2.5 cm cubes, sprinkle with salt, leave to stand for 30 minutes and rinse under cold water. Drain well.
7. Brush or spray pan with oil, heat, add garlic and onion and sauté until onion is golden brown.
8. Add zucchini, eggplant, mushrooms and capsicum and cook, stirring until vegetables are tender.
9. Remove vegetables from pan.
10. Melt margarine in pan, add flour and cook for 1 minute.
11. Gradually add milk and stir until sauce boils and thickens.
12. Add oregano, pepper and feta cheese and stir until cheese has melted.
13. Add vegetables, mix well and remove from heat and cool slightly.
14. Add lightly beaten eggs and mix well.
15. Put mixture into prepared rice base and sprinkle with mozzarella and paprika.
16. Bake in a moderate oven for 30 minutes or until pie is set and cheese is golden brown.

(Serves 4)

Fried Rice (China)

1 cup long grain rice
2 tablespoons oil
1–2 eggs
4 bacon rashers, diced
1 large onion, diced
2 or more shallots, sliced
**left over meat, ham or
prawns**
**½ green capsicum,
chopped**
½ stalk celery, chopped
**1 tablespoon soy sauce
(optional)**

1. Cook rice in boiling water for 12 minutes.
2. Drain and allow to cool and dry. Only cold, dry rice will fry well, so this step is best done the previous night.
3. Heat a little oil in a deep pan.
4. Add beaten eggs and fry until set.
5. Remove from pan and chop up.
6. Fry bacon lightly in the pan, with onion, until lightly browned.
7. Add extra oil if needed, then rice and fry quickly to coat each grain with oil.
8. Add prawns and ham and fry for a few minutes.
9. Add shallots, celery, capsicum and cooked eggs.
10. Heat thoroughly and add soy sauce.
11. Serve alone or with curries, steak or fish.

(Serves 4)

Bean Curry

1 tablespoon oil
1 onion, chopped
2 cloves garlic, crushed
**1 tablespoon fresh ginger,
grated**
1 teaspoon cumin
**2 teaspoons ground
coriander**
**¼ teaspoon ground
cinnamon**
**2 small hot chillies,
chopped**
1 tablespoon plain flour
2½ cups water
**4 tomatoes, peeled and
chopped**
1 415 g can kidney beans
**1 tablespoon lemon or lime
juice**
ground pepper

1. Heat oil in pan, cook onion and garlic gently until onion is transparent.
2. Add ginger, cumin, coriander, cinnamon and chillies and cook for 2 to 3 minutes.
3. Stir in flour and cook for 1 minute. Remove from heat and gradually add water and tomatoes, stirring continuously.
4. Add drained beans, lemon juice and pepper and simmer for 10 minutes.
5. Serve with a tossed salad, sambals and brown rice.

(Serves 4)

Bean and Potato Pie

Topping

1 kg potatoes, peeled and cubed

1 cup grated cheese

milk

Filling

300 g can kidney beans

2 tablespoons margarine

2 onions, diced

1 red or green capsicum, diced

3 tablespoons flour

1 teaspoon vegetable stock powder

1 tablespoon fresh basil, chopped

1 teaspoon dried oregano

1 teaspoon paprika

2 tablespoons fresh parsley, chopped

1 teaspoon soy sauce

bean liquid from can plus sufficient water to make 1½ cups

2 tablespoons tomato paste

1. Drain beans and reserve liquid.
2. Cook potatoes in boiling water until tender.
3. Drain and mash potatoes and add half of the grated cheese and sufficient milk to get a creamy consistency.
4. Melt margarine in pan, heat, add onions and cook until tender.
5. Add capsicum and flour and stir for 1 minute over moderate heat.
6. Take off the heat and add stock powder, basil, oregano, paprika, parsley and soy sauce and mix well.
7. Gradually add water and tomato paste and return to heat and bring to boil, stirring constantly.
8. Add beans and combine well.
9. Place bean mixture into a greased pie dish, cover with mashed potato and sprinkle remaining cheese over the top.
10. Bake in a moderate oven for 15 to 20 minutes or until top is well browned.
11. Serve with green vegetables.

(*Serves 4–6*)

Chilli Bean Nachos

oil

1 onion, finely chopped

1 clove garlic, crushed

1 cup finely diced vegetables (carrots, celery, capsicum, zucchini)

1 300 g can kidney beans

½–1 teaspoon chilli powder

1 400 g can tomatoes, chopped

2 tablespoons tomato puree

½ cup red wine or water

pepper

200 g corn chips

1 cup grated cheese

2 tablespoons fresh parsley, chopped

1. Brush or spray pan with oil, heat and cook onion and garlic for 2 to 3 minutes.
2. Add vegetables, beans and chilli powder and cook a further 2 to 3 minutes.
3. Add undrained tomatoes, tomato puree, wine and pepper.
4. Simmer for 15 to 20 minutes until it is a thick consistency.
5. Place corn chips on an ovenproof serving platter, top with the chilli bean mix and sprinkle with cheese.
6. Place under grill for 5 minutes or until cheese has melted.
7. Sprinkle with parsley and serve immediately.

(Serves 6)

Self Crusting Lentil and Tomato Quiche

½ cup brown lentils

1 cup water

1 bay leaf

oil

2 onions, sliced

2 cloves garlic, crushed

1 tablespoon lemon juice

ground pepper

3 eggs

1 cup milk

1 teaspoon fresh basil, chopped

½ teaspoon dried oregano

½ cup self-raising flour

½ cup grated tasty cheese

3 tomatoes, thinly sliced

2 tablespoons grated parmesan cheese

1. Simmer lentils in water with bay leaf for 20 to 30 minutes or until tender. Drain and remove bay leaf.
2. Brush and spray pan with oil, heat and add onions and garlic and cook until onion is transparent.
3. Remove from heat and add lemon juice and pepper.
4. In a large bowl, beat together eggs, milk and herbs and stir in flour and tasty cheese.
5. Combine lentils with onion and add to egg mixture.
6. Pour into a greased pie dish, top with tomato slices and sprinkle with parmesan cheese.
7. Bake in a hot oven for 25 to 30 minutes or until centre is firm when pressed.
8. Serve with salad or cooked vegetables.

(Serves 4–6)

Curried Lentils

250 g lentils
2 cups water
1–2 teaspoons oil
1 large onion, chopped
1 apple, chopped
1 clove garlic, crushed
2 teaspoons curry powder
2 tablespoons sultanas
pepper
1 tablespoon lemon juice
½ cucumber, chopped

1. Soak the lentils in water for several hours, overnight if possible.
2. Cook in the same water until soft.
3. Heat oil in a pan and add onion, apple, garlic, curry to taste and sultanas and fry for about 15 minutes.
4. Add the lentils, pepper and lemon juice to taste.
5. Add the cucumber and serve with boiled rice.

(*Serves 3–4*)

Lentil Burgers

1 cup cooked brown lentils, lightly mashed
1 cup cooked and mashed potato
½ cup grated carrot
½ cup rolled oats
½ cup fresh wholemeal breadcrumbs
1 onion, grated
1 egg, lightly beaten
½ teaspoon cumin
½ teaspoon turmeric
½ teaspoon ground coriander
2 tablespoons fresh parsley, chopped

Coating
3–4 tablespoons dry breadcrumbs, bran or wheat germ

1. Combine all ingredients except coating and mix well.
2. Divide into uniform pieces and make into round, flat patties.
3. Coat with breadcrumbs, bran or wheat germ and press coating on firmly.
4. Brush or spray a baking tray with oil and place patties on tray.
5. Bake in a 220°C oven for 20 minutes, turning once during this time.
6. Serve on a bread roll with salad.

(*Serves 4*)

Lentils with Cheese

1¾ cups lentils

2 cups water

1 bay leaf

½ teaspoon pepper

⅛ teaspoon marjoram

¼ teaspoon sage

¼ teaspoon thyme

3 medium onions, chopped

2 cloves garlic, chopped

500 g tomatoes, chopped

3 medium carrots, sliced

1 stalk celery, sliced

1 green capsicum, chopped

3 tablespoons fresh
parsley, chopped

1 cup grated cheese

1. Rinse the lentils in a colander under running water.
2. Mix lentils with water, bay leaf, pepper, marjoram, sage, thyme, onion, garlic and tomatoes.
3. Pour the mixture into a shallow greased baking dish and cover tightly with aluminium foil.
4. Bake in a moderate oven (190°C) for 30 minutes.
5. Uncover and add carrots and celery. Mix well. Continue to bake until the vegetables are tender, about 40 minutes.
6. Stir in the capsicum and parsley and sprinkle with the grated cheese.
7. Bake uncovered until the cheese melts.

(Serves 6–8)

Spicy Vegetable Couscous

oil

1 onion, diced

2 cloves garlic, crushed

1 tablespoon curry paste,
red or green

1 teaspoon orange rind,
finely grated

1 capsicum, diced

1 zucchini, cubed

1 carrot, diced

¼ cup sultanas

1½ cups couscous

3 cups water

1 large tomato, chopped

1 tablespoon fresh
coriander, chopped

1 tablespoon fresh parsley,
chopped

1. Brush or spray pan with oil, heat and sauté onion, garlic and curry paste.
2. Add rind, capsicum, zucchini and carrot and continue to cook for 2 to 3 minutes.
3. Add sultanas, couscous and water, bring to boil and remove from heat. Stand for 5 minutes.
4. Add tomato, coriander and parsley and warm through.
5. Serve with crusty bread.

(Serves 4)

Polenta and Herb Cakes with Tomatoes

750 mL chicken stock

1⅛ cups polenta

4 tablespoons fresh herbs, chopped

pepper

2 large tomatoes, sliced

1 tablespoon grated parmesan cheese

1. Place stock in a large saucepan and bring to boil. Remove from heat and gradually stir in polenta.
2. Return to moderate heat and cook for about 5 minutes, stirring constantly until the mixture begins to come away from the side of the pan.
3. Stir in herbs and pepper, spoon into a greased shallow tin (23 × 33 cm), spread evenly and leave to cool.
4. Cut the cooled polenta into 5 cm squares and arrange squares and tomato slices, alternately and overlapping in a greased, shallow, ovenproof dish.
5. Sprinkle with parmesan cheese and bake in a 200°C oven for 20 minutes or until golden brown.
6. Serve garnished with fresh herbs and a crisp green salad.

(Serves 4)

Falafel (Egypt)

1 450 g can chickpeas, drained and rinsed

1 onion, finely diced

2 slices bread, cubed

2 cloves garlic, crushed

1 tablespoon chopped fresh parsley

½ teaspoon cumin

pepper

pinch chilli powder

1 egg

¾ cup dry breadcrumbs

1 tablespoon oil

4 pita bread rounds, warmed

salad vegetables

1. Place chickpeas, onion, bread, garlic, parsley, cumin, pepper, chilli powder and egg in a food processor and process until smooth.
2. Shape mixture into 8 balls, flatten slightly and coat in breadcrumbs.
3. Shallow fry in hot oil until golden. Drain.
4. Cut each pita bread round in half and fill each half with falafel and salad vegetables and drizzle with yoghurt or tahini.

(Serves 4)

Gado Gado (Indonesia)

250 g cauliflower, chopped

250 g broccoli, chopped

oil

1 onion, sliced

1 capsicum, sliced

150 g green beans, cut into 4 to 5 cm lengths

¼ cabbage, shredded

1 310 g can chickpeas, drained and rinsed

1 cup bean sprouts

1 425 mL can coconut milk

¾ cup crunchy peanut butter

2 cloves garlic, crushed

2 tablespoons soy sauce

2 teaspoons lemon juice

⅛ to ¼ teaspoon chilli powder

1. Cook cauliflower and broccoli until just tender. Drain.
2. Brush or spray pan with oil, heat and add onion, capsicum and beans and cook until onion is soft.
3. Add cabbage and chickpeas and cook until cabbage is wilted.
4. Add cauliflower, broccoli and sprouts and cook until heated through. Remove and place in serving dish.
5. Add coconut milk, peanut butter, garlic, soy sauce, lemon juice and chilli powder to pan and stir over heat until sauce boils.
6. Pour over vegetables and serve.

(Serves 4)

Pesto Pasta

500 g fettucine

2 cups fresh basil leaves, washed

2 tablespoons pine nuts

2 cloves garlic, crushed

ground pepper

¼ cup olive oil

3 tablespoons grated parmesan cheese

1. Cook fettucine in a large pan of boiling water for 10 to 12 minutes or until tender. Drain.
2. Place basil, pine nuts, garlic and pepper in a food processor and process until mixture is smooth.
3. With processor still running, add oil in a thin stream and process a further few seconds. Stir in cheese.
4. Pour pesto sauce over fettucine and toss to combine well together.
5. Serve garnished with extra parmesan cheese.

(Serves 4)

Vegetable Lasagna

Tomato Sauce

oil

1 onion, chopped

250 g mushrooms, sliced

1 small green capsicum, chopped

1 tablespoon freshly chopped basil

½ teaspoon dried oregano

400 g can tomatoes, chopped

½ cup tomato paste

2 tomatoes, chopped

½ teaspoon sugar

200 g instant lasagna sheets

White Wine Sauce

30 g margarine

2 tablespoons plain flour

¾ cup milk

2 tablespoons white wine

½ cup grated tasty cheese

Spinach Layer

12 spinach leaves, chopped

1 clove garlic, crushed

2 shallots, chopped

Cheese Layer

400 g ricotta cheese

¼ cup parmesan cheese

2 eggs

Tomato Sauce

1. Brush or spray pan with oil, heat and add onion, mushrooms and capsicum and cook until onion is transparent.
2. Add herbs, undrained tomatoes, tomato paste, tomatoes and sugar and bring to boil. Reduce heat and simmer uncovered for 30 minutes, stirring occasionally.

White Wine Sauce

1. Melt margarine in a saucepan, stir in flour and cook for 1 minute, stirring.
2. Off heat, add milk and wine gradually to make a smooth liquid and stir over heat until sauce boils and thickens.
3. Add cheese and stir until melted.

Spinach Layer

Brush or spray pan with oil, add garlic, spinach and shallots and stir-fry gently until spinach is wilted. Drain.

Cheese Layer

Beat cheeses and eggs together until blended.

To Assemble

1. Pour half the tomato sauce into a greased, oven-proof dish (16 × 26 cm) and place a single layer of lasagna sheets over the tomato sauce.
2. Top with the spinach layer and then the cheese layer.
3. Add a second layer of lasagna sheets and then the remaining tomato sauce and finish with a layer of lasagna sheets.
4. Pour the white sauce over the tomato sauce and bake in a moderate oven until well browned. Stand 10 minutes before cutting.
5. Serve with salad and crusty bread.

(*Serves 6*)

Macaroni Cheese

1 cup macaroni

2 teaspoons butter or
  margarine

2 teaspoons flour

1 teaspoon dry mustard

300 mL milk

cayenne pepper

1 cup grated cheese

2 tablespoons dry
  breadcrumbs

extra grated cheese

1. Place macaroni in boiling water and boil for 12 minutes or until tender. Drain.
2. Melt butter in pan, add flour and mustard. Mix to a smooth paste and cook for 1 minute.
3. Remove from heat and gradually add milk, stirring continuously. Add cayenne pepper and mix well.
4. Place on heat, bring to boil and simmer for 1 minute, stirring continuously. Remove from heat.
5. Add the grated cheese and macaroni and mix well.
6. Pour into a pie dish. Sprinkle top with dry breadcrumbs and extra grated cheese.
7. Heat thoroughly in a moderate oven just before serving.

(*Serves 3–4*)

Curried Eggs

4 eggs

2 tablespoons margarine

1 onion

1 apple

2 teaspoons curry powder

2 teaspoons sugar

2 tablespoons flour

1 cup milk

1 cup water

a little lemon juice

1. Hard boil the eggs, cool and shell.
2. Melt margarine in a pan. Add diced onion and apple and fry lightly until golden in colour.
3. Add the curry powder, sugar and flour.
4. Gradually add milk and water stirring all the time.
5. Cook gently with lid on until apple and onion are soft.
6. Cut eggs into halves or quarters and add to sauce.
7. Heat gently and lastly add a little lemon juice.
8. Serve with boiled rice.

Non Vegetarian Variation

Cooked and sliced sausages or chicken can be substituted for eggs.

(*Serves 2–3*)

Cheesy Pumpkin Quiche

1 tablespoon margarine

16 plain savoury biscuits, crushed, e.g. Jatz

Filling

1 onion, finely chopped

1 cup cooked, mashed pumpkin, cooled slightly

4 eggs, lightly beaten

½ cup evaporated milk

80 g tasty cheese, grated

1 tablespoon fresh chives, chopped

1. Melt margarine, add to biscuit crumbs and mix well.
2. Press crumb mixture over the base of a 20 cm quiche dish.
3. Combine all filling ingredients in a bowl and pour carefully into the quiche dish.
4. Bake in a moderate oven for 30 to 35 minutes or until set.
5. Serve with a tossed salad.

(Serves 4)

Self-Crusting Zucchini Quiche

200 g zucchini, grated

1 medium onion, finely chopped

½ cup grated tasty cheddar cheese

½ cup self-raising flour

¼ cup oil

3 medium eggs

ground pepper

1. Combine zucchini, onion, cheese, flour, oil, lightly beaten eggs and pepper.
2. Pour into a greased, 23 cm pie dish and bake in a moderate oven for 25 to 30 minutes or until set.
3. Serve hot or cold with salad.

Variation

Other vegetables can be added or substituted, e.g. grated carrot, corn niblets, chopped capsicum.

(Serves 4)

Spinach and Cheese Flan

8 sheets filo pastry

500 g cottage cheese

150 mL sour cream

3 eggs

oil

1 onion, diced

8 spinach leaves, chopped

2 tablespoons plain flour

2 tomatoes, sliced

¼ cup parmesan cheese

1 teaspoon dried basil or
   1 tablespoon chopped
   fresh basil

1. Layer sheets of pastry into a 25 cm flan tin, brushing between each sheet with a little oil. Press flat and trim edge to about 1.5 cm higher than side of tin.
2. Place cottage cheese, sour cream and eggs into food processor and process until smooth.
3. Brush or spray pan with oil, heat and cook onion until transparent.
4. Add spinach, cook until just wilted and then remove pan from heat.
5. Add flour and cottage cheese mixture and pour into pastry case.
6. Place tomato slices around the edge and sprinkle with combined parmesan cheese and basil.
7. Bake in a hot oven for 15 minutes then reduce to moderate and cook a further 20 to 30 minutes until set.

(Serves 4)

Tofu and Vegetable Kebabs

1 small red chilli, de-seeded
   and finely chopped

⅓ cup olive oil

1 teaspoon grated lemon
   rind

20 mL lemon juice

1 teaspoon chopped fresh
   oregano

1 teaspoon chopped fresh
   dill

1 clove garlic, crushed

2 zucchinis, cut into 1 cm
   thick slices

300 g firm tofu, drained and
   cubed

12 cherry tomatoes

1 large red onion, cut into
   wedges

6 yellow squashes, halved

12 skewers, pre-soaked

1. Combine chilli, oil, rind, juice, herbs and garlic and mix well.
2. Thread zucchini, tofu, tomato, onion and squash onto pre-soaked skewers.
3. Grill the kebabs, brushing with the oil mixture until browned on both sides and vegetables are just tender, turning only once as the tofu breaks easily.
4. Serve with rice drizzled with any remaining oil mixture.

(Serves 4)

Peanut Tofu and Noodles

400 g firm tofu, cut into cubes

oil

1 clove garlic, crushed

½ teaspoon minced chilli

2 cups vegetable stock

80 g crunchy peanut butter

1 tablespoon soy sauce

1 packet Hokkien noodles

1. Place tofu onto greased baking tray and brush or spray with oil. Bake in a moderate oven for 20 minutes or until golden brown.
2. In a large saucepan, combine garlic, chilli, stock, peanut butter and soy sauce. Bring to the boil, lower heat and simmer for 5 minutes.
3. Prepare noodles as per packet directions and add to the sauce and stir.
4. Place noodles and sauce on plates, and top with baked tofu.

(Serves 4)

Tofu and Thai Vegetables

600 g firm tofu, cut into cubes

1 teaspoon peanut oil

2 teaspoons red curry paste

1 can low-fat coconut milk

3 teaspoons fish sauce (optional)

3 teaspoons brown sugar

2 tablespoons fresh coriander, chopped

2 carrots, cut into strips

2 cups broccoli pieces

1 cup green beans, chopped

2 yellow zucchini, sliced thickly

12 fresh baby corn

½ cup snow peas

1 tablespoon basil, chopped

1. Place tofu onto greased tray, brush or spray with oil and bake in a moderate oven for 20 minutes or until golden brown.
2. Heat oil in a large non-stick pan, add curry paste and stir over a low heat for 2 minutes. Add coconut milk, fish sauce, brown sugar and half of the coriander. Bring to boil, cover and simmer for 10 minutes.
3. Microwave or steam carrots, broccoli, beans and zucchini until tender.
4. Add the cooked vegetables to the curry sauce along with corn, snow peas and remaining herbs. Simmer for 2 minutes.
5. Place tofu onto plates and top with sauce and vegetables.

(Serves 4–6)

Vegetable Frittata (Italy)

1½ tablespoons oil

4 100 g potatoes, peeled
   and cubed

1 onion, chopped

1 clove garlic, crushed

½ capsicum, chopped

1 cup peas

½ cup corn kernels

2 tomatoes, chopped

¼ cup tomato paste

a few drops Tabasco sauce

1 tablespoon water

1 tablespoon chopped
   fresh parsley

ground pepper

6 eggs, beaten

1. Heat oil in pan, add potatoes and stir fry until brown. Remove from pan.
2. Add onion, garlic and capsicum and cook until onion is transparent.
3. Add peas, corn, tomatoes, tomato paste and Tabasco sauce, stir to combine and cook for 1 minute.
4. Return potato to the pan and add the water, parsley and pepper and continue to cook for a few minutes.
5. Place mixture into a greased, shallow, ovenproof dish, pour the beaten eggs over and bake in a moderate oven until set.
6. Serve immediately with a green salad.

(Serves 6)

Thai Vegetable Curry

450 g potato, peeled and
   cubed

350 g pumpkin, peeled and
   cubed

1 large carrot, peeled and
   sliced

1 large onion, chopped

2 cloves garlic, crushed

2 to 4 teaspoons Thai red
   curry paste

1 415 g can coconut cream

1 cup green beans, sliced
   in 4–5 cm lengths

2 zucchinis, sliced

½ cup peas

1 tablespoon chopped
   fresh basil

1 teaspoon fish sauce

1. Boil potatoes for 10 minutes, add pumpkin and carrot and continue to cook for 5 minutes.
2. Brush or spray another large saucepan with oil, heat and add onion and garlic and cook until onion is transparent. Add curry paste and fry for 1 minute.
3. Add coconut cream and bring to the boil, stirring constantly.
4. Add potato, pumpkin, carrot, beans, zucchini and peas and simmer uncovered until vegetables are tender.
5. Add fish sauce and basil, stir through and serve over rice.

(Serves 4)

Pad Thai

500 g thick fresh rice noodles
¼ cup sugar
⅓ cup chilli sauce
1 tablespoon soy sauce
¼ cup fish sauce
1 tablespoon tomato sauce
oil
2 eggs, lightly beaten
1 small onion, thinly sliced
5 shallots, thinly sliced
2 cloves garlic, crushed
½ cup chopped roasted peanuts
2 cups bean sprouts
1 tablespoon fresh, chopped coriander leaves

1. Place noodles in ovenproof bowl, cover with hot water and stand for 30 seconds. Gently separate noodles and drain well.
2. Combine sugar and sauces.
3. Spray or brush pan with oil, heat and add egg and swirl pan to make a thin omelette. Cook until set, remove from pan, roll up and cut into thin strips.
4. Brush or spray pan with oil if required, heat and add onion, shallots and garlic and cook until onion is transparent.
5. Add noodles, sauce mixture, peanuts, sprouts, coriander and egg and stir-fry gently until heated through.
6. Serve garnished with peanuts, coriander and lemon wedges.

Variation

Cubed firm tofu or prawns can be added in step five.

(Serves 4)

Vegetable Rissoles

2 medium potatoes, grated and well drained with paper towels
1 large carrot, grated
1 onion, finely chopped
1 zucchini, grated and drained on paper towel
80 g grated tasty cheese
ground pepper
2 eggs, beaten
½ cup flour
1 tablespoon oil

1. In a large bowl, mix the potato, carrot, onion, zucchini, cheese, pepper, eggs and flour.
2. Divide into uniform pieces and make into round, flat patties.
3. Heat oil in pan and fry until golden brown on both sides.
4. Serve with a green salad.

(Serves 4)

Vegetarian Delight Pasta Sauce

oil

6 shallots, chopped

10 mushrooms, sliced

½ red capsicum, diced

½ green capsicum, diced

2 cloves garlic, crushed

6 small tomatoes, chopped

350 g feta cheese, cubed

ground pepper

**1 tablespoon chopped
fresh parsley**

**500 g cooked pasta, any
variety**

1. Brush or spray pan with oil, heat and cook shallots, mushrooms, capsicum and garlic for 5 minutes.
2. Add tomatoes and cook until tomatoes are soft.
3. Reduce heat and add feta cheese and cook for 1 minute or until feta starts to melt.
4. Add pepper and parsley and mix well.
5. Serve with pasta and crusty bread.

(Serves 4)

Vegetable Cheese Pie

1½ cups cooked macaroni

1 onion, diced

**3 tomatoes, skinned and
diced**

2 zucchini, sliced

**1 tablespoon chopped
parsley**

1 cup grated cheese

pepper

Topping

1 cup cooked pumpkin

½ teaspoon margarine

½ cup self-raising flour

1. Arrange macaroni, onion, tomatoes, zucchini, parsley and cheese in a well-greased ovenproof dish.
2. Add pepper, cover and bake in a moderate oven for 40 to 45 minutes.
3. To mashed pumpkin add margarine and flour to make a stiff paste. If mixture is too dry add more milk; if too moist, add more flour.
4. Press out on a floured board and cut out as for scones.
5. Place on top of vegetables.
6. Brush with milk and bake for 15 to 20 minutes.

(Serves 5–6)

Vegetable Slice

3 medium potatoes
5 sheets filo pastry
1–2 tablespoons oil
pepper
**2 eggs, hard boiled and
sliced**
**1 440 g can asparagus
spears, drained**
50 g sliced gouda cheese
**1 tablespoon sesame
seeds**

1. Peel potatoes, slice and cook in water until just tender.
   Drain.
2. Place a sheet of filo pastry on a baking tray and brush
   sparingly with oil. Place a second sheet on top and brush
   again with oil. Repeat until five layers are in place, leaving
   the last sheet unoiled.
3. Arrange potato slices over half the pastry and place egg
   slices on top. Season with pepper.
4. Next arrange asparagus spears in a row close together.
   Top with cheese slices.
5. Fold pastry over the filling and tuck ends under.
6. Brush with a little oil and sprinkle with sesame seeds.
7. Bake in a moderately hot oven (190° to 200°C) for 15 to
   20 minutes or until pastry is golden brown.

(Serves 4)

Caballasas con Queso (Mexico)

(Zucchini with Cheese)
oil
1 onion, chopped
**1 clove garlic, finely
chopped**
**3 tomatoes, skinned and
chopped**
**1 vegetable stock cube,
crumbled**
1 kg zucchini, diced
½ cup corn
**1 small ball mozzarella
cheese, diced**
pepper

1. Brush or spray pan with oil, heat and cook onion, garlic
   and tomatoes for 5 minutes. Add the stock cube.
2. Add the zucchini and corn and simmer gently for
   20 minutes, stirring occasionally.
3. Gradually add diced cheese. As it melts and settles into
   the mixture add more.
4. Cook for about 40 minutes altogether.
5. Serve hot.

(Serves 4)

Asparagus Mornay

1 can asparagus spears
½ quantity mornay sauce
(see Sauces section)
1 tablespoon soft
breadcrumbs
1 tablespoon grated cheese

1. Heat asparagus in its own liquid. Drain well and arrange in a dish.
2. Pour sauce over allowing asparagus to show at each end.
3. Sprinkle with a mixture of crumbs and cheese.
4. Bake in a moderate oven until sauce bubbles and cheese melts.
5. Serve hot as a vegetable accompaniment or as a main dish with a green salad.

(Serves 4)

Variation

Zucchini Mornay

Add 250 g sliced zucchini cooked in boiling water until tender. Proceed as for asparagus mornay.

(Serves 4)

BOILED VEGETABLES

Boiling is a popular method of cooking vegetables as almost all vegetables may be cooked this way.

Overcooking and the use of excess water are the common faults.

Use saucepans with tight-fitting lids so that a minimum of water may be used. Cooking procedures may vary according to the type of vegetable being used.

The water that remains after boiling or steaming vegetables may be used as a vegetable stock.

STEAMED VEGETABLES

Any vegetables suitable for boiling may also be steamed.
1. Wash vegetables and peel, if necessary.
2. Cut into even-sized pieces.
3. Place in a steamer.
4. Stand steamer over a saucepan of boiling water and cook until tender.
5. Lift out and serve hot.
6. Serve with sauce if required.

BAKED VEGETABLES

When baking meat some of the vegetables may be cooked with it. Suitable vegetables are potatoes, pumpkin, parsnips, carrots, sweet potatoes and onions.
1. Prepare vegetables, wash well and cut into even-sized pieces.
2. Dry each piece well.
3. Place oil in baking pan and heat in oven. When hot, add vegetables and baste. Cook for about 1 hour before serving, turning when half the cooking time has expired.
4. Lift out onto absorbent paper to drain.
5. Serve in a hot dish.

Note: Young carrots and sweet potatoes require a shorter cooking time than potatoes and pumpkin. These should be added when 15 minutes have elapsed.

BAKED VEGETABLES — LOW FAT

Quantities of vegetables to suit.

1. Peel potatoes, pumpkin, sweet potato, carrots, onions and cut into wedge sized pieces. Dry well.
2. Brush each piece with oil and place on baking paper on a baking tray and bake in a moderate oven for between 45 minutes and 1 hour or until tender. Brush again with oil as needed.

FROZEN VEGETABLES

1. Place sufficient water in a saucepan.
2. Bring to boiling point.
3. Drop frozen vegetables into water. Do not allow to thaw out before cooking.
4. Cook for the time stated on the packet. Do not overcook.
5. Drain immediately and add flavourings if desired.

COOKING OF VEGETABLES

Beans (Broad)
Shell beans. Drop into boiling water and cook for 10 to 15 minutes until just tender.

Beans (French)
Wash, top and tail and string beans. Slice finely, cut in half or leave whole. Drop beans a few at a time into a saucepan of boiling water and cook rapidly without the lid for 5 to 10 minutes until just tender. Drain and add pepper to flavour if desired.

Bok Choy
Cut bok choy into 5 cm lengths or chop roughly, discarding any old or withered leaves or tips. Steam or stir-fry until just wilted. Serve as is or drizzled with sweet chilli sauce or a little soy sauce.

Broccoli
Break into flowerets, trim stalks and cook in boiling water until tender, about 5 to 7 minutes. Drain and serve.

Brussels Sprouts
Remove ragged outside leaves and some of the stalk. Make a cross on the bottom of each stalk. Cook in a small quantity of water with lid on the saucepan. Drain and serve.

Button Squash
Trim stalks and flower ends. Steam or boil until tender. Drain and serve. They may also be stuffed, sprinkled with cheese and baked.

Cabbage

Remove outside leaves and most of the hard core. Cut into 4 pieces then shred finely with a sharp knife. Cook with a small quantity of water with the lid on the saucepan. Cook for 3 to 5 minutes or until tender, drain and sprinkle with pepper and a little melted margarine if desired.

Carrots

Scrape lightly and cut into slices or strips. Cook in boiling water until tender. Serve with chopped parsley or sesame seeds.

Cauliflower

Divide head into sprigs, removing excess stalks. Cook rapidly in boiling water. Drain and serve, may be served with white, parsley or cheese sauce.

Chokoes

Peel, cut in half, remove seed. Cut into even-sized pieces. Cook in boiling water until tender. Serve with a little melted margarine or white sauce and pepper if desired.

Corn-on-the-Cob

Wash well, strip outer husks. Open inner husks and remove silk. Cook in boiling water for 20 minutes or until tender. Drain and serve.

Onions

Remove outer layer and trim ends. Cook in boiling water until tender. Brown onions will require a longer cooking time than white onions. Serve.

Parsnips

Peel and cut into pieces. Parsnips are most satisfactory when baked with roast meats. They may also be cooked in boiling water, drained and mashed with a little margarine.

Peas

Shell peas. Place sufficient water to cover peas in a saucepan and bring to boiling point. Add a little sugar and 2 or 3 sprigs of mint. Add the peas a handful at a time so water is off the boil for only a short time. Cook for 5 to 7 minutes. Drain and serve.

Potatoes

Peel and wash potatoes and cut into even-sized pieces. If new potatoes leave skin on. Place in a saucepan and barely cover with boiling water. Cook for 15 to 20 minutes. When tender, drain and allow to steam until potatoes are dry. Serve immediately with a little butter or margarine.

Potatoes (Sweet)

Peel and cut into even-sized pieces. They are usually baked with meat but may be boiled and mashed or parboiled and then cooked in a frying pan that has been brushed or sprayed with oil.

Pumpkin

Peel, remove seeds and cut into even-sized pieces. Cover with boiling water and cook until tender. Drain, add a little butter or margarine, pepper and mash well. Pumpkin may also be baked with roast meats.

Spinach/Silverbeet

Remove stalks and wash leaves under a running tap. Chop or shred if desired and place in a heavy pan and cover with a tight-fitting lid. Cook for about 5 to 10 minutes. Shake saucepan frequently. Drain off any liquid remaining, chop finely and serve.

Squash, Marrow

Peel and cut into pieces. Steam or boil in water until tender — 10 to 15 minutes. Drain and serve. The skin may be left on while cooking and removed before serving.

Swede

Peel thickly and cut into small pieces. Place in boiling water and cook for 30 to 45 minutes or until tender depending on the age of the swedes. Drain and mash. Add butter and pepper if desired.

White Turnip

Peel and cut into 2 or 3 pieces. Place in boiling water and cook for 15 minutes or until tender. Drain and serve. White turnips are usually used in casseroles.

Zucchini

Wash and trim ends of zucchini. Leave whole or slice or cube. Boil water. Drop whole unpeeled zucchini into water. Cook for 5 to 10 minutes or until tender. Drain, add a little butter or margarine and toss lightly. Sprinkle with pepper.

MICROWAVING VEGETABLES

Cooking of Fresh Vegetables

Vegetables should be covered and cooked on HIGH power for best results. Time will depend on whether vegetables are to remain crisp or be well cooked, and the size of individual pieces.

Allow 2 minutes standing time for the more solid vegetables.

The following are approximate times for the more common vegetables. It is always advisable to follow the instructions given for each make of microwave.

Vegetable	Quantity	Procedure	Approximate cooking time in minutes
Asparagus	500 g	Cover with water.	7–10
Beans, sliced	250 g	Cook with ½ cup water.	8–10
Butter beans, sliced	250 g	Cook with ½ cup water.	10–12
Beetroot	4 whole	Cover with water. Stand in water 5 minutes after cooking.	16–20
Broccoli	500 g	Cook with ¼ cup water. Flowerets only.	4–6
Brussels sprouts	250 g	Cook with 2 tablespoons water.	4–5
Cabbage, shredded	500 g	Cook with 1 tablespoon water.	4–5
Carrots, finely sliced	4	Cook with 2 tablespoons water.	4–5
Cauliflower	500 g	Cook flowerets with ¼ cup water.	6–8
Celery	6 stalks	Cook with 1 tablespoon water.	4–6
Corn	2 cobs	Cook with 1 tablespoon water.	4–6
	4 cobs	As above.	8–12
Mushrooms, sliced	250 g	Cook	2–4
Onions	2 (175 g)	Cook, cut in quarters, with ¼ cup water.	4–6
Parsnips	500 g	Cook, cut into wedges, with ¼ cup water.	8–10
Peas	250 g	Cook with ¼ cup water.	3–5
Potatoes	4 (500 g)	Cook, peeled and quartered, with ¼ cup water.	10–12
Pumpkin	500 g	Cook, in uniform pieces with ¼ cup water.	8–10
Snow peas	100 g	Cook with 1 tablespoon water.	3–4
Spinach	250 g	Remove stems, cut leaves into small pieces. Cook with 1 tablespoon water.	4–6
Squash, sliced	250 g	Cook with 2 tablespoons water.	4–5
Tomatoes	2 (300 g)	Cook sliced as is or pierce skin and cook whole.	2–4
Zucchini	500 g	Cut in 2 cm pieces. Cook with 2 tablespoons water.	4–6

PRESSURE COOKING OF VEGETABLES

Prepare vegetables as for other methods of cooking and cut into even-sized pieces. Selected vegetables should have similar cooking times but small differences may be overcome by cutting into smaller or larger pieces. Place ¼ cup hot water into the pressure cooker for greens such as cabbage, peas, beans, celery and spinach. For the more solid vegetables, such as potatoes, beetroot, parsnips and carrots, use ½ cup hot water. Generally it is better to season after cooking.

Avoid overloading the pressure cooker. Vegetables may be cooked with the rack but generally it is used for larger pieces.

Place lid on pressure cooker and cook over a very moderate heat. Time the cooking from the moment the correct pressure is reached, turning the control back to the lowest number. Reduce pressure immediately.

Finish vegetables as for boiling and steaming.

The following are approximate times for the more common vegetables. It is always advisable to follow the instructions given for each make of pressure cooker.

Peas	½–1 minute
Cabbage, sliced	1–1½ minutes
Spinach	
Beans, French	1½–2 minutes
Broccoli	
Cauliflower, sections	
Celery, diced	2–4 minutes
Marrow	
Pumpkin	
Onions	4–6 minutes
Turnips	5–6 minutes
Parsnips	7–8 minutes
Potatoes	9–11 minutes
Beetroot, whole unpeeled	10–15 minutes

Mashed Potatoes

3–4 potatoes
1 teaspoon butter or
  margarine
warm milk

1. Prepare and cook potatoes.
2. Mash well with a potato masher.
3. Add butter and sufficient milk to make potatoes creamy.
4. Beat well with a wooden spoon.
5. Serve immediately.

(Serves 4)

Dry Baked Potatoes

potatoes of even size
pepper
butter or margarine
oil

1. Scrub potatoes well and allow to dry.
2. Grease skins well with cooking oil.
3. Bake in a moderate to hot oven for about 1 hour. Test with a skewer.
4. Cut a cross in the top of each potato and open out a little to allow steam to escape.
5. Sprinkle with pepper and place a little butter or sour cream on top if desired.
6. Serve immediately.

Note: Cooking time may be reduced by threading potatoes on skewers.

Rosemary Roast Potatoes

750 g potatoes (desiree
  give best results)
3 cloves garlic, whole or
  crushed
1 sprig rosemary, leaves
  only
3 tablespoons olive oil
freshly ground pepper

1. Cut the potatoes into bite-size pieces, leaving skin on and place in a lightly greased baking tray.
2. Combine the garlic, oil, rosemary and pepper and drizzle over potatoes.
3. Bake in a moderate oven for 1 to 1½ hours until tender, basting if needed with oil mixture.
4. Serve with grilled meats and a green salad.

(Serves 4–6)

Potato Wedges

6 medium, unpeeled, scrubbed potatoes
4 cloves garlic, crushed
¼ cup olive oil

1. Cut each potato into 8 wedges and place into a large greased baking dish.
2. Combine oil and garlic and brush over wedges and bake in a moderate oven for 1 hour or until tender, turning twice during cooking.
3. Serve immediately.

(Serves 4–6)

Duchesse Potatoes

3–4 potatoes (peeled)
1 egg
a little beaten egg for glaze
½–1 teaspoon butter or margarine (optional)
pepper

1. Boil the potatoes in water, drain and toss over heat for 1 minute to dry them.
2. Mash potatoes well then add butter and beaten egg.
3. Add pepper and beat well.
4. Fill a forcing bag with a large star pipe attached to it.
5. Lightly grease a baking tray and pipe rosettes of mixture in rows on the tray (about 36 rosettes).
6. Allow to stand until quite cold.
7. Brush lightly with beaten egg.
8. Just before they are required place in a moderately hot oven (190°C) for 15 to 20 minutes.

(Serves 6–8)

Scalloped Potatoes

1 kg potatoes
1 onion, finely chopped
pepper
¼ cup cream
1 cup milk
chopped parsley

1. Peel potatoes, wash and slice thinly.
2. Dry slices carefully.
3. Arrange potatoes in layers in a greased pie dish with a little chopped onion and pepper between the layers.
4. Mix milk and cream and pour over the top.
5. Spray top with a little cooking oil if desired.
6. Bake in a moderate oven for 1½ hours or until potatoes are tender and well browned.
7. Chop parsley finely and sprinkle over the top just before serving.

(Serves 6–8)

✳ Scalloped Potatoes

1 kg potatoes
1 onion
pepper
½ cup cream
¾ cup milk
chopped parsley

1. Peel potatoes, wash and slice thinly.
2. Dry slices carefully.
3. Arrange potatoes in layers in microwave-safe dish with a little chopped onion and pepper between the layers.
4. Mix milk and cream and pour over the top.
5. Cook on MEDIUM for 16 to 18 minutes or until potatoes are tender.
6. Chop parsley finely and sprinkle over the top just before serving.

(Serves 6–8)

Potato Lorraine

500 g potatoes
1 cup grated cheddar cheese
2 eggs
½ cup milk
pinch nutmeg
pepper

1. Boil potatoes in water until cooked. Drain, cool and slice.
2. Sprinkle half of grated cheese on the base of a greased ovenproof dish. Arrange sliced potatoes on top.
3. Beat eggs, milk and nutmeg together and season well with pepper.
4. Pour over the potatoes. Sprinkle with remainder of cheese, and bake in a moderate oven (190°C) for about 30 minutes. Mixture will become bubbly and brown.
5. Serve hot with meats or warm as an accompaniment to salads.

(Serves 4–6)

Potato Chips

potatoes
cooking oil

1. Peel potatoes and cut into 12 mm strips.
2. Place in a bowl and cover with hot water.
3. Allow to stand for 30 minutes then drain and dry thoroughly.
4. Half fill a saucepan with oil and heat.
5. When oil is hot add chips carefully and fry until brown.
6. Drain on absorbent paper.
7. Serve hot.

Crispy Potatoes

500 g even-sized new potatoes

2–3 tablespoons butter or margarine

¾ cup parmesan cheese, grated

1. Scrub potatoes and boil in water until tender. Drain, cool and remove skins.
2. Melt butter in a pan and toss potatoes until they are thoroughly coated.
3. Place the cheese in a plastic bag. Taking a few potatoes at a time shake them in the bag until they are coated with cheese.
4. Place potatoes on a greased tray and bake in a hot oven until golden brown and crisp.

(Serves 4)

Anna Potatoes

3–4 potatoes

2 tablespoons butter or margarine (optional)

pepper

chopped parsley or chives

1. Peel and wash potatoes.
2. Cut into thin slices.
3. Arrange a layer of potato in bottom of a greased pie dish.
4. Sprinkle with pepper and spoon on a little melted butter or spray with a little cooking oil.
5. Repeat layers until all potatoes have been used.
6. Cover with a lid and bake for 45 minutes in a moderate oven.
7. Remove lid and bake for another 15 minutes to crisp the top.
8. Sprinkle a little chopped parsley or chives over the top before serving.

Note: A no fat version can be made by deleting butter and pouring 1 cup of beef, chicken or vegetable stock over potatoes before baking.

(Serves 4)

Cheesy Potatoes with Topping

500 g potatoes
½ cup grated cheese
¼ cup milk
¼ cup sour cream
3–4 shallots
pepper
1 cup fresh white breadcrumbs
1 tablespoon parmesan cheese

1. Prepare potatoes and boil in water until tender. Drain and mash well then add grated cheese and sour cream. Add milk if required to bring to a good consistency.
2. Add chopped shallots and pepper to taste.
3. Turn into a greased, ovenproof dish and smooth the surface.
4. Combine breadcrumbs and cheese and sprinkle over the top.
5. Bake in a moderate oven for about 20 minutes or until top has browned.
6. If browning is slow, place under hot griller for a few minutes.
7. Serve hot with meats and poultry.

(*Serves 4–6*)

✳ Stuffed Potatoes with Corn and Cheese

6 medium potatoes
¾ cup grated cheddar cheese
1 130 g can creamed corn
1 tablespoon chopped chives

1. Pierce unpeeled potatoes in several places with a fork, rub with oil, place around the outside edge of the turntable and cook for approx. 13 minutes on HIGH or until just tender. Stand for 5 minutes.
2. Slice tops off the potatoes and scoop out potato, taking care not to break the outside skin.
3. Mash potato pulp, mix in cheese, corn and chives until well combined.
4. Spoon potato mixture back into the potato shells and cook on HIGH for 3 minutes or until heated through.
5. Serve garnished with fresh chives.

(*Serves 6*)

✳ Stuffed Potatoes with Tomato and Onion Filling

6 medium potatoes
1 onion, chopped finely
2 medium tomatoes, chopped
1 tablespoon chopped fresh basil
freshly ground pepper

1. Complete steps 1 and 2 for Stuffed Potatoes with Corn and Cheese.
2. Brush or spray a pan with oil, heat and add the onion and cook until transparent.
3. Add tomato, basil and pepper and cook gently until tender.
4. Combine potato pulp with the tomato mixture and spoon back into the potato shells.
5. Cook on HIGH for approximately 3 minutes or until heated through.
6. Serve garnished with basil.

(Serves 6)

Cajun Spiced Sweet Potato

4 small, orange-coloured, sweet potatoes
3 egg whites
1 teaspoon cumin
1 tablespoon cajun seasoning
⅛ to ¼ teaspoon chilli powder

1. Peel sweet potatoes and cut in half lengthwise and score-cut side in criss-cross pattern.
2. Combine egg whites with cumin, seasoning and chilli in a bowl.
3. Add half of sweet potato to bowl, toss until well coated with egg mixture and repeat with the remaining sweet potato.
4. Place sweet potato cut side up on a greased wire rack in a baking dish and bake uncovered in a moderate oven for 45 minutes or until tender.

(Serves 4–6)

✳ Sweet Potato with Ginger

2 sweet potatoes, peeled and sliced

¼ cup orange juice

1 tablespoon honey

1 tablespoon brown sugar

2 teaspoons ginger, finely grated

1 orange, thinly sliced

Topping

¼ cup fresh breadcrumbs

1 tablespoon brown sugar

¼ teaspoon cinnamon

60 g pecan nuts, chopped

1. Place sweet potatoes in a single layer over base of a greased shallow dish.
2. Combine orange juice, honey, sugar and ginger and pour over potatoes and cook on HIGH for 6 minutes or until potatoes are tender.
3. Arrange orange slices between potato slices.
4. Combine topping ingredients, sprinkle over potatoes and cook on HIGH for 3 minutes or until heated through.
5. Serve with any roast meal.

(Serves 4)

Vegetable Patties

3 cups dry mashed potatoes

2 cups cooked mixed vegetables

pinch cayenne pepper

pinches dry oregano, basil, sage

1 egg, beaten

oil

1 small onion

light-coloured dry breadcrumbs

1. Place potatoes, mixed vegetables, cayenne, herbs and beaten egg in a bowl.
2. Brush or spray pan with cooking oil and heat, add onion and cook until transparent, then add to the mixture and mix well.
3. Using a tablespoon, divide mixture into even portions.
4. Flatten each into a cake and coat with breadcrumbs.
5. Heat a small quantity of oil in a non-stick pan and brown patties on both sides.
6. Lift onto absorbent paper.
7. Serve hot as required.

(Serves 6)

Corn and Potato Cakes

oil

½ cup chopped onion

¼ cup chopped celery

1 340 g can corn kernels, well drained

3 cups mashed potatoes

1 egg yolk

pepper

oil for frying

1. Brush or spray pan with cooking oil, heat and add onion and celery and cook for 1 minute.
2. Add corn and mix well. Remove from heat.
3. In a bowl combine mashed potatoes, onion and corn mixture, egg yolk and seasoning.
4. With floured hands and using a ⅓ cup measure, shape into 7.5 cm flat cakes.
5. Fry in hot oil until well browned on both sides.
6. Lift onto a paper-lined plate to absorb any oil.
7. Arrange in a serving dish and garnish with tomato wedges and parsley or bean sprouts.

(Serves 6)

Glazed Carrots

6 medium sized carrots

½–1 tablespoon butter or margarine

1 tablespoon brown sugar

¼ cup macadamia nuts or almonds, slivered

1 teaspoon finely chopped ginger

1. Prepare carrots and slice or cut into matchstick-sized pieces. Cook in a small amount of water until barely tender. Drain off water and set aside.
2. Melt butter in a saucepan, add sugar, nuts and ginger.
3. When hot add carrots and simmer for 1 to 2 minutes turning frequently to glaze all sides.

(Serves 4)

Variations

Honey Glazed Carrots

Cut the carrots in slices or matchstick-sized pieces and cook. For 3 large carrots, heat 1 tablespoon honey and ½ tablespoon butter or margarine and toss carrots over low heat until well coated.

Orange Flavoured Carrots

Prepare as above. Mix together 1 tablespoon butter, margarine or cream and 1 tablespoon orange juice and a little grated orange rind. Add the carrots and heat through.

(Serves 4)

Broccoli with Lemon Butter Sauce

300 g broccoli
1 tablespoon butter or
  margarine
1 tablespoon lemon juice
pepper

1. Divide broccoli into four equal-sized pieces.
2. Cook gently in steamer for 10 to 12 minutes or until tender.
3. Melt butter in a saucepan and when it begins to foam add lemon juice and pepper.
4. Lift broccoli onto a serving dish and pour the sauce over.

(Serves 4)

Cauliflower au Gratin

1 small cauliflower
1½ cups white sauce
2 tablespoons
  breadcrumbs
2 tablespoons grated
  cheese

1. Divide cooked cauliflower into flowerets and arrange in an ovenproof dish.
2. Pour white sauce over cauliflower, sprinkle with breadcrumbs and grated cheese.
3. Bake in moderate oven until browned.

Note: Marrow and zucchini may be used instead of cauliflower.

(Serves 4–6)

Stuffed Zucchini (1)

4 zucchini
1 onion, finely chopped
1 tomato, finely chopped
chopped mint
pepper
grated cheese

1. Trim zucchini and cook in boiling water for 6 to 7 minutes or until barely tender.
2. Drain and cut each zucchini in half lengthwise. Scoop out centre with a spoon.
3. Chop pulp finely and mix with onion and tomato, mint and pepper.
4. Spoon filling into each shell and sprinkle with grated cheese.
5. Brown under the griller.

(Serves 4)

Stuffed Zucchini (2)

6 medium zucchini

oil

2 bacon rashers, finely chopped

2 teaspoons margarine

1 onion, finely chopped

1 clove garlic, crushed

1 tablespoon flour

½ cup milk

½ cup grated tasty cheese

250 g frozen mixed vegetables, cooked and drained

1 tablespoon chopped fresh dill

2 tablespoons grated parmesan cheese

1. Trim zucchini and cook in boiling water for 4 minutes. Drain and cover with cold water until cool enough to handle.
2. Cut in half lengthwise and scoop out pulp.
3. Brush or spray pan with oil, heat and add bacon and fry until crisp. Drain.
4. Melt margarine in pan and cook onion and garlic until onion is transparent.
5. Add flour and cook for 1 minute, stirring.
6. Remove from heat and gradually stir in milk.
7. Return to heat, bring to boil and allow to simmer for 1 minute, stirring continuously.
8. Remove from heat, add tasty cheese, vegetables and dill.
9. Fill zucchini with vegetable mixture, place on a greased ovenproof tray and sprinkle with bacon and parmesan cheese.
10. Bake in a moderate oven until heated through.

(Serves 6)

Button Squash with Topping

8 small button squash

½ cup prepared dry stuffing mix

2 tablespoons soft breadcrumbs

1 teaspoon butter or margarine

⅓ cup finely grated cheese

1. Steam or boil button squash in water until at least half cooked.
2. Drain squash and scoop a small amount out of tops.
3. Mix the dry stuffing mix with extra crumbs and melted butter and moisten with water.
4. Place a spoonful of stuffing on each squash and sprinkle with cheese.
5. Stand squash in a well-greased ovenproof dish and bake in a moderate oven to melt and brown the cheese.
6. Serve hot with meats and poultry.

(Serves 4)

Beans Greek Style

oil

2 large onions, sliced

2 cloves garlic, crushed

**300 g fresh green beans
cut into 5 cm lengths**

3 ripe tomatoes, diced

1 pinch cinnamon

1. Brush or spray pan with oil, heat and cook onion and garlic until onion is transparent.
2. Place beans and tomatoes on top of onions, cover and cook slowly for about 20 minutes until beans are tender.
3. Add cinnamon and serve.

(Serves 4)

Ratatouille

1–2 eggplants

salt

3 medium tomatoes

2–3 zucchini

**1 large red or green
capsicum**

2 onions

2 medium carrots

oil

¼ teaspoon sugar

2 cloves garlic, crushed

**1 tablespoon chopped
parsley**

**½ teaspoon basil or
chopped fresh basil**

freshly ground pepper

1. Cube unpeeled eggplants, sprinkle liberally with salt, set aside for ½ hour and then wash, drain and dry.
2. Peel and chop tomatoes, slice zucchini, seed and slice capsicum, slice onions and carrots.
3. Brush or spray pan with cooking oil, heat and brown eggplant. Remove with a slotted spoon and place in a lightly greased ovenproof dish. Cover with tomatoes.
4. Add zucchini, capsicum, onions, carrots and sugar to pan and sauté for 2 to 3 minutes. Remove with a slotted spoon and place on top of tomatoes, sprinkling with garlic, parsley, basil and pepper.
5. Cover and cook at 190°C to 200°C for about 1 hour or until vegetables are tender.

(Serves 6)

Asian Style Vegetables

6–8 cups of any or all of the following, cut into slices: carrots, cauliflower, celery, capsicum, zucchini, shallots, leeks, bean sprouts, Chinese cabbage, mushrooms, broccoli, snow peas

oil

piece of fresh root ginger, finely grated

1 clove garlic, crushed

3 onions, quartered

½ cup water

1 chicken stock cube

1 tablespoon soy sauce

1. Prepare vegetables, keeping carrots and cauliflower separate from the others.
2. Brush or spray pan with oil, heat and sauté ginger, garlic and onion for 2 minutes. Add carrots and cauliflower, water, stock cube and soy sauce and cook for 5 minutes.
3. Add the remaining vegetables, and cook for a further two minutes.
4. Test for a cooked but crunchy taste.
5. Serve immediately with boiled rice and meat, chicken or fish.

(Serves 6–8)

Stuffed Tomatoes (1)

4 tomatoes, firm and ripe

oil

1 small onion, diced or 2 shallots, chopped

2 bacon rashers, diced

½ cup corn kernels

½ cup fresh breadcrumbs

¼ cup grated cheese

pepper

1. Cut off a slice from the top of each tomato and carefully scoop out pulp and reserve.
2. Brush or spray pan with oil, heat and sauté onion and bacon until a golden colour. Add corn, breadcrumbs, cheese, chopped tomato pulp and pepper.
3. Spoon filling into tomato cases and heat through in a moderate oven.
4. Garnish with parsley.
5. Serve hot with meat and poultry.

(Serves 4)

Stuffed Tomatoes (2)

6 tomatoes, firm and ripe

oil

4 shallots, chopped

1 clove garlic, crushed

2 zucchinis, grated

2 teaspoons tomato paste

1 tablespoon chopped fresh basil

1 tablespoon grated parmesan cheese

1. Cut top from tomatoes, scoop out the pulp and reserve.
2. Brush or spray pan with oil, heat and cook shallots and garlic for 1 minute.
3. Add zucchini, tomato paste, basil and chopped tomato pulp and cook for another minute.
4. Spoon filling into the tomatoes, sprinkle with cheese and bake in a moderate oven until heated through.

(Serves 6)

Tomato and Onion Pie

2 large tomatoes
2 white onions
pepper
½ cup soft breadcrumbs
1 teaspoon butter or
    margarine
parsley

1. Wash and skin tomatoes. Cut into thick slices.
2. Peel onions and slice thinly.
3. Arrange tomatoes and onions in layers, in a greased pie dish sprinkling each layer with pepper.
4. Sprinkle with breadcrumbs and dot with butter.
5. Bake until vegetables are tender.
6. Garnish with fresh herbs.

Note: A little grated cheese may be added to the breadcrumb topping and butter omitted.

(*Serves 4–5*)

Grilled Capsicum

2 red capsicums
2 yellow capsicums
1 tablespoon olive oil
juice of 1 lime
2 sprigs oregano, leaves
    only
freshly ground pepper

1. Cut capsicums lengthwise into quarters and place in a shallow dish.
2. Combine the remainder of the ingredients and drizzle over the capsicum slices.
3. Grill the capsicum, basting frequently with the oil mixture until cooked.
4. Serve with grilled beef or chicken and crusty bread.

(*Serves 4–6*)

Stuffed Capsicums

6 green capsicums
1 cup soft breadcrumbs
1 egg, beaten
1 onion, diced
1 tomato, diced
250 g steak mince
pepper
1 tablespoon fresh
    chopped parsley
1 teaspoon Worcestershire
    sauce
butter or margarine

1. Wash capsicums and parboil for 5 minutes then drain and place in cold water until cool enough to handle.
2. Cut off tops and remove centres.
3. Mix most of the breadcrumbs, onion, tomato, egg, mince, pepper, parsley and Worcestershire sauce.
4. Fill capsicums with the mixture and sprinkle tops with remainder of the crumbs.
5. Place a little butter on top and put capsicums in a pie dish with a little water in the bottom.
6. Bake slowly for about 1 hour.
7. Serve immediately.

(*Serves 6*)

Roasted Capsicum and Tomatoes

2 medium red capsicums

2 medium green capsicums

2 medium yellow capsicums

6 large roma tomatoes, halved

2 cloves garlic, crushed

2 tablespoons olive oil

1 teaspoon sugar

freshly ground pepper

1 tablespoon freshly chopped thyme

1 tablespoon balsamic vinegar (optional)

1. Slice capsicums into 3 cm strips and combine with tomatoes and garlic in a large, greased baking dish.
2. Combine oil, sugar, pepper and thyme and drizzle over vegetables.
3. Bake uncovered in a hot oven for 45 minutes or until vegetables are tender.
4. Drizzle with vinegar if desired and serve.

(Serves 6)

Sweet and Sour Vegetables

1 carrot

4 sticks celery

2 onions

1 green capsicum

1 red capsicum

Sauce

1 cup chicken stock

1–2 tablespoons soy sauce

4 tablespoons brown sugar

⅔ cup white vinegar

1 tablespoon cornflour

1. Prepare vegetables. Cut capsicums into small squares and onions in quarters. Slice carrots and celery.
2. Drop all vegetables into boiling water and cook for 5 to 6 minutes.
3. Mix together stock, sauce, sugar, vinegar and cornflour in a saucepan.
4. Stir over heat until mixture boils. Cook for 2 to 3 minutes.
5. Add drained vegetables and heat through.

(Serves 4)

Vegetable Medley

2 carrots, sliced
2 potatoes, sliced
1 choko, sliced
2–3 zucchini, sliced
3–4 tomatoes, sliced
1 stalk celery, sliced
2 onions, sliced
bunch of herbs (parsley, marjoram, basil), chopped
pepper

1. Place carrots, potatoes and choko in a saucepan, cover with water and boil for 4 or 5 minutes. Drain immediately.
2. Brush or spray pan with oil and fry onion until golden in colour. Drain on absorbent paper.
3. Grease a deep ovenproof dish and arrange vegetables in layers, sprinkling each with pepper and herbs.
4. Cover with a lid and bake until vegetables are partly cooked, about 20 minutes.
5. Top with potato soufflé and bake in a fairly hot oven until top is crisp and golden brown.
6. Serve as an accompaniment to meat or chicken.

Note: Select vegetables according to availability — others are parsnips, eggplant, capsicums, mushrooms, beans.

(Serves 6)

Cheese Topped Vegetable Pie

Filling
oil
4 small zucchini, sliced
2 onions, chopped
3 sticks celery, sliced
125 g mushrooms, quartered
1 carrot, sliced
pepper
1 teaspoon curry powder

Cheese Sauce
60 g margarine
⅓ cup plain flour
pepper
¼–½ teaspoon dry mustard
1½ cups milk
125 g grated cheddar cheese
2 teaspoons chopped fresh parsley

Filling
1. Brush or spray pan with oil, heat and add vegetables and sauté for 3 minutes.
2. Add pepper and curry powder, mix well and place vegetables into a greased, ovenproof dish.
3. Pour sauce over vegetables and bake in a moderate oven for 35 to 40 minutes.

Cheese Sauce
4. Melt margarine in saucepan, stir in flour and cook for 1 minute. Remove from heat.
5. Add pepper and mustard, mix well and gradually add milk.
6. Return to heat, stirring constantly until mixture boils and thickens. Remove from heat.
7. Stir in cheese and parsley and continue to stir until cheese melts.

(Serves 4)

Roasted Mediterranean Vegetables

4 small zucchini, halved
  lengthwise

4 small baby eggplants,
  halved lengthwise

2 roma tomatoes, quartered

1 red capsicum, cut into
  3 cm wide strips

1 yellow capsicum, cut into
  3 cm wide strips

1 onion cut into thin wedges

2 tablespoons olive oil

fresh ground pepper

2 tablespoons chopped
  fresh parsley or basil

1. Lightly grease a large baking dish and arrange all
   vegetables in a single layer.
2. Drizzle vegetables with oil and sprinkle with pepper and
   bake in a hot oven for 20 to 25 minutes until just browned
   and softened.
3. Serve sprinkled with parsley or basil.

(Serves 4–6)

Skewered Vegetables

1½ tablespoons balsamic
  vinegar

3 teaspoons olive oil

1 clove garlic, crushed

1 teaspoon dried oregano
  leaves

½ teaspoon dried basil
  leaves

½ teaspoon dried
  rosemary leaves

freshly ground pepper

6 cherry tomatoes, whole
  or halved

1 medium red onion cut
  into 12 wedges

1 zucchini, thickly sliced

1 green capsicum, cut into
  3 cm strips then halved

1 yellow capsicum, cut into
  3 cm strips then halved

6 wooden skewers,
  pre-soaked

1. Combine vinegar, oil, garlic, herbs and pepper.
2. Thread vegetables alternately onto skewers.
3. Brush vegetables with dressing mixture.
4. Grill or bbq until golden brown and cooked through.

(Serves 6)

Paella Salad

1 tablespoon oil

1 onion, chopped

½ red capsicum, thinly sliced

½ green capsicum, thinly sliced

2 rashers bacon, diced

1 clove garlic, crushed

250 g long-grain rice

1 tomato, roughly chopped

1 stick celery, sliced

½ cup frozen peas

½ teaspoon saffron or turmeric

1½ teaspoons curry powder

2½ cups water

2 chicken stock cubes

2 to 5 cm piece cinnamon stick (optional)

freshly ground pepper

3 shallots, sliced

60 g small mushrooms, sliced

60 g stuffed green olives, sliced (optional)

½ tablespoon chopped fresh parsley

1 tablespoon French dressing

1. Heat oil in a large pan and sauté onion, capsicum, bacon and garlic for 2 minutes.
2. Stir in rice, tomato, celery, peas, saffron, curry powder, water, crumbled stock cubes, cinnamon stick and pepper.
3. Cover pan and simmer gently for 15 to 20 minutes or until almost all the liquid has been absorbed.
4. Remove lid, add shallots, mushrooms and olives and stir into rice mixture.
5. Cover, simmer gently for 3 minutes. Remove lid and check if rice is cooked and all liquid has evaporated. If rice needs further cooking, add extra ½ cup of boiling water, cover and cook for a further 2 to 3 minutes.
6. Stir in parsley and French dressing and serve hot or cold.

Note: Cooked seafood, beef or chicken strips may be added to this dish.

(*Serves 4*)

Potato Salad

500 g potatoes

3 bacon rashers, trimmed and diced

6 shallots, finely sliced

chopped parsley

1 cup mayonnaise

½ red capsicum, diced

1 tablespoon chopped fresh basil

1 tablespoon chopped fresh chives

1. Peel potatoes, cut into cubes and place in saucepan.
2. Add boiling water and cook until tender but firm.
3. Drain and allow to cool.
4. Sauté bacon in pan, or microwave between 2 sheets of paper towel for 2 minutes on HIGH or until crisp. Crumble when cool.
5. Add bacon, shallots, parsley and mayonnaise to bowl with potato.
6. Mix lightly and place in a serving bowl and sprinkle with fresh herbs.

Variation

Add ½–¾ teaspoon curry powder to the mayonnaise. Add chopped yolks of two hard boiled eggs. Substitute sour cream for half the mayonnaise.

(Serves 4–6)

Hot Potato Salad

500 g new potatoes

½ cup chopped celery

1 small red capsicum, chopped finely

1 onion, chopped finely

1 medium carrot, grated

2 bacon rashers, diced and cooked

Dressing

1 cup low fat yoghurt

1 teaspoon dry mustard

½ teaspoon paprika

black pepper

1 tablespoon parmesan cheese

1. Cook potatoes in their skins, drain and cool.
2. Skin potatoes if desired and cut up roughly.
3. Add celery, capsicum, onion and carrot.
4. Add bacon, reserving about a quarter of it for sprinkling over the top.
5. Combine the dressing ingredients and pour over potato mixture.
6. Spoon into an ovenproof dish and sprinkle with cheese.
7. Bake in a hot oven for about 20 minutes or until the cheese is beginning to brown.
8. Sprinkle remaining bacon over top and serve immediately.

Note: A tablespoon of chopped ginger may be added to the dressing if desired.

(Serves 4–6)

Coleslaw

½ **young cabbage heart**
1 **red capsicum, chopped**
1 **cup celery, sliced**
1 **carrot, grated**
½ **cup mayonnaise**
1 **tablespoon lemon juice**
parsley

1. Shred cabbage very finely.
2. Add capsicum, carrot, celery, mayonnaise and lemon juice.
3. Mix lightly together.
4. Serve sprinkled with parsley.

(Serves 6–8)

Carrot and Raisin Salad

2 **carrots, grated**
1 **cup chopped celery**
1 **cup seeded raisins**
½ **cup mayonnaise**
fresh herbs

1. Grate the carrot on a medium grater. Chop the celery.
2. Separate raisins and mix with carrot and celery. Add mayonnaise to taste and mix lightly.
3. Place in a bowl and chill well.
4. Serve garnished with fresh herbs.

(Serves 6)

Mango and Orange Salad

2 **mangoes, peeled and sliced *or* 500 g canned and drained mango slices**
3 **oranges**
3 **sticks celery, sliced**
6 **shallots, sliced**
1 **cucumber, peeled and sliced**

Dressing

⅓ **cup mayonnaise**
⅓ **cup cream**
pepper
2 **tablespoons chopped parsley**
½ **teaspoon grated orange rind**
1 **teaspoon French mustard**

1. Peel oranges, remove pith, divide oranges into segments.
2. Combine mangoes, oranges, celery, cucumber and shallots.
3. Refrigerate until ready to serve.
4. Add dressing to salad ingredients and toss gently to mix.
5. Serve with roast meat or ham.

Dressing

6. Combine all ingredients in a bowl and mix well. Allow to stand for 15 minutes.

(Serves 6–8)

Greek Salad

1 small red capsicum
1 small green capsicum
1 large onion
2 ripe tomatoes
2 sticks celery
1 cucumber
1 small lettuce
125 g black olives
¼ cup French dressing
125 g fetta cheese, cubed

1. Cut red and green capsicums into rings, remove any seeds.
2. Peel onion, cut into wedges, separate in pieces. Cut tomatoes into wedges.
3. Cut celery into slices and cucumber into cubes.
4. Wash and dry lettuce, tear into pieces.
5. Put all vegetables into a salad bowl, add olives and fetta cheese and cover and refrigerate until ready to serve.
6. Add dressing, toss well and serve.

(Serves 6–8)

Layered Salad

½ lettuce, shredded
1½ cups frozen peas, lightly cooked and cooled
250 g mushrooms, sliced
2 hard-boiled eggs, chopped
125 g grated cheese
½ cup mayonnaise
¾ cup natural yoghurt
1 tablespoon lemon juice
2 teaspoons French, grain or German mustard
4 shallots, sliced
1 clove garlic, crushed
1 large tomato, cut into 8 wedges
2 bacon rashers, chopped finely and cooked
1 tablespoon chopped fresh parsley

1. Layer the vegetables in the following order: lettuce, peas, mushrooms, eggs and cheese.
2. Combine mayonnaise, yoghurt, lemon juice, mustard, shallots and garlic and pour over the top of the salad.
3. Cover and refrigerate for several hours or overnight.
4. Serve garnished with tomato wedges, bacon and parsley.

Note: A layer of cooked, chopped chicken can be added to this dish to make it suitable for a main course.

(Serves 6–8)

Mixed Green Salad

large serve of a variety of lettuce

25 g baby spinach leaves

1 small bunch rocket

1 stick celery, sliced

2 shallots, sliced

1 Lebanese cucumber, halved lengthwise and sliced

1 punnet cherry tomatoes, halved

1 sprig fresh oregano, leaves only, chopped finely.

Dressing

3 tablespoons olive oil

1 tablespoon red wine vinegar

freshly ground pepper

1. Wash lettuce leaves and break into bite-sized pieces. The inner, tender leaves can be left whole.
2. Trim the stems from spinach and rocket leaves.
3. Place all leaves in a large serving bowl and add celery, shallots, cucumber, tomatoes and oregano.
4. Place oil, vinegar and pepper in a screw-top jar and shake well to mix.
5. Pour dressing over salad and toss gently. Serve immediately.

(*Serves 6*)

Sweet Corn and Red Capsicum Salad

250 g can corn kernels, drained

1 red capsicum, cut into thin strips

1 cup bean shoots

1 large avocado, halved lengthwise and sliced

Dressing

2 tablespoons lemon juice

3 tablespoons French dressing

3 tablespoons olive oil

1. In a large bowl mix gently together the corn, capsicum, bean shoots and avocado.
2. Place dressing ingredients in a screw-top jar and shake well to mix.
3. Pour dressing over salad and serve.

(*Serves 4*)

Caesar Salad

Croutons

1 clove garlic, crushed

1 tablespoon olive oil

3 slices thick bread, crusts removed

Salad ingredients

2 rashers bacon, diced

1 cos lettuce, torn into pieces

4 anchovies, chopped

100 g freshly shaved parmesan cheese

Dressing

3 tablespoons olive oil

1 tablespoon lemon juice

1 tablespoon sour cream

½ teaspoon Worcestershire sauce

Variation

Cooked and sliced chicken breast may be added for a main meal option.

1. Combine garlic and oil and brush over bread.
2. Cut bread into small cubes and place on a lightly greased oven tray and bake in a moderate oven for 10 minutes until golden brown.
3. Remove from oven and leave to cool.
4. Brush or spray pan with oil and fry bacon until crisp. Drain on absorbent paper.
5. Place oil, lemon juice, sour cream and Worcestershire sauce in a screw-top jar and shake well to mix.
6. Place lettuce, bacon, croutons, anchovies and parmesan cheese into a large bowl and drizzle over dressing. Serve immediately.

(Serves 4–6)

Caesar Salad — Low fat

4 thick slices bread, crusts removed and cubed

2 bacon rashers, trimmed and diced

¼ × 45 g can anchovies, rinsed and drained

1 cos lettuce, torn into pieces

30 g fresh parmesan cheese, shaved and chopped

Dressing

100 g low fat ricotta cheese

½ teaspoon Dijon mustard

1 tablespoon lemon juice

¼ cup skim milk

1. Place bread cubes on a lightly greased baking tray and bake in a moderate oven for 10 minutes or until browned.
2. Brush or spray non-stick pan with oil, heat and cook bacon until crisp. Drain.
3. Reserve half of the anchovies for dressing and chop the remainder.
4. Blend reserved anchovies with the ricotta cheese, mustard, lemon juice and milk until smooth.
5. Arrange lettuce, bacon and half the croutons in a large bowl. Toss gently. Sprinkle with the remaining croutons, parmesan cheese and remaining anchovies and drizzle with dressing.

(Serves 4)

Coconut Pineapple Salad

fresh or canned pineapple pieces
coconut
mint sprigs

1. Drain pineapple pieces very well.
2. Sprinkle lightly with coconut and toss.
3. Turn into a bowl and garnish with sprigs of mint.
4. Chill well and serve with other salads.

Waldorf Salad (U.S.A.)

2 cups sliced red apples
2 tablespoons lemon juice
½ cup mayonnaise
1 cup thinly sliced celery
¾ cup seeded raisins
½ cup coarsely chopped walnuts

1. Prepare apples, leaving skins on.
2. Mix together lemon juice and 1 tablespoon mayonnaise.
3. Add the apples and toss lightly.
4. Add celery, raisins, walnuts and remaining mayonnaise.
5. Toss well and serve garnished with slices of red apple and parsley sprigs.

(Serves 6–8)

Warm Bean Salad

500 g green beans
2 onions, finely chopped
4 large tomatoes, cut in wedges
10 small potatoes, cooked with skins on and quartered
10 small anchovies, sliced (optional)

1. Cut beans into 4 cm lengths and blanch in sufficient water to barely cover. Drain.
2. While still hot, place beans in a bowl, add onion, tomato, potato and anchovies.
3. Place dressing ingredients in a small screw-top jar and shake well until evenly mixed.
4. Drizzle dressing over salad and toss gently to mix through.
5. Serve warm or at room temperature.

Dressing

1 to 2 teaspoons mustard paste
4 tablespoons peanut or corn oil
2 tablespoons red wine vinegar
1 teaspoon fresh chopped oregano
fresh ground pepper

(Serves 6–8)

Mexican Red Bean and Chicken Salsa Salad

Chicken

3 chicken breasts (approximately 400 g)

2 tablespoons olive oil

1 clove garlic, crushed

1 teaspoon grated lime zest

pepper

Salad

1 410 g can kidney beans, drained

½ to 1 green chilli, finely chopped

1 red onion, chopped

juice of 1 lime

3 tablespoons olive oil

pinch sugar

1 punnet cherry tomatoes, halved

1 tablespoon fresh coriander, chopped

1 large avocado, chopped

1 230 g packet corn chips

Chicken

1. Mix oil, garlic, lime zest and pepper and brush over chicken.
2. Grill chicken, basting frequently with oil mixture. Slice diagonally into ½ cm slices and keep warm.

Salad

3. Mix beans and the rest of the salad ingredients, except corn chips.
4. Pile salad onto 4 individual plates and top with sliced chicken.
5. Serve with corn chips and garnished with fresh coriander.

(Serves 4)

Bean Salad

1 440 g can beans (red kidney beans or 3 bean mix)

2 tomatoes, cut into 1 cm cubes

½ cup green and red capsicum, diced

1 small onion, diced

½ cup diced celery

2 tablespoons wine vinegar

1 tablespoon olive oil

1 clove garlic, crushed

1 tablespoon chopped fresh parsley

freshly ground pepper

1. Drain beans and place in bowl with tomatoes, capsicum, onion and celery and mix well.
2. Place vinegar, oil, garlic, parsley and pepper in a screw top jar and shake to combine.
3. Pour dressing over salad, toss to mix and serve garnished with parsley.

(Serves 4)

Tabouli (Lebanon)

½ cup fine cracked wheat

½ cucumber, finely chopped

4 tomatoes, finely chopped

3 shallots, finely sliced

4 tablespoons finely chopped parsley

2 tablespoons finely chopped fresh mint

juice of 2–3 lemons

2 tablespoons olive oil

shallots

1. Rinse the cracked wheat in a bowl several times until the water runs clean. Squeeze out any excess or prepare according to instructions on packet.
2. Put the chopped vegetables, parsley and mint into a large mixing bowl and add the cracked wheat.
3. Stir in the lemon juice and olive oil. Mix well, leave for 15 minutes, then taste and adjust the seasoning if necessary.
4. Chill and serve garnished with shallots.

(Serves 6–8)

Hot Thai Salad

2 carrots, peeled and grated

1 bunch radish, grated

½ continental cucumber, grated

½ bunch coriander, chopped

2 tablespoons soy sauce

2 tablespoons fish sauce

2 tablespoons mirin (rice wine)

3 tablespoons lemon juice

assorted lettuce leaves

400 g chicken breast strips, pork strips, lean beef strips (rump or fillet steak) or seafood

1 to 2 small, hot red chillies, seeded and finely chopped

1. Toss all vegetables together in a large bowl.
2. Place soy sauce, fish sauce, mirin, lemon juice and chillies in a screw-top jar and shake well.
3. Pour dressing over the salad.
4. Stir-fry meat or seafood until cooked.
5. Serve salad on a bed of assorted lettuce leaves and top with meat or seafood and sprinkle with freshly chopped coriander.

(Serves 4)

Noodle Salad with Tofu and Chilli

300 g packet firm tofu, chopped

1 large (180 g) carrot, cut into long thin strips

1 (130 g) Lebanese cucumber, cut into long thin strips

4 shallots, sliced

1 to 2 teaspoons grated fresh ginger

250 g bean thread noodles

½ cup (75 g) cashews, toasted

2 tablespoons fresh coriander leaves, chopped

2 tablespoons fresh mint leaves, chopped

2 tablespoons fresh basil, chopped

1 small red fresh chilli, seeded and sliced (optional)

Chilli Dressing

½ cup (60 mL) lime juice

2 tablespoons sweet chilli sauce

1 tablespoon fish sauce

2 tablespoons soy sauce

1. Combine the tofu with half of the chilli dressing in a small bowl. Cover and refrigerate for 1 hour.
2. Place the noodles in a medium, heat-proof bowl, cover with boiling water and stand until tender then drain.
3. Combine the undrained tofu with the noodles, vegetables, remaining ingredients and chilli dressing in a large bowl and toss.

Chilli Dressing

4. Combine lime juice and sauces in a screw-top jar and shake well.

(Serves 4)

Asian Beef Salad

2 teaspoons oil

2 × 200 g pieces fillet steak (eye or rib)

2 zucchini

1 red onion, sliced thinly

1 red capsicum, cut into long thin strips

mixed salad greens

snow pea sprouts

Dressing

3 tablespoons black bean sauce

1/4 cup peanut oil

1 tablespoon lemon juice

Variation

Alternative Dressing

1/4 cup lemon juice

2 cloves garlic, crushed

2 tablespoons freshly chopped coriander

2 tablespoons freshly chopped mint

1 tablespoon fish sauce

1 tablespoon soy sauce

1 tablespoon brown sugar

1 to 2 teaspoons chopped fresh chilli

1. Brush or spray pan with oil and heat. Cook steak until medium-rare (steak will be a medium firmness, and have some resistance when pressed).
2. Remove meat from pan and allow to cool before cutting into thin slices.
3. Trim ends of zucchini, cut in half crosswise and using a potato peeler cut lengthwise strips from zucchini halves.
4. Place zucchini, onion, capsicum, salad greens and meat in a bowl and toss to mix.
5. Place all dressing ingredients together in a screw-top jar and shake to mix.
6. Drizzle dressing over the salad and garnish with sprouts.

Place all ingredients in a screw-top jar and shake well to combine.

(Serves 4)

Couscous, Tomato and Rocket Salad

oil

1 red onion, diced

1 to 2 cloves garlic, crushed

2 cups couscous

2 cups boiling water

2 tablespoons chopped fresh basil

1 tablespoon chopped fresh parsley

1 tablespoon grated lemon rind

¼ cup olive oil

2 tablespoons lemon juice

4 medium tomatoes, chopped

½ cup pine nuts, toasted

100 g baby rocket leaves, chopped

1. Brush or spray pan with oil, heat and sauté onion and garlic until soft. Remove from heat.
2. Place couscous in a large heat-proof bowl, add boiling water and stand approximately 5 minutes or until water is absorbed. Fluff with a fork. Cool.
3. Combine basil, parsley, rind, oil and lemon juice in a screw-top jar and shake well to mix.
4. Just before serving, combine couscous, onion mixture, tomatoes, pine nuts and rocket.
5. Pour dressing over the salad and toss gently.

(Serves 6–8)

Melon and Prawn Salad with Chilli Coconut Dressing

½ rockmelon

½ honeydew melon

½ small champagne melon

small piece watermelon

500 g medium sized prawns, peeled and de-veined

Dressing

1 cup coconut milk

2 tablespoons sweet chilli sauce

2 tablespoons chopped mint

1. Peel and cut melons into small chunks.
2. Mix all dressing ingredients.
3. Place melons and prawns into a large bowl, gently mix and pour dressing over.
4. Serve immediately.

(Serves 4–6)

SALAD ACCOMPANIMENTS

Mayonnaise (1)

½ cup condensed milk
4 tablespoons vinegar
1 teaspoon mustard
a little fresh milk

1. Place condensed milk in a bowl.
2. Add vinegar and mustard blended with a little vinegar and mix well.
3. Add a little milk to thin mixture to pouring consistency.

Mayonnaise (2)

2 hard boiled eggs
1 teaspoon mustard
½ cup cream
3 tablespoons sugar
2 tablespoons vinegar

1. Rub egg yolks through a sieve.
2. Add mustard, cream, sugar and mix well.
3. Gradually add vinegar to taste and mix until smooth.

Mayonnaise (3)

2 tablespoons sugar
1 teaspoon mustard
2 teaspoons butter
1 egg
½ cup milk
3 tablespoons vinegar

1. Place sugar, mustard and butter in small saucepan.
2. Add beaten egg and milk gradually and mix well.
3. Gradually add the vinegar.
4. Stand saucepan in another pan of water and cook until mixture coats the spoon.
5. Take care not to overcook the mixture.
6. Cool before serving.

French Dressing

2 tablespoons wine vinegar
  (or tarragon vinegar)
2 tablespoons olive oil
pepper
1 small clove garlic,
  crushed
a little dry mustard

1. Place vinegar in a small bowl with seasonings.
2. Gradually blend in the oil, whisking with a fork.
3. Store in a jar and use for tossed salads.

Vinaigrette

½ **cup olive oil**

1½ **tablespoons white wine**
  vinegar

¼ **teaspoon Dijon mustard**

½ **teaspoon caster sugar**

1 **clove garlic, crushed**

freshly ground pepper

1 **tablespoon chopped**
  fresh herbs (optional)

Combine ingredients in a bowl and whisk until combined or place ingredients in a screw-top jar and shake well.

Variation

Lime and Chilli Vinaigrette

Omit vinegar and Dijon mustard and add:

½ **teaspoon finely grated lime rind**

1 **tablespoon lime juice**

1 **tablespoon sweet chilli sauce.**

Herb Butter

250 g **butter**

1 **tablespoon chopped**
  fresh parsley

1 **tablespoon chopped**
  fresh chives

1 **tablespoon chopped**
  fresh dill

2 **cloves garlic, crushed**

pepper

1. Beat butter until creamy.
2. Add chives and parsley, dill, garlic and pepper to taste.
3. Form into a roll in baking paper.
4. Refrigerate until firm. Use, cut into thin slices, on grills, vegetables or bread.

Herb Bread

1. Slice a French loaf or any crusty bread leaving lower side of crust uncut. Spread each side of each slice with herb butter. Roll in aluminium foil and bake shortly before required, in a moderate oven, for about 15 minutes.
2. Serve in a basket lined with cloth or paper serviettes.

Basic White Sauce

80 g butter or margarine
4 tablespoons flour
2 cups milk

1. Melt butter in a saucepan.
2. Remove from the heat and mix in the flour, using a wooden spoon. Return to heat and cook for 1 minute, stirring continuously.
3. Remove from heat.
4. Add milk gradually, stirring all the time.
5. Return to heat and bring to boil stirring continuously and boil for 1 to 2 minutes.
6. Use as required.

Variations

Parsley Sauce

Add 2 tablespoons finely chopped parsley.

Serve with fish and vegetables.

Onion Sauce

Add 2 boiled and chopped white onions.

Serve with hot corned beef.

Cheese Sauce

Add 2 tablespoons finely grated cheese and a pinch of cayenne.

Serve with vegetables and fish.

Egg Sauce

Chop the whites of 2 hard boiled eggs finely and add to white sauce. Pour over steamed fish. Rub yolks of eggs through a sieve and use as a garnish.

Anchovy Sauce

Add 2 teaspoons anchovy sauce or paste and 1 teaspoon lemon juice. Serve with fish.

* Basic White Sauce

80 g margarine or butter
4 tablespoons flour
2 cups milk

1. Melt butter in a microwave-safe dish on HIGH for 30 seconds.
2. Mix in the flour, using a wooden spoon.
3. Add milk gradually, stirring until well combined.
4. Return to microwave and cook on HIGH for 2 to 3 minutes, stirring every minute, until boiling and thickened.

White Sauce — Low fat

4 tablespoons plain flour
2½ cups skim milk
freshly ground pepper
(optional)

1. Place flour in saucepan and add milk gradually using a whisk to keep the mixture smooth.
2. Place over heat and continue to whisk until mixture boils and thickens.
3. Add pepper to taste and remove from heat.

✗ White Sauce

4 tablespoons maize
cornflour (gluten free)
600 mL milk
2 tablespoons margarine

1. Place cornflour in a bowl and blend with 60 mL milk to make a smooth paste.
2. Heat the remaining milk in a saucepan over medium heat until boiling, then pour onto the blended cornflour mixture, whisking continuously.
3. Return mixture to saucepan and bring to boil, stirring continuously, until the sauce thickens. Simmer for 1 minute then stir in the margarine until melted.
4. Season to taste and serve.

Note: Gluten-free flavourings, e.g. grated cheese, chopped mixed fresh herbs, lightly sautéed onions or cooked sliced mushrooms, can be added for extra flavour.

(Makes 600 mL)

Mint Sauce

½ cup finely chopped mint
3 tablespoons sugar
3 tablespoons boiling water
3 tablespoons vinegar

1. Prepare mint and place in a bowl.
2. Add sugar and boiling water and stand until cold.
3. Add vinegar and stir well.
4. Make about 2 hours before serving.
5. Serve with roast lamb.

Mornay Sauce

60 g butter or margarine
4 tablespoons flour
2½ cups milk
1 cup grated cheese
cayenne
nutmeg

1. Melt butter, add the flour and cook over gentle heat, stirring constantly with a wooden spoon. Cook for 2 minutes.
2. Remove saucepan from heat and gradually add milk. Stir constantly until well blended.
3. Return saucepan to the heat and cook until mixture thickens. Continue to stir so sauce will be smooth. Cook for 2 minutes longer.
4. Remove from heat and add grated cheese, cayenne and nutmeg to taste.

* Mornay Sauce

60 g butter or margarine
4 tablespoons flour
2½ cups milk
1 cup grated cheese
cayenne
nutmeg

1. Place butter in a microwave-safe dish and cook on HIGH for 30 to 60 seconds, add the flour and stir and cook on HIGH for 30 seconds.
2. Remove from microwave and gradually add milk, stirring constantly until well blended.
3. Return to microwave and cook on HIGH for 2 to 3 minutes, stirring every minute until mixture thickens.
4. Add grated cheese, cayenne and nutmeg to taste. Stir until smooth.

Apple Sauce

2 cooking apples
2 tablespoons water
1 tablespoon sugar

1. Peel and slice apples and place in a saucepan.
2. Add water and cook gently until apples are quite soft.
3. Add sugar and beat until smooth or process in a blender.
4. Serve with roast pork.

* Apple Sauce

2 cooking apples
2 tablespoons water
1 tablespoon sugar

1. Peel and slice apples and place in a microwave-safe dish.
2. Add water and cook on MEDIUM for 3 to 5 minutes until apples are soft.
3. Add sugar and beat until smooth or process in a blender.
4. Serve with roast pork.

Tartare Sauce

1 tablespoon each of gherkins and capers, chopped finely

1 teaspoon chopped parsley

½ teaspoon mustard

2 teaspoons lemon juice

1 cup mayonnaise

1. Prepare gherkins, capers and parsley.
2. Mix mustard with the lemon juice.
3. Blend all ingredients.
4. Serve with fish.

Brown Sauce

1 onion

1 carrot

1 stalk celery

2 tablespoons margarine or butter

1 bacon rasher

3 tablespoons flour

2 cups beef stock

1 bay leaf

pepper

1. Prepare vegetables and chop finely.
2. Melt margarine or butter in a small saucepan, add vegetables and chopped bacon.
3. Cook for 4 to 5 minutes until soft. Blend in the flour and stir continuously for about 2 minutes.
4. Gradually add the stock and stir until thickened. Add the bay leaf and pepper.
5. Simmer for 10 minutes then strain.
6. Serve with rissoles, meat loaves, sausages.

Note: A little tomato paste may be added if desired.

Tomato Sauce

1 onion

1 bacon rasher

1 tablespoon margarine or butter

4–5 ripe tomatoes

1 cup chicken stock or water

2 teaspoons sugar

1–2 tablespoons tomato paste

pepper

few drops lemon juice

pinch mixed herbs or basil

1. Chop bacon and onion finely.
2. Fry in heated margarine until soft.
3. Add skinned and chopped tomatoes and cook for 2 to 3 minutes.
4. Add stock, sugar, tomato paste, pepper, lemon juice and herbs. Simmer for 15 to 20 minutes without a lid or until liquid has evaporated and is a thick consistency.
5. Check taste and add more seasoning if needed.
6. Blend until smooth in a blender, strain through a sieve or leave sauce as it is.
7. Serve with meat loaf, sausages, rissoles or pasta.

*Tomato Sauce

1 onion
1 bacon rasher
4–5 tomatoes
¼ cup water
½ teaspoon sugar
1 teaspoon tomato paste
pepper
few drops of lemon juice
basil

1. Chop bacon and onion finely.
2. Cook on HIGH for 2 to 3 minutes in microwave-safe dish.
3. Add skinned and chopped tomatoes. Cook on HIGH for 3 to 4 minutes.
4. Add water, sugar, tomato paste, pepper, lemon juice and basil. Cook on HIGH for 4 to 5 minutes.
5. Check taste and add more seasoning if needed.
6. Blend until smooth in blender.

Barbecue Sauce

4 tablespoons brown sugar
4 tablespoons soy sauce
4 tablespoons malt vinegar
2 tablespoons tomato sauce
2 tablespoons French mustard
1 tablespoon Worcestershire sauce
½ cup orange juice
black pepper

1. Place all ingredients in a jar and shake vigorously to mix.
2. Chill until required.
3. Serve with barbecue meats.

Sweet and Sour Sauce

2 tablespoons lemon juice
1 tablespoon white sugar
2 teaspoons tomato sauce
1 teaspoon soy sauce
2 teaspoons cornflour
oil
½ teaspoon fresh grated ginger
1 cup pineapple pieces
½ red capsicum, diced
1 medium carrot, cut into thin strips
3 shallots, thinly sliced
1½ cups water

1. Place lemon juice, sugar, tomato sauce, soy sauce and cornflour in a bowl and mix well.
2. Brush or spray pan with oil, heat, cook ginger, pineapple, capsicum, carrot and shallots for 2 to 3 minutes.
3. Add water to pan and stir to mix. Add sauce mixture stirring constantly.
4. Bring to the boil and simmer for 1 to 2 minutes.

Curry Sauce

2 onions
1 cooking apple
1 ripe banana
2 tomatoes
2 tablespoons butter or margarine
4 tablespoons flour
1 tablespoon curry powder
1 tablespoon coconut
2 cups stock
1 cup milk
2 tablespoons chutney
juice 1 lemon

1. Peel and chop onions, apple, bananas and tomato.
2. Heat butter or margarine in a pan, add onions and fruit and fry gently until brown, stirring frequently.
3. Add flour, curry powder (add curry cautiously and taste) and coconut.
4. Cook for a few minutes. Gradually add stock and then milk. Cook, stirring all the time, until boiling.
5. Stir in chutney. Simmer for about 30 minutes. Lastly add lemon juice.
6. Rub through a sieve, blend in a blender or leave sauce as it is.
7. If too thick add more stock or water.
8. Serve with chicken, meat or vegetables.

Mushroom Sauce

1 tablespoon butter or margarine
125 g mushrooms, sliced finely
1 tablespoon cornflour
½ cup milk
½ cup cream
freshly ground pepper

1. Melt butter in pan, add mushrooms and cook until tender.
2. Add flour, stir in and cook for 1 minute. Remove from heat.
3. Add milk and cream, return to heat and stir until sauce boils and thickens.
4. Season with pepper and serve with beef, chicken or sausages.

Seafood Sauce

¾ cup mayonnaise
½ cup whipped cream
⅓ cup tomato sauce
¼ teaspoon Worcestershire sauce
2–3 drops Tabasco sauce

Place all ingredients in a bowl and combine well.

Hollandaise Sauce

2 egg yolks
pinch cayenne pepper
pepper
**1–2 tablespoons lemon
juice or white wine
vinegar**
**60–120 g butter or
margarine**

1. Use a double saucepan if possible; if not, a basin over a saucepan can be used. Put the egg yolks, seasonings and vinegar into the top of the pan or basin.
2. Whisk over hot water until sauce begins to thicken.
3. Add butter in small pieces, whisking in each piece until completely melted before adding the next — do not allow to boil, as it will curdle.
4. If too thick add a little cream.

Béarnaise Sauce

This is made the same way as Hollandaise Sauce except that the vinegar is flavoured. Use tarragon vinegar or infuse a chopped shallot, chopped fresh tarragon and thyme and a bay leaf in the white vinegar. Heat, simmer for 2 to 3 minutes and strain. Proceed as above. The shallot may be left in the sauce.

Chilli Plum Sauce

oil
1 large onion, sliced
1 stalk celery, chopped
2 tablespoons soy sauce
1 tablespoon chilli sauce
1 tablespoon dry sherry
½ teaspoon ground ginger
1 cup plum jam

1. Brush or spray with oil, heat and cook the onion and celery until soft but not browned.
2. Remove from heat and stir in the sauces, sherry and ginger. Lastly add the plum jam.
3. Return to heat and stir until bubbling, being careful not to burn the sauce.
4. Serve with fried chicken, pork or veal, meat balls and kebabs.

Lemon and Honey Sauce

oil
1 onion, finely chopped
1 clove garlic, crushed
1 tablespoon cornflour
200 mL dry white wine
1 lemon, rind and juice
1 tablespoon honey
few drops Tabasco sauce

1. Brush or spray pan with oil, heat and add onion and garlic and cook for 1 minute.
2. Stir in cornflour blended with other ingredients. Bring to boil, stirring constantly.
3. Serve with beef, lamb or veal.

Sweet White Sauce

600 mL milk
2 tablespoons sugar
2½ tablespoons cornflour
vanilla

1. Place milk in a saucepan and bring to boiling point.
2. Add sugar and cornflour blended with a little milk.
3. Allow to cook for 2 minutes, stirring constantly.
4. Remove from heat and flavour with vanilla.
5. Serve with steamed puddings.

✳ Sweet White Sauce

2½ tablespoons cornflour
2 tablespoons sugar
600 mL milk
vanilla

1. Blend cornflour and sugar with a little milk then gradually add remaining milk, stirring well.
2. Cook on HIGH for 3 to 4 minutes, stirring every minute.
3. Remove from microwave and flavour with vanilla.
4. Serve with steamed puddings.

Caramel Sauce (1)

3 tablespoons brown sugar
2 tablespoons butter
2½ tablespoons flour
600 mL milk

1. Place brown sugar in a saucepan and allow to melt over gentle heat.
2. Remove from heat and add butter. Heat until melted then stir in flour.
3. Very gradually add milk.
4. Return to heat and stir all the time until mixture thickens.
5. Allow to boil for 1 minute.
6. Pour into a jug to serve.
7. Serve with baked apples or steamed puddings.

Caramel Sauce (2)

¾ cup brown sugar (packed)
3 tablespoons butter
2 tablespoons cream
2 tablespoons milk
2 tablespoons condensed milk
vanilla
lemon juice

1. Place sugar, butter, cream and milk in a small saucepan.
2. Stir over gentle heat for 10 minutes.
3. Remove from heat, add condensed milk.
4. Flavour with vanilla and lemon juice.
5. Serve as a topping on ice-cream.

Chocolate Sauce (1)

155 g dark chocolate, broken into small pieces
½ cup cream

1. Place chocolate in a small saucepan with cream.
2. Heat gently, stirring continuously, until chocolate melts and continue to stir until smooth.
3. Serve warm or at room temperature with baked pears or profiteroles.

Chocolate Sauce (2)

600 mL sweet white sauce
vanilla
60 g plain chocolate

1. Grate chocolate and stand over a saucepan of boiling water until very soft.
2. Make sweet white sauce and allow to become almost cold.
3. Stir in melted chocolate and mix well.
4. Flavour with vanilla.
5. Serve with steamed puddings.

Brandy Sauce

1 cup water
1 tablespoon sugar
1 tablespoon cornflour or arrowroot
2 tablespoons cold water
3 tablespoons brandy

1. Place sugar and water in a saucepan and heat.
2. Stir in blended cornflour and cook for 2 to 3 minutes.
3. Just before serving add the brandy.
4. Serve with steamed Christmas pudding.

Mocha Sauce

2 tablespoons instant coffee powder
½ cup water
¾ cup firmly packed brown sugar
¾ cup caster sugar
¾ cup golden syrup
¼ cup butter or margarine
⅓ cup evaporated milk
½ teaspoon vanilla

Into a saucepan place coffee, water, sugars, syrup and butter. Stir over low heat until sugar has dissolved. Boil to 115°C or until a little will form a soft ball in cold water. Remove from heat, cool for a few minutes then stir in the evaporated milk. Add vanilla to taste. Bottle and use as required as a topping for ice-cream.

Orange Sauce

2 oranges
3 tablespoons sugar
¾ cup water
2 tablespoons cornflour
a little orange rind

1. Squeeze juice from oranges and place in a saucepan with sugar and water.
2. Blend cornflour with a little water.
3. Bring liquid to boiling point then stir in blended cornflour.
4. Stir until thickened then remove from the heat. Add rind.
5. Pour over steamed orange pudding just before serving.

Hard Sauce

120 g butter or margarine
½ cup icing sugar
2 tablespoons brandy

1. Beat butter and sugar together until creamy.
2. Add the brandy gradually. Chill well.
3. Serve with steamed Christmas pudding.

Pineapple Sauce

1 440 g can crushed pineapple
½ cup sugar
2–3 sprigs mint
1 tablespoon cornflour

1. Drain pineapple. Measure juice and add water to make 1 cup liquid. Combine juice and sugar and boil for 5 minutes.
2. Thicken with cornflour blended with a little cold water.
3. Remove from heat and add sprigs of mint. Allow to stand until cold.
4. Remove mint and add pineapple. Chill well.
5. Use as a topping for ice-cream.

Jam Sauce

4–5 tablespoons red jam
4 cups water
1½ tablespoons arrowroot
2 tablespoons sugar
a little lemon juice

1. Place jam, water, sugar and lemon juice in a saucepan.
2. Bring to boiling point and stir in blended arrowroot.
3. Boil for 1 minute then remove from heat.
4. Strain if desired and serve with plain steamed pudding.

Variation

Brandy may be added and the sauce served with steamed Christmas pudding.

Toasted Muesli

2 cups rolled oats

1½ cups mixed grain flakes

1 cup unprocessed bran

½ cup coconut

½ cup flaked almonds

½ cup skim milk powder

½ cup sunflower seeds

½ cup honey

¼ cup cold pressed oil

1 cup (or more) chopped dried fruits, including apples, apricots and prunes

½ cup sultanas

1. In a large bowl mix oats, flakes, bran, coconut, almonds, milk powder and sunflower seeds.
2. Place honey and oil in a small saucepan and heat until combined.
3. Mix into dry ingredients and bake in moderate oven for about 20 minutes. Stir frequently during baking.
4. Cool then add prepared fruit and mix well.
5. Store in an airtight container in the refrigerator, if possible.

(Approx. 8 cups)

✗ Toasted Muesli

2 cups rice flakes

2 cups chopped mixed nuts and/or sunflower seeds

1 cup soy flakes or soy grits

1 cup coconut

½ cup honey

⅓ cup vegetable oil

1. Place all dry ingredients in a bowl and mix well.
2. Place honey and oil in a saucepan and heat until well warmed.
3. Pour honey mixture over dry ingredients and combine.
4. Spread on a greased tray and toast in a slow oven until dry and light brown, taking care to mix and stir ingredients often.
5. Cool and store in an airtight container.

Traditional Oats

1 cup traditional rolled oats

1 cup cold water

3 cups boiling water

1. Place rolled oats in a saucepan with cold water. Mix well.
2. Add boiling water and mix well.
3. Place over heat and bring to boiling point and simmer for 8 to 10 minutes, stirring occasionally.
4. Pour into individual bowls and serve with milk.

(Serves 4)

* Rolled Oats Porridge

1½ cups quick cooking rolled oats

4 cups hot water

½ teaspoon salt

1. Place oats, water and salt in 2 to 3 litre bowl.
2. Cook on HIGH for 10 to 12 minutes, stirring several times during cooking.
3. Allow to stand for 2 to 3 minutes before serving in bowls with milk, and sugar if liked.

Note: Porridge may be made in serving bowls. Place ¼ cup oats, pinch salt and ⅔ cup water in a bowl and cook on HIGH for 2 to 3 minutes. Allow to stand for 2 minutes.

Muesli

2 cups quick cooking or traditional rolled oats

½ cup rye flakes

½ cup barley flakes

½ cup wheat flakes

½ cup rice flakes

½ cup oat bran

½ cup (or more) chopped mixed dried fruit medley containing apricots, pears, apples and peaches

½ cup sultanas

½ cup skim milk powder

1. Mix all ingredients.
2. Store in an airtight container in a cool place.

Additional optional ingredients

1 tablespoon sunflower seeds

1 tablespoon pumpkin seeds

2 to 3 tablespoons flaked almonds

Note: Quantities may be varied according to availability.   *(Approx. 6 cups)*

✴ Muesli

90 g rice puffs or flakes

2 cups gluten-free cornflakes

½ cup rice bran

¼ cup soy grits or soy flakes

1 cup flaked coconut

2 cups raisins or sultanas

125 g chopped dried pawpaw

1 cup chopped dried apples

¼ cup sunflower seeds

1½ cups chopped dried apricots

Mix all ingredients well and store in an airtight container.

Eggs Cooked in Shells

This may be done in three ways:

Boiling — Soft

Half fill a small saucepan with water and bring to boiling point. Lower eggs into water gently and simmer for 3 to 4 minutes.

Boiling — Hard

As above, cooking for 10 to 15 minutes. So that the yolks will be in the centre of eggs when cooked, stir the eggs gently during the first 5 minutes of cooking. Cool under running cold water and shell as soon as possible to prevent a dark ring forming around the yolks.

Coddling

Place in a saucepan of boiling water, remove from the heat and allow to remain in water for 10 minutes. When eggs are ready, remove at once from water and serve in egg cups with pepper and toast.

Note: To avoid eggs cracking, eggs should be at room temperature when immersed in boiling water.

Poached Eggs

boiling water

eggs

toast

1. Pour water into frying pan to a depth of 18 mm.
2. Bring to boiling point.
3. Crack eggs one at a time and pour into egg rings in the pan.
4. Simmer for approximately 3 minutes. Lift rings when eggs are partly set.
5. Remove with an egg-lifter, drain off water and serve on hot toast. Garnish with parsley.

* Poached Eggs

½ cup water

vinegar

2 eggs

toast

1. Place ¼ cup water and a dash of vinegar into each of two small ramekin dishes or bowls.
2. Heat on HIGH for 1½ minutes or until boiling.
3. Break egg into boiling water, pierce yolk and white with a cocktail stick. Cover with plastic wrap.
4. Cook on MEDIUM for 30 to 40 seconds. Allow to stand for 1 minute before serving.
5. Drain and serve on toast.

(Serves 2)

Scrambled Eggs

2 eggs

1–2 tablespoons milk

parsley (optional)

toast

1. Beat eggs well then add milk. Chop parsley finely.
2. Brush or spray pan with oil and heat.
3. Add egg mixture and stir over gentle heat until thick. Do not overcook.
4. Add a little chopped parsley and spoon onto toast.
5. Serve on a hot plate.

(Serves 1–2)

Baked Eggs in Tomatoes

2 firm ripe tomatoes
pepper
2 eggs
1 teaspoon butter
2 slices toast

1. Cut a thick slice off tops of tomatoes and scoop out most of the centres.
2. Sprinkle pepper in the bottom of each tomato.
3. Break eggs into tomato cups.
4. Grease a small pie dish very well.
5. Stand tomatoes in pie dish and cover with alfoil.
6. Bake in a moderate oven until eggs are set — approximately 20 minutes.
7. Lift onto toast and garnish with parsley.
8. Fried or grilled bacon may accompany this dish.

(Serves 1–2)

Fried Eggs and Bacon

2 bacon rashers
a little oil
2 eggs

1. Remove rind. Cut bacon rashers into 2 or 3 pieces.
2. Brush or spray non-stick pan with oil, heat and cook bacon until crisp.
3. When cooked, drain on paper towels and keep warm.
4. Add a little extra oil to pan if necessary and heat until hot.
5. Breaks eggs on a saucer, one at a time, and slide carefully into pan.
6. Cook slowly, until eggs are set.
7. When ready lift out with an egg-lifter, drain on paper towels and serve on a hot plate with the bacon.

(Serves 1–2)

✳ Bacon

bacon rashers

1. Remove rind from rashers.
2. Place between four layers of absorbent paper on a dinner plate.
3. Cook on HIGH allowing 1 minute per rasher, longer for crisper bacon. Time will vary with thickness and size of rashers. Bacon will continue to brown on standing.
4. Serve as required.

Scrambled Eggs with Tomato

oil

1 tomato, skinned and chopped

¼ teaspoon sugar

pepper

2 eggs

1–2 tablespoons milk

parsley

1. Brush or spray pan with oil and heat. Place tomato, pepper and sugar in a small saucepan and cook until soft. If very juicy, allow to simmer until excess liquid evaporates.
2. Prepare scrambled eggs as previous recipe and serve.
3. Spoon tomato over the top.
4. Garnish with parsley.

(Serves 1–2)

French Omelette

2 eggs

pepper

1. Break eggs into a bowl, add pepper.
2. Beat eggs with a whisk for about 30 seconds.
3. Brush or spray non-stick pan with oil and heat.
4. Pour in eggs and stir briskly for a few seconds.
5. As the omelette begins to set lift edges to cause unset egg to run onto the bottom of pan. This will give irregular edges and a rippled surface.
6. When egg no longer runs freely but is still creamy in the centre, remove from heat and fold omelette in three.
7. Lift onto a hot plate and serve at once garnished with parsley.

Variations

Bacon Omelette

Add a little very finely chopped cooked bacon and a teaspoon of finely chopped shallot to the egg mixture.

Cheese Omelette

Stir a little finely grated cheese into the egg mixture.

Mushroom Omelette

Fry some chopped mushrooms in a little oil then add to the mixture.

Note: Fillings may also be put into the centre of the omelette before folding.

(Serves 1–2)

Soufflé Omelette

2 eggs
2 teaspoons water
pepper
parsley

1. Separate whites from yolks of eggs.
2. Beat yolks with water until creamy.
3. Whisk egg whites to a stiff but not dry froth.
4. Lightly fold yolks into whites. Add pepper to taste.
5. Brush or spray omelette pan with oil, heat and pour in egg mixture.
6. Cook over very moderate heat for about 3 minutes.
7. Set top by placing under griller for a minute.
8. Fold in half and place on a hot plate.
9. Garnish with parsley and serve immediately.

Variations

Fillings

Cheese Omelette

Sprinkle grated cheese on top of omelette just before folding.

Asparagus Omelette

Warm some asparagus in a saucepan. Drain well and place in omelette before folding.

Avocado Omelette

Fill with cubes of avocado. Fold over.

(Serves 1–2)

Catalan Omelette (Spain)

olive oil for frying
1 large onion, finely chopped
1 clove garlic, crushed
2 potatoes, boiled in skins, skinned and diced
black pepper
6 eggs, beaten

1. Heat a little olive oil in a large frying pan and fry onion and garlic gently until golden.
2. Add the potatoes and season with pepper.
3. Cook until the potatoes are golden, stirring occasionally.
4. Pour eggs into the pan and cook until the bottom sets and is lightly browned when lifted with a spatula.
5. Transfer to a hot griller and cook for a few minutes or until top is set and browned.
6. Slide onto a hot platter and serve immediately cut into wedges.

Note: Spanish Omelettes are never folded.

(Serves 4)

Fried Sausages with Gravy

500 g sausages, pork, beef
   or chicken
1–2 tablespoons flour
2 pinches pepper
1 cup water

1. Prick sausages with a fork.
2. Roll in a mixture of flour and pepper.
3. Brush or spray non-stick pan with oil, heat and add sausages. Fry gently until well browned, turning frequently.
4. Drain on absorbent paper.
5. Pour any oil out of pan and sprinkle pan with remainder of flour. Mix flour with pan sediment.
6. Stir until browned, add water gradually, blending to a smooth consistency. Stir until boiling.
7. Serve over sausages.

(Serves 3–4)

Crumbed Sausages

500 g sausages
1–2 tablespoons flour
pepper
1 egg
milk
dry breadcrumbs
oil for frying

1. Place sausages in a saucepan and cover with warm water.
2. Bring to boiling point slowly and simmer for 30 minutes.
3. Drain and when cool peel skins off.
4. Roll in flour seasoned with pepper.
5. Dip in a mixture of egg and milk.
6. Toss in light-coloured dry breadcrumbs.
7. Deep fry until a rich brown colour.
8. Drain on absorbent paper.
9. Serve hot with tomato sauce.

(Serves 3–4)

Sausages with Tomatoes

sausages
oil for frying
tomatoes
pepper
a little sugar
flour

1. Prick sausages with a fork.
2. Brush or spray pan with oil and heat.
3. Place sausages in pan, and cook gently for about 10 minutes.
4. When half cooked add tomatoes, each cut into three slices.
5. Turn sausages frequently and tomato slices once.
6. Sprinkle tomatoes with pepper and sugar.
7. Serve on a hot plate.

Preparation of Brains

1. Wash brains under running water.
2. Soak in cold or tepid water with salt for 1 hour.
3. Keep changing water during soaking.
4. Divide lobes carefully with a knife.
5. Remove skin very carefully with fingers.
6. Place in cold water in a saucepan. Add a little lemon juice or vinegar.
7. Bring to boiling point and strain immediately.

Cooking of Brains

1. (a) Place brains in a saucepan with very little water.
   (b) Simmer very gently for 20 minutes.
   (c) Drain off water.   or

2. (a) Place brains in a small basin.
   (b) Cover and stand in a saucepan of water.
   (c) Bring to boiling point and allow water to boil for 30 minutes.

Crumbed Brains

1 set brains
flour
pepper
beaten egg
dry breadcrumbs
oil for frying

1. Divide cooked brains into pieces and roll in flour seasoned with pepper.
2. Dip in beaten egg then toss in breadcrumbs.
3. Deep or shallow fry until golden brown.
4. Drain on absorbent paper.
5. Serve hot garnished with parsley.

(*Serves 1*)

Welsh Rarebit (Wales)

1¼ cups grated cheddar cheese
2–3 tablespoons milk
1 egg
pepper
2 slices bread

1. Place cheese in a saucepan with milk and stir over heat until cheese has melted.
2. When quite hot, stir in beaten egg, continue to stir until the mixture is smooth. Do not boil.
3. Season with pepper.
4. Serve on toast.

(*Serves 2*)

Bean and Sausage Bake

500 g pork sausages

oil

1 onion, chopped

2 medium carrots, sliced

1 425 g can chopped tomatoes

½ cup water

1 stock cube

250 g can haricot beans, drained and rinsed

pepper

½ cup grated cheese

1. Grill sausages and cut into slices.
2. Brush or spray pan with oil and heat.
3. Sauté onion and carrot for 3 minutes.
4. Add chopped tomatoes, stock cube and water and simmer until vegetables are tender.
5. Add beans and sausages and pepper to taste.
6. Place in an ovenproof dish and top with grated cheese.
7. Bake in a moderate oven for 15 minutes.
8. Serve hot.

(Serves 6–8)

Cheese Soufflé

2 teaspoons margarine

1 tablespoon plain flour

150 mL milk

3 eggs

pinch white pepper

pinch cayenne pepper

¾ cup grated cheese

1. Cut a piece of foil or baking paper 5 cm longer than the circumference of the soufflé dish. Fold paper in half lengthwise and wrap around the outside edge of the dish extending 5 cm above the rim. Secure paper with string.
2. Grease soufflé dish well.
3. Melt margarine in a saucepan, add flour and mix until smooth.
4. Add the milk gradually and stir continuously over the heat until thickened. Remove from heat.
5. Add the egg yolks and beat well.
6. Add pepper and cayenne to taste.
7. Mix in the grated cheese.
8. Whisk egg whites to a stiff froth and fold into mixture.
9. Pour into greased dish and bake for approximately 30 minutes.
10. Serve immediately.

(Serves 3)

French Toast and Bacon

oil
4 bacon rashers
4 slices toasting bread
1 egg
1–2 tablespoons milk
pepper

1. Brush or spray pan with oil, heat and add bacon.
2. Cook until crisp then remove from pan.
3. Remove crusts from bread if desired.
4. Beat egg and milk together, dip bread quickly in egg mixture and fry until golden brown. Add extra oil if necessary.
5. Drain on absorbent paper then serve on hot plates with bacon on top.

(Serves 2)

Liver and Bacon

4 bacon rashers
500 g calves liver *or* lambs fry
2 tablespoons plain flour
pepper
1½ cups water
½ lemon
parsley

1. Cut bacon rashers in half, and remove rind.
2. Put bacon into a hot frying pan and fry in its own fat.
3. When cooked remove, drain and keep warm.
4. Remove skin from liver and cut downwards into slices about 12 mm thick.
5. Roll each piece in a mixture of flour and pepper.
6. Fry for 5 to 6 minutes in a small amount of the hot bacon fat, turning once.
7. Lift out onto a plate and pour oil out of pan.
8. Sprinkle in remainder of flour, stir well until browned, add water and stir until boiling. Add lemon juice.
9. Strain if necessary then return to pan and add liver and reheat.
10. Serve on a hot dish with bacon around it.
11. Garnish with parsley.

(Serves 4)

Reiberkuchen (Germany)

(Potato Cakes)

500 g potatoes
1 medium onion
1 egg
1 tablespoon flour
pepper
oil for frying

1. Peel potatoes and grate finely. Press between paper towels to remove excess liquid.
2. Chop or grate onion finely and add to the potato. Drain off any liquid which may have collected.
3. Add beaten egg, flour and pepper to taste.
4. Heat oil in a frying pan. Spoon mixture into the pan to make circular cakes about 15 cm in diameter.
5. Cook until golden brown on each side making sure they are cooked through. Ensure that the pan has sufficient oil to prevent the cakes from sticking.
6. Continue until all the mixture has been used.
7. Serve Reiberkuchen immediately while fresh and hot. Serve with apple sauce.

Note: This is a traditional German dish and is eaten at any time of the day or evening.

(Serves 3–4)

Mushroom, Ham and Zucchini Slice

(Crustless Quiche)

4 eggs
½ cup oil
1 cup self-raising flour
1 cup grated zucchini
1 cup chopped ham
1 onion, chopped
1 cup sliced mushrooms
1 cup grated cheddar cheese
pepper

1. Beat eggs, add oil, then the flour and mix well.
2. Add the other ingredients and mix.
3. Pour into a greased deep-sided square dish.
4. Bake in a moderate oven for about 40 minutes until brown.
5. Serve hot cut into slices.

(Serves 4–6)

Tomato Savoury

1 kg tomatoes
oil
4 bacon rashers, diced
1 onion, sliced
100 g mushrooms, sliced
1 cup grated cheese

1. Place tomatoes in a deep bowl and scald with boiling water. Leave 2 minutes then plunge into cold water and drain.
2. When cool enough to handle remove skins and cut into slices.
3. Brush or spray pan with oil, heat and sauté bacon, onion and mushrooms until onions are transparent.
4. Place half the tomatoes in a greased ovenproof dish.
5. Spread with bacon mixture and half the cheese.
6. Add remaining tomatoes and sprinkle with cheese.
7. Bake in a moderate oven for 25 to 30 minutes. Do not overcook.

(Serves 5–6)

Quick Mix Savoury Flan

1 cup fresh breadcrumbs (optional)
3 large eggs
1 onion, chopped
4 bacon rashers, diced
1 cup grated cheese
1 cup milk
1 tablespoon chopped parsley
pepper
1 tomato, sliced (optional)

1. Grease a 20 to 22 cm flan or pie dish and sprinkle base with breadcrumbs.
2. Beat eggs lightly then add all ingredients except tomato.
3. Carefully pour the mixture into the dish over the back of a spoon.
4. Arrange tomato slices over the top.
5. Stand dish on a baking tray and bake in a moderate oven (180°C) for 40 to 45 minutes or until set in the centre.
6. Serve hot or warm garnished with parsley.

Variation

Add 1 zucchini, grated, and/or 1 cup corn kernels, drained.

(Serves 6–8)

Batters

French Frying Batter

1 cup plain flour
1 tablespoon melted butter or margarine
½ cup warm water
2 egg whites

1. Sift flour into a bowl.
2. Add melted butter, then the tepid water and beat well.
3. Allow to stand 1 hour.
4. Just before frying fold in stiffly beaten egg whites.
5. Use for sweet or savoury fritters.

Note: The yolks may be added with the butter and water if a richer colour is required.

Plain Batter

½ cup plain flour
½ cup self-raising flour
1 small egg
1 cup milk

1. Sift flour into a bowl.
2. Add the well-beaten egg and then the milk.
3. Beat or process until smooth.
4. Allow to stand for 1 hour if possible.
5. Use as required for sweet or savoury fritters.

✗ Batter

1 cup maize cornflour (gluten free)
⅓ cup soy flour
2 teaspoons gluten-free baking powder
½ cup instant baby rice cereal, gluten free
1 egg, beaten
½ cup milk
½ cup water
2 teaspoons vegetable oil

1. Sift together cornflour, soy flour and baking powder. Add rice cereal and mix well.
2. Make a well in the centre, add egg, milk, water and oil and beat well until smooth.
3. Use as required.

Note: If a thinner batter is required, add a little extra milk.

Fritters

Apple

1. Peel, core and slice apples into rings about 6 mm thick.
2. Sprinkle with lemon juice and sugar.
3. Dip in batter then shallow fry in hot oil.
4. Allow to become a rich brown on both sides.
5. Place on absorbent paper to drain.
6. Sprinkle with sugar.
7. Serve at once.

Banana

1. Peel bananas, cut into slices and stir into batter.
2. Spoon into hot, shallow oil and cook until a rich brown on both sides.
3. Place on absorbent paper to drain.
4. Sprinkle with sugar.
5. Serve at once.

Meat

1. Dice any cold meat, e.g. corned beef, and add to batter.
2. Add chopped parsley.
3. Spoon into hot, shallow oil and fry until a rich brown on both sides.
4. Drain on absorbent paper.
5. Serve at once with tomato sauce.

Crepe Batter

125 g plain flour (1 cup)
2 egg yolks
125 mL milk
125 mL water
2 tablespoons melted butter
oil
2 teaspoons caster sugar, for sweet crepes

1. Sift flour into a bowl and make well in centre.
2. Add yolks to milk and mix well.
3. Gradually add milk and egg mixture, water and melted butter, beating well.
4. Beat until smooth and allow to stand for 30 minutes to 1 hour.
5. Brush or spray pan with oil and heat.
6. Pour in enough batter to coat base of pan thinly and cook until the edges of the crepe turn golden brown.
7. Flip it over and cook on the other side for 1 minute.
8. Brush pan with a little more oil and repeat for each crepe.

(Makes 12 crepes)

Crepes

2 eggs

3/4 cup milk

6 tablespoons maize cornflour (gluten free)

1 tablespoon canola oil

3/4 teaspoon gluten-free baking powder

1. Place all ingredients in bowl and beat or process until smooth.
2. Cook as for traditional Crepe recipe.

FILLINGS FOR CREPES

Savoury

- To a cup of white sauce add 120 g finely chopped ham, grated cheese and a little mustard. Reheat to melt cheese. Garnish with parsley.
- To a cup of white sauce add 105 g can drained salmon. Flavour with a little chopped shallot. Serve with a spoonful of sour cream and garnish with fresh herbs.

Sweet

- Four peeled and sliced apples cooked with brown sugar, cinnamon and a little butter. Sprinkle top with cinnamon and sugar.
- A small can of apricots pureed and thickened with arrowroot. Add chopped almonds. Top with whipped cream.
- 1 tin crushed pineapple in natural juice thickened with 2 tablespoons of custard powder. Top with whipped cream.
- Two or three bananas mashed with lemon juice and a little icing sugar. Top with whipped cream.
- Equal parts of honey and butter creamed together with walnuts added.
- Lemon juice and sugar sprinkled over rolled pancakes or crepes.

Pancakes

1 cup plain flour
2 eggs
½ cup milk
½ cup water
1 tablespoon melted butter or margarine

1. Sift flour into a bowl.
2. Make a well in the centre, drop in well-beaten eggs.
3. Gradually add milk, water and melted butter, beating all the time.
4. Beat or process until smooth then allow to stand for 1 hour.
5. Grease a small pan very lightly and heat.
6. Pour in sufficient batter for one pancake.
7. When edges are set turn to brown the other side.
8. Spread with filling and roll.

Pancakes

½ cup buckwheat flour
½ cup rice flour
1 egg
300 mL milk

1. Place flour in bowl and make well in centre.
2. Add egg to milk and beat well.
3. Gradually beat milk mixture into flour until smooth.
4. Cook as for basic pancakes.

Yorkshire Pudding

1 cup plain flour
1 egg
½ cup milk
½ cup water
a little oil

1. Sift flour into a bowl.
2. Hollow out centre of flour and drop egg into it.
3. Pour half of liquids onto egg.
4. Using a wooden spoon, mix batter from centre, first mixing eggs and liquids together, then gradually working in flour from round the sides.
5. Beat the batter well until smooth and shiny.
6. Stir in remainder of liquids and allow to stand for 1 hour.
7. Place a small amount of oil in each of 12 deep patty tins and heat in a hot oven.
8. Pour batter from a jug into each tin until almost full.
9. Put into hot oven (230°C) on top shelf and bake 10 minutes.
10. Reduce heat and bake for a further 10 to 15 minutes.
11. Serve with roast beef.

Yorkshire Pudding

2 eggs (55 g each)
125 g rice flour
150 mL milk

1. Place all ingredients in bowl and beat or process until smooth.
2. Allow to stand for 30 minutes then beat batter well.
3. Place into lightly greased patty tins and bake in a hot oven (220°C) for 10 to 15 minutes.

Pikelets

1 egg
3 tablespoons sugar
½ cup milk
1 cup self-raising flour
2 teaspoons butter or
** 1 tablespoon cream**

1. Place egg, sugar and half the milk in a bowl.
2. Whisk well with a rotary beater.
3. Sift flour and add to mixture.
4. Add remaining milk until batter is the consistency of thick cream. Add melted butter or cream.
5. Beat until smooth then pour tablespoonfuls onto a preheated and greased griddle iron or frypan.
6. When surface is bubbly turn with a spatula and cook on the other side.
7. Remove and place in a tea towel to cool.

(Makes approximately 12)

Pikelets

2 eggs, beaten
2 tablespoons sugar
1¼ cups pourable,
** prepared, gluten-free**
** custard**
1 tablespoon vegetable oil
2 cups maize cornflour
** (gluten free)**
4 teaspoons gluten-free
** baking powder**

1. Place eggs, sugar, custard and oil in a bowl.
2. Sift cornflour and baking powder and beat into the egg mixture until smooth.
3. Continue as for traditional Pikelet recipe.

Baked Custard

3 eggs
600 mL milk
2–3 tablespoons sugar
vanilla
nutmeg

1. Beat eggs well then add milk, sugar and vanilla.
2. Stir until sugar has dissolved.
3. Pour into a greased pie dish.
4. Sprinkle with nutmeg.
5. Stand in a baking dish filled with one centimetre of water and bake in a slow oven until set.
6. Serve chilled with fruit.

(Serves 4–6)

Bread and Butter Custard

Prepare custard as above. Spread sliced bread lightly with margarine or butter. Remove crusts if desired and cut slices into squares or triangles. Arrange on top of custard mixture. Add a few sultanas for flavour. Make sure bread is saturated with custard before baking.

Rice Custard

Boil 2 tablespoons of rice in water until soft. Drain and add to custard mixture.

Quick Custard

2 tablespoons custard powder
600 mL milk
1–2 tablespoons sugar
vanilla

1. Blend custard powder with a little of the milk to make a smooth paste.
2. Place remainder of milk in a saucepan with sugar and bring to the boil. Remove from heat.
3. Stir in custard powder mixture, return to heat and continue to stir until sauce boils and thickens.
4. Add vanilla and serve as required.

Boiled Custard

2 tablespoons cornflour
600 mL milk
2 egg yolks
2 tablespoons sugar
vanilla

1. Blend cornflour with a little of the milk.
2. Beat egg yolks and sugar with a little milk.
3. Place remainder of milk in a saucepan and bring to boiling point.
4. Stir in the cornflour and allow to boil for 2 minutes.
5. Remove from heat and cool.
6. Pour over egg yolks and beat well.
7. Return to saucepan and cook until mixture coats the spoon. Take care mixture does not boil. Stand pan in water while cooking or use a double saucepan.
8. Add vanilla.
9. Pour into a jug to serve.

(Serves 5–6)

✳ Boiled Custard

2 tablespoons cornflour
600 mL milk
2 egg yolks
2 tablespoons sugar
vanilla

1. Blend cornflour with a little of the milk, add beaten egg yolks, sugar and remaining milk. Beat well.
2. Cook on HIGH for 4 to 5 minutes, stirring every minute until mixture coats the spoon.
3. Take care mixture does not boil.
4. Add vanilla.
5. Pour into a jug to serve.

(Serves 4–5)

Junket

600 mL milk
2 tablespoons sugar
vanilla
2 junket tablets

1. Pour milk into a saucepan.
2. Add sugar and warm mixture.
3. Remove from heat, add vanilla and pour into a glass dish.
4. Crush junket tablet and mix with a little cold water.
5. Stir into milk and mix well.
6. Allow to stand until set.
7. Chill and serve with fruit.

(Serves 4–5)

Crème Caramel (France)

Caramel

1 cup sugar

¼ cup water

Custard

2 teaspoons sugar

600 mL milk

3 eggs

vanilla

Caramel

1. Place sugar and water in a small saucepan.
2. Stir over heat until sugar has dissolved.
3. Boil without stirring until light caramel colour.
4. Remove from heat and pour hot caramel into greased moulds and swirl to cover base. When quite cold add custard.

Custard

5. Place sugar and milk in saucepan and gently stir over low heat until sugar has dissolved.
6. Whisk eggs and vanilla for 1 to 2 minutes and stir in warm milk mixture.
7. Pour into moulds.
8. Stand moulds in a dish of water and bake in a slow oven (140°C) until firm.
9. When cold turn out onto a dish.
10. Serve with whipped cream and strawberries.

(Serves 4–5)

Blancmange

3–4 tablespoons sugar

3 tablespoons cornflour

600 mL milk

vanilla

1. Blend cornflour and sugar with a little milk.
2. Place remaining milk in a saucepan and bring to boiling point. Remove from heat.
3. Add blended sugar and cornflour, stirring well the whole time.
4. Place over heat and boil for 2 to 3 minutes.
5. Flavour with vanilla then pour into a wet mould to set. Sprinkle with coconut.

Note: Blancmange may be made in two colours: while and pale pink. Pour half mixture into a mould, colour the remainder with cochineal and pour on top of white.

Variation

Chocolate Blancmange

Add 2 tablespoons cocoa and 4 tablespoons sugar.

(Serves 5–6)

Baked Rice

3 tablespoons short-grain rice
300 mL water
600 mL milk
3 tablespoons sugar
nutmeg

1. Place rice in a pie dish and add water.
2. Cook slowly in the oven (150°C) until rice absorbs the water.
3. Add milk and sugar and mix well. Sprinkle with nutmeg.
4. Bake in a very slow oven for about 1 hour.
5. Serve cold with stewed fruit.

(Serves 4–5)

Creamed Rice

3 tablespoons short-grain rice
600 mL milk
3 tablespoons sugar

1. Place rice in a saucepan with milk.
2. Cook over low heat until grains are soft, stirring frequently.
3. Add sugar and stir to dissolve.
4. Pour into a serving dish to cool.
5. Serve with fruit.

Note: The cooked mixture will be very thin. It will thicken on cooling.

Variations

Extra Creamy Rice with Fruit

Add a little whipped cream to the cooled rice and serve in individual dishes. Top with canned or stewed fruit.

Banana and Coconut Rice

Add 1 tablespoon coconut and a few drops of coconut essence to creamed rice. Just before serving add sliced bananas and fold in. Serve in individual dishes and decorate with 2 or 3 slices of banana and a cherry.

Chocolate Rice

When creamed rice is almost cooked add 50 g grated cooking chocolate. Serve in individual dishes topped with sliced fresh or canned peaches.

(Serves 5–6)

Queen Pudding

3 egg yolks
3 tablespoons sugar
1 teaspoon vanilla
2½ cups milk
1½ cups soft white breadcrumbs
⅓ cup apricot jam

Meringue
3 egg whites
3 tablespoons caster sugar

1. Beat egg yolks with sugar and vanilla.
2. Pour into a saucepan with milk. Heat until very warm.
3. Add breadcrumbs and pour into an ovenproof dish.
4. Stand dish in a baking tray of hot water and bake in a slow to moderate oven until set.
5. Allow to cool then spread with jam.
6. Whisk egg whites until stiff peaks form then gradually add sugar, whisking until dissolved.
7. Pile on top of pudding and bake in a slow oven until meringue is golden brown.
8. Chill well before serving.

(Serves 4–5)

Apple Crumble

Fruit
4–6 cooking apples
1–2 tablespoons sugar
⅓ cup water

Crumble
1 cup plain flour
3 tablespoons butter or margarine
3 tablespoons brown sugar
3 tablespoons coconut
½ teaspoon cinnamon

1. Peel and core apples and slice thinly.
2. Place in a saucepan with water and simmer gently until soft. Add sugar to taste and stir to dissolve.
3. Allow to cool then pour into a pie dish, keeping back excess juice.
4. Place flour in a bowl then rub in butter with the fingertips.
5. Add sugar, coconut and cinnamon and mix well.
6. Sprinkle lightly on top of apples.
7. Bake in a moderate oven until lightly browned on top.
8. Serve hot or cold with boiled custard or caramel sauce.

Variations of Fruit

Rhubarb and apple
Pie peaches
Stewed dried apricots
Crushed pineapple, thickened with custard powder

Variations of Crumble

Rolled oats can be added and refined flour replaced by wholemeal flour.

(Serves 5–6)

Apple Crumble

Fruit Layer

Proceed as in the traditional recipe.

Crumble

¾ cup brown rice flour

4 tablespoons margarine

¼ cup buckwheat flakes

¼ cup millet flakes

¼ cup almonds, walnuts or hazelnuts, chopped

¼ cup brown sugar

1 teaspoon ground cinnamon

1. Place brown rice flour in bowl and rub in margarine until mixture resembles breadcrumbs.
2. Stir in buckwheat and millet flakes, nuts, brown sugar and cinnamon. Mix well.
3. Continue as per traditional recipe.

(Serves 4)

Lemon Delicious Pudding

2 tablespoons butter or margarine

¾ cup sugar

2 large eggs, separated

1 cup milk

3 tablespoons flour

juice and rind 2 lemons

1. Cream butter and sugar.
2. Add the egg yolks and a little of the milk and beat to combine.
3. Add the flour and mix until smooth. Add remainder of milk.
4. Add grated rind of 1 lemon and the juice of both lemons.
5. Lastly fold in the stiffly-beaten egg whites.
6. Pour into a greased pie dish.
7. Stand in a dish of warm water.
8. Bake in a moderate oven for about 20 minutes, reduce heat and bake slowly for another 25 minutes.
9. Serve cold with cream.

(Serves 5–6)

Lemon Delicious

1 tablespoon butter or margarine

4 tablespoons caster sugar

2 eggs, separated

2 tablespoons maize cornflour (gluten free)

juice of 2 lemons

rind of 1 lemon (optional)

1¼ cups milk

1. Cream butter and sugar.
2. Add egg yolks, sifted cornflour, lemon juice and rind and mix well.
3. Gradually add milk and stir thoroughly.
4. Beat egg whites until stiff and fold into pudding mixture.
5. Pour into a greased ovenproof dish and bake in a slow to moderate oven for 30 to 40 minutes.

(Serves 4–6)

Pineapple Upside-Down Cake

Cake Mixture

60 g butter or margarine

⅓ cup caster sugar

1 large egg

3 tablespoons milk

1 cup self-raising flour

1 teaspoon cinnamon (optional)

1 teaspoon ginger (optional)

Caramel

⅓ cup brown sugar

3 tablespoons butter or margarine

Fruit

1 small can sliced peaches, sliced pineapple or pears

glacé cherries

1. Cream the caramel mixture together and spread on the base of an 18 cm sandwich tin.
2. Arrange well-drained peaches, pineapple or pears in a pattern on top of caramel. Decorate with cherries.
3. Beat butter and sugar to a cream.
4. Add the egg and beat well.
5. Add sifted flour and spices alternately with milk.
6. Pour over caramel and fruit and spread evenly.
7. Bake in a moderate oven for 30 to 35 minutes.
8. Turn out of tin and place upside-down on a plate.
9. Serve hot with custard or cream.

(Serves 6)

✳ Pineapple Upside-Down Cake

Caramel

⅓ cup brown sugar

2 tablespoons butter or margarine

Fruit

3 slices canned pineapple

9 glacé cherries

Cake Mixture

60 g butter or margarine

⅓ cup caster sugar

1 large egg

¼ cup milk

1 cup self-raising flour

1 teaspoon cinnamon (optional)

1 teaspoon ginger (optional)

1. Grease an 18 cm round dish and place a greased circle of paper in the base.
2. Cream brown sugar and butter and spread over base.
3. Arrange a slice of pineapple in the centre with half circles round it. Fill spaces with cherries.

Cake Mixture

4. Beat butter and sugar to a cream. Add egg and mix in carefully without beating.
5. Add the sifted dry ingredients alternately with milk and mix.
6. Pour mixture over caramel and fruit.
7. Cook on MEDIUM-HIGH for 6 to 7 minutes or until just firm in the centre.
8. Allow to stand for 2 to 3 minutes before turning out onto a plate.
9. Serve hot with custard or cream, or warm for morning tea.

Note: For a larger cake use the Apple Tea Cake recipe, page 244, and increase caramel and fruit quantities. Cook in a 21 to 22 cm dish.

Basic Steamed Pudding

120 g butter or margarine
²/₃ cup caster sugar
2 large eggs
2 cups self-raising flour
vanilla
½ cup milk

1. Beat butter and sugar to a cream.
2. Add the eggs one at a time and beat well. Add vanilla.
3. Sift flour and add to mixture alternately with milk.
4. Grease pudding basin well and pour pudding mixture in.
5. Cover with lid or alfoil.
6. Place in a steamer or saucepan of simmering water with the water level halfway up basin. Cook for 1 to 1¼ hours.
7. Serve hot with boiled custard or sweet white sauce.

Variations

Steamed Fruit Pudding

Add ¾ cup chopped raisins, sultanas or dates to the mixture.

Steamed Jam or Syrup Pudding

Pour 1 cup thin jam or golden syrup into the base of the basin before filling with mixture.

Steamed Chocolate Pudding

Sift 3 teaspoons cocoa with the flour and increase milk to ¾ cup.

Steamed Orange Pudding

Add the grated rind of 1 orange and replace 1 tablespoon of milk with 1 tablespoon of juice.

Steamed Ginger Pudding

Add: 3 teaspoons ground ginger
      3 tablespoons treacle
      1 teaspoon baking soda
      Use plain flour.

(Serves 6–8)

✷ Steamed Pudding

125 g margarine or butter
½ cup caster sugar
2 eggs
1½ cups maize cornflour (gluten free)
1½ teaspoons gluten-free baking powder
¼ cup milk or water
⅓ cup jam or golden syrup

1. Cream margarine and sugar.
2. Add eggs and beat well after each egg addition.
3. Add sifted flour and baking powder alternately with milk or water.
4. Mix gently until well combined.
5. Place jam or syrup into base of greased pudding dish.
6. Pour pudding mixture in and cover with a lid of alfoil.
7. Place in a steamer or simmering water and cook for 40 to 45 minutes.
8. Serve hot with custard.

(Serves 4–6)

✗ Steamed Plum Pudding

1 cup milk

1½ cups mixed dried fruit

1 tablespoon margarine or butter

2 tablespoons sugar

2 eggs, beaten

1½ teaspoons cinnamon

1 cup maize cornflour (gluten free)

2 teaspoons bicarbonate of soda

1. Combine milk, dried fruit, margarine and sugar in a saucepan and bring to the boil. Allow to cool.
2. Place eggs, spices, cornflour and bicarbonate of soda in a medium bowl and mix well.
3. Fold fruit mixture into flour until well combined.
4. Pour into a greased pudding basin, cover with lid or alfoil and steam for 1½ hours.
5. Serve hot with custard or cold and sliced as a fruit cake.

(Serves 6–8)

Sticky Date Pudding

1 cup pitted dates, chopped

1 teaspoon bicarbonate of soda

1 cup water

90 g margarine or butter

½ cup brown sugar, firmly packed

2 eggs, beaten

1 teaspoon vanilla

1½ cups self-raising flour, sifted

Sauce

300 mL cream

1 cup brown sugar

90 g margarine or butter

¼ teaspoon vanilla essence

1. Place dates, bicarbonate of soda and water in a saucepan, stir and bring to boil. Remove from heat and allow to cool.
2. Cream margarine and sugar and add eggs, beating well after each. Add vanilla.
3. Sift flour and add to the creamed mixture alternately with dates.
4. Pour into a greased 20 cm square or round cake tin or ovenproof dish and bake in a moderate oven for 40 to 45 minutes.
5. Serve cut into slices and covered with warmed sauce.

Sauce

6. Combine cream, sugar, margarine and vanilla in a saucepan and heat until simmering, stirring continuously.
7. Simmer until slightly thicker and golden.

(Serves 6–8)

✗ Sticky Date Pudding

1½ cups rice flour

3 teaspoons gluten-free baking powder

60 g margarine or butter

¾ cup brown sugar, firmly packed

1 teaspoon vanilla

2 eggs

1 cup pitted dates

1 teaspoon bicarbonate of soda

1½ cups boiling water

Caramel Sauce

1 cup brown sugar, firmly packed

100 g margarine or butter

½ cup cream

½ teaspoon vanilla

Pudding

1. Sift rice flour and baking powder together.
2. Cream margarine, sugar and vanilla.
3. Beat in eggs, one at a time.
4. Fold in flour mixture.
5. Combine dates and bicarbonate of soda in a small bowl and pour boiling water over.
6. Stir date mixture into pudding and pour into a greased, 20 cm baking dish.
7. Bake in a 160°C oven for 35 to 40 minutes.
8. Pour ¼ cup of caramel sauce over pudding and bake a further 5 minutes.
9. Remove from oven and allow to stand for 10 minutes.
10. Serve with remaining caramel sauce.

Caramel Sauce

1. In a small saucepan, combine sugar, margarine, cream and vanilla.
2. Heat until boiling and simmer for 2 minutes.

Note: If sauce is too thick, thin with a little milk.

(Serves 6–8)

Apple Windsor

4 cooking apples
½ cup water
1–2 tablespoons sugar

Sponge

60 g butter or margarine
⅓ cup caster sugar
1 large egg
vanilla
3 tablespoons milk
1 cup self-raising flour

1. Peel and core apples and cut into eighths.
2. Place in a saucepan with water and cook gently until soft. Add sugar to taste and stir to dissolve.
3. Pour into a pie dish, keeping back excess juice.
4. Beat butter and sugar to a cream.
5. Add the egg and beat well. Add vanilla.
6. Add sifted flour and milk alternately and mix into a soft dough.
7. Pour on top of apples and spread evenly.
8. Bake in a moderate oven for 30 to 40 minutes or until sponge is well cooked.
9. Serve hot or cold with boiled custard.

Note: Packet cake mixture may be substituted for the above sponge mixture.

Variations

Stewed peaches
Canned peach pie filling
Rhubarb and apple
Mulberries thickened with arrowroot
Crushed pineapple, thickened with cornflour

(Serves 4–6)

Self-Saucing Chocolate Sponge

60 g butter/margarine
½ cup sugar
1 egg
1 cup self-raising flour
2 tablespoons cocoa
½ cup milk

Sauce

½ cup sugar
1½ cups hot water
2 tablespoons cocoa

1. Cream butter and sugar.
2. Add beaten egg and beat in.
3. Sift flour and cocoa, add flour and milk alternately. Pour into a greased 6-cup ovenproof dish.
4. Combine sugar and cocoa for sauce and sprinkle over batter in dish.
5. Pour hot water gently over the top and bake in 180°C oven for 35 to 40 minutes.
6. Serve warm with ice-cream.

(Serves 4–6)

Self-Saucing Chocolate Pudding

1 cup white rice flour

¾ cup caster sugar

2 tablespoons pure, unsweetened cocoa, extra

2 teaspoons gluten-free baking powder

½ cup milk

2 tablespoons vegetable oil

1 teaspoon vanilla

1 cup chopped nuts (optional)

1 cup brown sugar

¼ cup pure, unsweetened cocoa

1¾ cups very hot water

1. Place rice flour, sugar, extra cocoa and baking powder in a bowl and mix well.
2. Add milk, oil and vanilla and beat well until smooth. Stir in nuts.
3. Turn into a lightly greased, deep, ovenproof dish.
4. Mix together sugar and cocoa and sprinkle over batter.
5. Pour hot water gently over batter. Do not stir.
6. Bake in a moderate oven for 35 to 40 minutes.

(Serves 6)

Self-Saucing Caramel Pudding

Sponge Mixture

60 g butter or margarine

⅓ cup caster sugar

1 egg

¾ cup self-raising flour

3 tablespons milk

⅓ cup raisins

Sauce

1 cup brown sugar

1 cup water

1. Place sugar and water in a saucepan and boil for 3 minutes. Set aside to cool while sponge is made.
2. Cream butter and sugar. Add the egg and beat well.
3. Add sifted flour and milk alternately and mix into a soft dough. Add chopped seeded raisins.
4. Turn into a small, greased ovenproof dish. Pour the sauce over the top.
5. Bake in a moderate oven for 30 to 40 minutes.
6. Serve hot with boiled custard.

(Serves 4–6)

Steamed Christmas Pudding

120 g butter or margarine

½ cup caster sugar

2 large eggs

rind and juice ½ orange

1 tablespoon rum

1½ cups plain flour

½ teaspoon baking soda

¾ cup raisins

¾ cup sultanas

⅓ cup dates

8 or 10 cherries, chopped

1 tablespoon mixed peel

1½ teaspoons mixed spice

½ teaspoon nutmeg

½ teaspoon cinnamon

1. Beat butter and sugar to a cream.
2. Beat the eggs well and add gradually to mixture.
3. Add the rind and juice of orange and the rum.
4. Sift flour and soda onto a sheet of paper.
5. Cut raisins in half, dates and cherries into small pieces and mix with small amount of flour. Add sultanas and mix well.
6. Add prepared fruit and spices to flour and mix together.
7. Add gradually to creamed mixture and mix well.
8. Pour into a greased pudding basin, leaving 5 cm of space at the top.
9. Cover with a lid or greased alfoil and steam for 3 hours.
10. Steam for another hour on day of serving. Stand for a few minutes before turning out.
11. Serve with boiled custard.

Note: If desired additional fruit may be added.

(Serves 6–8)

Lemon Sago

½ cup sago

600 mL water

2 lemons

4 tablespoons sugar

4 tablespoons golden syrup

1. Wash sago and soak for 2 hours in 300 mL of water.
2. Put the remainder of water in a saucepan and bring to boiling point.
3. Add soaked sago and cook until transparent, stirring occasionally.
4. Remove from heat and add lemon juice and rind, sugar and syrup.
5. Mix well to blend ingredients.
6. Pour into a mould to set.
7. Serve cold with custard or cream.

Variation

Reduce water by ½ cup and add 1 cup grated pineapple.

(Serves 4–5)

Apple Cake

125 g butter or margarine
1–2 tablespoons sugar
1 egg
vanilla
1 tablespoon milk
1½ cups self-raising flour

Filling

4 large cooking apples
½ cup sugar
¼ cup water

Decoration

1 tablespoon icing sugar
strawberries

1. Peel, core and slice apples thinly.
2. Place in a saucepan with water and cook slowly until tender. Add sugar to taste and stir until dissolved.
3. Cream butter and sugar. Add the egg and vanilla and beat well.
4. Add milk and flour and mix into a soft paste. If too soft add a little more flour.
5. Turn onto a floured board, knead and cut into two pieces, one a little larger than the other.
6. Press larger piece into a greased springform tin. Make the sides high enough to enclose the apples.
7. Fill with cooled, drained apples.
8. Roll remainder of the pastry on a sheet of baking paper and cover apples.
9. Brush with milk. Bake in a moderate oven for about 30 minutes.
10. Before serving sift icing sugar over the top.
11. Decorate with strawberries.
12. Serve with boiled custard or cream.

(Serves 8)

Apple Slice with Topping

cake mixture as for apple cake

Filling

6–7 cooking apples
⅔ cup sugar
½ cup water

Topping

4 tablespoons sugar
2 tablespoons coconut
2 tablespoons walnuts, chopped
4 tablespoons flour
60 g butter or margarine, melted

1. Prepare and stew apples. Drain off any surplus juice. Allow to cool.
2. Mix together ingredients for the topping.
3. Press cake mixture into a lamington tin, making sides deep enough to accommodate the filling and topping.
4. Fill with cooked apple then sprinkle with topping.
5. Bake in a moderate oven for about 20 minutes.
6. Serve warm or cold cut into squares.

(Serves 8)

Apple Cream Pie (Italy)

Pastry

1¼ cups plain flour

½ teaspoon baking powder

½ teaspoon cinnamon

¼ cup caster sugar

120 g butter or margarine

2 tablespoons grated
    lemon rind

1 egg yolk

2 tablespoons sherry or
    substitute milk or water

Topping

2 apples

250 g cream cheese

½ cup caster sugar

2 eggs

3 tablespoons plain flour

2 tablespoons grated
    lemon rind

½ cup cream

1 tablespoon chopped
    mixed peel (optional)

¼ cup chopped raisins or
    sultanas (optional)

Pastry

1. Sift together dry ingredients.
2. Rub in butter. Add lemon rind.
3. Beat egg yolk and sherry together.
4. Add to flour mixture and mix well, forming a smooth ball.
5. Roll out dough between 2 sheets of baking paper and line 20 cm square sandwich tin and trim edges.

Topping

6. Peel and core apples, cut into quarters. Slice thinly.
7. Arrange in overlapping lines in pastry shell.
8. Beat cheese and sugar together until creamy then gradually add beaten eggs.
9. Gradually add flour, rind, cream, mixed peel and raisins.
10. Pour over apples.
11. Bake in moderate oven for 1¼ to 1½ hours.
12. Serve slightly warm or cold with whipped cream.

(Serves 8)

Chocolate Whip

1 small can evaporated
    milk (150 mL)

1 tablespoon gelatine

110 g dark chocolate

3 tablespoons water

2 teaspoons instant coffee

3 tablespoons caster sugar

1 teaspoon vanilla

1. Chill milk for several hours.
2. Soak gelatine in a little water and dissolve over boiling water.
3. Place chocolate, water and coffee in a bowl and melt over hot water.
4. Allow both this mixture and gelatine to cool.
5. Beat milk until thick and foamy.
6. Continue beating, gradually adding gelatine, chocolate, sugar and vanilla.
7. Pour into a bowl or individual serving dishes.
8. Chill then decorate with cream and grated chocolate.

(Serves 6–8)

Fruit Flummery

½ **cup sugar**

1½ **tablespoons plain flour**

2 **tablespoons gelatine**

1½ **cups water**

½ **cup orange and lemon juice**

pulp of 1 passionfruit

1. Mix sugar, flour and gelatine together in a saucepan.
2. Add water and mix well.
3. Bring to boiling point then pour into large bowl to cool.
4. Whisk until white and fluffy, adding fruit juice gradually.
5. Lastly add passionfruit.
6. Pour into a glass dish to set.
7. Serve with custard or cream.

(Serves 6–8)

Chocolate Mousse

125 **g dark chocolate**

4 **eggs, separated**

1 **cup cream**

1. Chop chocolate roughly and put into top of double saucepan.
2. Stir over hot water until melted, remove from heat and cool slightly.
3. Beat egg yolks and gradually add to chocolate and beat until the mixture is smooth and thick.
4. Whip cream until thick and fold in gently to the chocolate mixture.
5. Beat egg whites until soft peaks form and fold half the egg whites into the chocolate mixture, then fold in remaining egg whites.
6. Spoon the mixture into individual dishes or one large dish and refrigerate until firm.
7. Top with whipped cream and grated chocolate.

(Serves 4–6)

Orange Fluff

3 **eggs**

1 **cup caster sugar**

juice of 2 oranges

1 **tablespoon gelatine**

1. Beat egg yolks with half the sugar till thick.
2. Beat egg whites until soft peaks form. Gradually add remaining sugar and beat until dissolved.
3. Dissolve gelatine in juice and add to egg yolk mixture.
4. Fold in egg whites.
5. Pour into a bowl and set in refrigerator.
6. Serve with fruit or ice-cream.

(Serves 4–6)

Milk Jelly

600 mL milk
2–4 tablespoons sugar
1½ tablespoons gelatine
3 tablespoons boiling water
vanilla
pink colouring

1. Place milk and sugar in a saucepan.
2. Heat until sugar has dissolved.
3. Dissolve gelatine in hot water.
4. Flavour milk to taste. Colour pink.
5. When both milk and gelatine are cool mix together.
6. Pour into a wet dish and stand in refrigerator until set.
7. Serve with fruit and ice-cream.

Variations

Flavour of milk jelly may be varied by adding either 2 teaspoons of instant coffee or 2 tablespoons of melted chocolate. For a richer flavour fold in ½ cup cream, whipped, when jelly is partly set.

(*Serves 4–5*)

Trifle

1 single sponge or jam roll
⅓ cup raspberry or strawberry jam
juice 1 orange
2 tablespoons sherry (optional)
1 raspberry or strawberry jelly, pre-set
600 mL boiled custard
whipped cream

1. Split cake through the centre and spread with jam. Cut into cubes.
2. Arrange cake in a serving dish.
3. Sprinkle with orange juice and sherry.
4. Chop jelly and arrange half of it between pieces of cake.
5. Pour custard over the top.
6. Decorate top with remainder of jelly and whipped cream.

Variations

Add sliced canned peaches, pears or lychees to the trifle, reserving some of the fruit for decorating the top. The fruit should be well drained. Very small meringues may be used to decorate the top of the trifle. In this case make trifle in a fairly shallow dish to allow room for at least one meringue per serving.

(*Serves 6–8*)

Banana Custard

600 mL boiled custard
4–6 bananas
1 tablespoon lemon juice
nutmeg

1. Make custard and allow to cool.
2. Peel bananas, slice and sprinkle with lemon juice. Place in a bowl.
3. Pour custard over and mix lightly.
4. Sprinkle with a little nutmeg.
5. Serve with jelly and ice-cream.

(Serves 4–6)

Fruit Salad

1 small pineapple, peeled and cubed
1 small papaw, peeled and cubed
3 bananas, sliced
3 apples cubed
grapes, plums, peaches, apricots, seeded and chopped
2 passionfruit
juice 2 oranges
sugar to taste

1. Mix all fruit well and add, if desired, sugar to taste.
2. Serve in individual glasses with cream or ice-cream and topped with strawberries.

Note: Any fruit in season may be used. Have a variety of fruits. No one fruit flavour should predominate.

(Serves 8–10)

Baked Apples

4 cooking apples
½ cup sugar
cloves (optional)
2 teaspoons butter or margarine
a little water

1. Wash apples and remove cores.
2. Slit skin around the middle line.
3. Place in a pie dish and fill centre with sugar. Press clove into apple.
4. Place butter on top and water in the dish.
5. Bake in moderate oven until tender.
6. Serve warm or cold with boiled custard.

Note: A date or a few sultanas or raisins may be placed in the base of the hole in the apple before filling with sugar.

Baked Apples with Meringue

Allow cooked baked apples to cool. Make meringue by beating 1 egg white stiffly, then beating in 2 tablespoons caster sugar gradually. Pile a spoonful on top of each apple. Return to the oven and allow meringue to brown lightly.

Serve cold with boiled custard.

Alternatively coat apples completely with meringue and spike all over with almonds cut into thin strips. (Three egg whites would be required.)

(Serves 4)

Baked Bananas

4 bananas
40 mL lemon juice
¼ cup golden syrup
¼ cup brown sugar
¼ teaspoon cinnamon
30 g butter or margarine, melted

1. Slice bananas in half, lengthwise and place in shallow, greased, ovenproof dish.
2. Combine juice, syrup, sugar, cinnamon and butter and pour over bananas.
3. Bake in a moderate oven for approximately 15 minutes or until bananas are tender.
4. Serve with ice-cream or whipped cream.

(Serves 4)

Stewed Rhubarb

1 bundle rhubarb (4–6 sticks)
¼–½ cup sugar
water

1. Remove leaves, trim stalks and wash.
2. Cut into lengths of about 2.5 cm.
3. Place in saucepan, with water half covering the pieces.
4. Simmer gently until tender then add sugar and allow to dissolve.
5. Pour into a serving dish to cool and serve with custard or ice-cream.

(Serves 6–8)

Stewed Prunes

250 g prunes
water
lemon rind
sugar to taste

1. Place prunes in a saucepan and cover with water. Add lemon rind.
2. Cook very slowly until tender.
3. Add sugar to taste.
4. Chill and serve with custard or ice-cream.

(Serves 4–5)

Apple Compote

3 cooking apples
1–2 tablespoons sugar
1½ cups water
strip of lemon rind or 2 cloves (optional)
1 teaspoon lemon juice
cochineal (optional)

1. Prepare apples and cut into eighths.
2. Place sugar, water and rind or cloves in a saucepan and bring to boiling point. Add lemon juice.
3. Place pieces of apple in carefully without overlapping.
4. Simmer gently without the lid until apples are clear.
5. Allow to cool in the syrup.
6. Arrange apple slices carefully in a serving dish.
7. Add a few drops of cochineal to syrup and pour over apples.
8. Serve cold with custard, ice-cream or cream.

(Serves 3–4)

Dried Fruit Compote

1 cup dried apricots
1 cup prunes
1 450 g can pineapple pieces, undrained
2 cups water

1. Place all ingredients in a large saucepan and cook on low for 30 to 40 minutes or until tender.
2. Serve warm or cold with a dollop of sour cream and a dash of cinnamon or nutmeg.

Variation

Other dried fruits can be added, e.g. apples, peaches, pears or sultanas.

Poached Pears

½ cup sugar
½ cup water
½ cup orange juice
6 firm pears
6 cloves (optional)
lemon juice

1. Place sugar, water and orange juice in a saucepan and bring to boiling point.
2. Peel pears leaving the stalk intact.
3. Insert a clove in the base of each pear.
4. Stand the pears side by side in the saucepan.
5. Cover and cook gently until soft.
6. Lift pears out carefully and place in a serving dish or individual dishes.
7. Thicken the syrup by boiling uncovered for about 10 minutes.
8. Add a few drops of lemon juice and spoon over the pears.
9. Chill well and serve. Pears may be decorated with toasted almonds if desired.

(Serves 6)

Fruit Flan

Cake Base

Basic one-bowl cake cooked in a lamington tin

Filling

600 mL very thick, cold vanilla custard

Mock Cream

2 tablespoons butter or margarine

4 tablespoons caster sugar

6 tablespoons milk

vanilla

or substitute fresh whipped cream

Fruit

Select from:
  sliced peaches, strawberries, rockmelon balls, kiwi fruit, mangoes or any tinned and drained fruit

Glaze

apricot jam

1. Prepare a flat surface such as a board covered with aluminium foil and not much bigger than the cake.
2. Split cake and place lower half on the board. Make a slight recess in the top of the cake.
3. Fill cake with half the custard and place remainder on the top. Try to keep the cake as neat as possible, avoiding custard spilling over the sides.
4. Decorate sides with mock cream stars. Use whipped cream if preferred.
5. Prepare and dry pieces of fruit. Arrange in rows on the surface so custard is covered. Use four or five fruits for colour contrast.
6. Brush fruits with sieved, warmed apricot jam.
7. Decorate base with strawberry leaves and a few whole strawberries.
8. Serve with a bowl of whipped cream.

Note: This is a large cake suitable for a function. For ordinary use halve the quantities. It is advisable to make the custard on the previous day to allow for thorough chilling and thickening.

(Serves 10–12)

Pavlova

4 large egg whites
1 cup caster sugar
2 teaspoons cornflour
½ teaspoon vanilla
1 teaspoon vinegar

1. Beat egg whites until very stiff peaks form.
2. Very gradually add the sugar while beating vigorously.
3. Fold in cornflour with the last of the sugar. Add vanilla and vinegar and mix lightly.
4. Line a flat baking tray with baking paper and draw a 18 to 20 cm circle onto paper. Spread mixture to fill circle. Smooth the surface.
5. Place in oven pre-heated to 200°C then reduce heat to 150°C and bake undisturbed for 1¼ to 1½ hours. Cool in oven.
6. When cold top pavlova with whipped cream, chocolate shavings, and fruit such as strawberries, passionfruit or fruit salad.

Note: Turn oven off and allow pavlova to cool in the oven with the door ajar.

(Serves 8–10)

Fillings for Pavlova

Pineapple

1 small can crushed pineapple
2 tablespoons sugar (optional)
1–2 tablespoons arrowroot
1–2 egg yolks (optional)

1. Place pineapple and sugar in a saucepan and heat.
2. Thicken with arrowroot and egg yolks blended with a little of the pineapple juice.
3. Allow to become quite cold before filling pavlova.
4. Decorate with cream.

Passionfruit

3 egg yolks
½ cup sugar
125 g cream cheese
3 teaspoons gelatine
2 tablespoons water
2 bananas
1 tablespoon lemon juice
4 passionfruit
1 cup cream, whipped

1. Beat egg yolks and sugar then cook over boiling water in a double saucepan for 5 minutes. Cool.
2. Beat cream cheese and gradually add egg mixture.
3. Dissolve gelatine in water and add mashed bananas, lemon juice and passionfruit.
4. Fold in whipped cream and spoon into pavlova.
5. Decorate with whipped cream and passionfruit.

Mango

1 440 g can mango slices

2 tablespoons sugar

2 teaspoons gelatine dissolved in 1 tablespoon water

1 cup cream, whipped

1. Drain mango and reserve syrup. Chop or puree mango and place in a saucepan with reserved syrup, sugar and dissolved gelatine.
2. Heat to dissolve sugar and when cool place in refrigerator.
3. When beginning to set fold in whipped cream and spoon into pavlova.
4. Allow to set and decorate with piped cream.

Strawberry

1 punnet strawberries

½ cup strawberry jam

1 teaspoon brandy or rum

300 mL cream, whipped

1. Hull strawberries and cut each in half unless very small.
2. Heat jam then rub through a sieve and add brandy or rum.
3. Toss fruit in the jam and allow to drain.
4. Fill pavlova with whipped cream and pile the strawberries on top.

Lemon Cheesecake

Crust

2 cups sweet biscuit crumbs

½ teaspoon cinnamon

½ teaspoon nutmeg

125 g butter or margarine

Filling

250 g cream cheese

1 400 g tin condensed milk

½ cup lemon juice

1. Place biscuit crumbs, cinnamon and nutmeg in a bowl.
2. Melt butter, add to crumb mixture and combine well.
3. Press mixture into a greased pie dish or springform tin and stand in refrigerator until set.
4. Beat cream cheese until smooth.
5. Gradually add condensed milk then lemon juice and beat until smooth.
6. Pour into prepared shell and chill until firm.
7. Decorate with finely cut slices of lemon and lime and serve with ice-cream or whipped cream.

(Serves 8)

✷ Crumb Crust

1½ cups crushed gluten-free cornflakes

½ cup desiccated coconut

125 g margarine or butter, melted

1 tablespoon caster sugar

1 tablespoon milk

1. Place cornflakes and coconut in a bowl.
2. Mix margarine, sugar and milk in a saucepan and stir over low heat until margarine melts and ingredients are mixed well.
3. Add to cornflake mixture and mix well.
4. Press into a greased springform tin.

Black Forest Cheesecake

Base

250 g plain chocolate biscuits

125 g butter or margarine

Filling

250 g cream cheese

¾ cup sugar

1 tablespoon lemon juice

1 tablespoon gelatine

½ cup water

300 mL thickened cream

1 425 g can black cherries

Topping

1 tablespoon sugar

1 tablespoon cornflour

¾ cup cherry syrup

1 tablespoon rum

Base

1. Crush biscuits finely, add melted butter and mix well.
2. Press onto the base and sides of a greased 20 cm springform tin and refrigerate while preparing filling.

Filling

3. Beat cream cheese, sugar and lemon juice until smooth.
4. Sprinkle gelatine over water then dissolve over hot water. Allow to cool.
5. Add gelatine to cream cheese mixture and beat well.
6. Whip cream and fold into the mixture.
7. Drain and pit cherries, reserve syrup.
8. Spoon one-third of the filling onto the crust and arrange half the cherries over it. Spoon on another third of the filling and arrange the remainder of the cherries on top.
9. Top evenly with the remainder of the filling and refrigerate until firm.

Topping

10. Place sugar and cornflour into a saucepan. Gradually stir in the syrup.
11. Stir over heat until boiling. Remove from heat and add rum. Stir for a few minutes to cool slightly.
12. Spread over cheesecake and swirl lightly into cheese mixture.
13. Refrigerate until set.
14. To decorate pipe cream around the edge.

Note: This recipe may be made as a slice using a 28 × 18 cm lamington tin.

(*Serves 8*)

Mango Cheesecake

Crust

200 g sweet biscuits

80 g butter or margarine

Filling

1½ tablespoons gelatine

2 tablespoons water

grated rind 1 lemon

1 tablespoon lemon juice

½ cup orange juice

⅓ cup sugar

2 egg yolks

250 g cream cheese

1 cup sour cream

1 cup fresh mango pulp or tinned mango

2 egg whites

whipped cream for decoration

extra mango pulp

1. Crush biscuits and add melted butter. Press firmly into a 20 cm springform tin.
2. Place in refrigerator to become firm while preparing filling.
3. Soak gelatine in cold water.
4. Into a saucepan place rind, juice, water, sugar and egg yolks.
5. Cook over low heat. Remove from heat and add softened gelatine. Allow to cool.
6. Beat cream cheese until smooth then gradually add cooked mixture and beat well.
7. Add mango pulp and sour cream and mix well. Lastly fold in beaten egg whites.
8. Pour into prepared crumb case and refrigerate until set.
9. Before serving spread top with mango pulp and decorate with whipped cream.

Note: It is essential to use mangoes with good flavour.

(*Serves 8*)

Baked Cheesecake

250 g packet plain sweet biscuits, finely crushed

125 g margarine or butter, melted

3 250 g packets cream cheese

3 eggs

1 cup caster sugar

¾ cup sour cream

2 teaspoons finely grated lemon rind

¼ cup lemon juice

fresh fruit slices to garnish (e.g. strawberries or peaches)

1. Add margarine to crushed biscuits and mix well.
2. Press the mixture evenly over the base and sides of a 20 cm springform tin and refrigerate for 30 minutes.
3. In a large bowl, beat cream cheese until soft, add eggs, sugar, sour cream, rind and juice and continue beating until smooth.
4. Pour the cheese mixture into the biscuit crust and bake in a moderate oven for about 1 hour or until set. Leave in oven to cool.
5. Refrigerate for several hours before serving.
6. Garnish with fresh fruit slices.

(*Serves 8–10*)

✳ Cheesecake

125 g butter
125 g crushed sweet biscuits
200 g cream cheese
2 eggs, beaten
2 teaspoons grated lemon rind
1 tablespoon lemon juice
⅓ cup caster sugar
⅓ cup plain flour
450 g can crushed pineapple, drained
300 mL cream, whipped
pulp of 2 passionfruit

1. Place butter in a bowl and heat on HIGH for 1 minute.
2. Add biscuit crumbs and mix well.
3. Press mixture into a 24 cm pie plate. Use a metal spoon to make firm and even. Refrigerate while preparing filling.
4. Place cream cheese in a mixing bowl and soften on HIGH for 45 to 60 seconds. Add eggs, lemon rind, juice, sugar, flour and pineapple and mix well.
5. Pour into biscuit shell.
6. Cook on MEDIUM for 12 to 14 minutes, elevated on a stand.
7. Allow to cool then decorate with passionfruit and whipped cream.

(Serves 6–8)

Hazelnut Torte

Meringue

4 large egg whites
¾ cup caster sugar
60 g ground hazelnuts
1½ tablespoons melted butter or margarine
¼ cup plain flour

Coffee Cream

300 mL cream
1 tablespoon caster sugar
1 teaspoon instant coffee
2 teaspoons rum

Chocolate Cream

300 mL cream
¼ cup caster sugar
½ teaspoon vanilla
2 tablespoons cocoa

1. Mark five 20 × 9 cm rectangles on baking paper and place paper on scone trays.
2. Beat egg whites until stiff. Gradually add the sugar and beat until dissolved. The mixture should be of good meringue consistency.
3. Carefully fold in nuts, butter and sifted flour.
4. Divide evenly between the trays and spread to fit the rectangles.
5. Bake in a slow oven (150°C) for 30 minutes.
6. Remove from the trays immediately, taking care not to break the wafers. Cool on wire racks on greaseproof paper.

Coffee Cream

7. Whip all ingredients together until thick. Sandwich meringue layers together with the cream.

Chocolate Cream

8. Mix ingredients together and whip until thick. Cover top and sides with the cream.
9. Decorate with whole hazelnuts and piped cream.
10. Refrigerate for several hours before serving.

(Serves 8–10)

Lemon and Passionfruit Cream Sponge

1 single sponge
400 mL thickened cream,
  whipped
¾ cup toasted coconut
  (optional)
extra passionfruit

Filling

⅓ cup sugar
2 eggs
2 tablespoons lemon juice
60 g butter or margarine
1 passionfruit
extra passionfruit

1. Mix the sugar and beaten eggs together in the top portion of a double saucepan.
2. Add lemon juice and butter and cook over simmering water until the mixture coats the spoon.
3. Remove from heat and stir in passionfruit pulp.
4. Check flavour and add a little more lemon juice if necessary.

To assemble

5. Cut cake horizontally into three layers and place bottom layer on a serving plate.
6. Spread with half the filling and some of the cream. Repeat with next layer of cake. Place third layer on top.
7. Coat the sides and top with cream, reserving sufficient to pipe decoration.
8. Carefully coat sides with coconut using a knife or spatula if desired.
9. Decorate as required and drizzle passionfruit on the top.
10. Refrigerate until required.

(Serves 8)

Tiramisu

225 g mascarpone cheese,
  at room temperature
3 tablespoons icing sugar
60 mL Kahlua or other
  coffee liqueur
45 g chocolate, grated
200 mL whipping cream
2 teaspoons coffee
  essence
1 tablespoon water
18 sponge fingers
1 tablespoon cocoa powder

1. Place mascarpone, sugar, 30 mL liqueur and ¾ chocolate into a bowl and beat until well combined.
2. Place cream in a separate bowl and beat until stiff peaks form.
3. Fold cream into cheese mixture.
4. Mix coffee essence, remaining liqueur and water.
5. Place 6 sponge fingers in the bottom of a 21 × 21 × 8 cm dish and brush with coffee essence mixture.
6. Top with one third of the cheese mixture and repeat with another layer of sponge fingers brushed with coffee essence and top with another third of the cheese mixture.
7. Top with the remaining sponge fingers brushed with the coffee essence and spoon in remaining cheese mixture.
8. Smooth over the top and sift cocoa powder all over. Cover and chill for at least 4 hours or overnight.
9. Sprinkle with extra cocoa powder and grated chocolate before serving.

Note: 1 teaspoon instant coffee powder dissolved in 2 teaspoons boiling water and cooled may be substituted for coffee essence.

Pastry

Short Pastry

1 cup plain flour (125 g)
1 cup self-raising flour (125 g)
125 g shortening
⅓ cup cold water (approx.)

1. Sift flours into a bowl.
2. Rub shortening through the flour with the fingertips.
3. Make a well in the centre and stir in water gradually to make a dry dough.
4. Turn onto a lightly floured board and knead until smooth.
5. Wrap in plastic wrap and refrigerate until required.

✳ Short Pastry

1¾ cups warm mashed potato
2 tablespoons oil
1 cup maize cornflour (gluten free)
½ cup potato flour
2 teaspoons gluten-free baking powder
1 egg, lightly beaten

1. Place potato, oil and sifted dry ingredients into a large bowl.
2. Mix well and knead into a smooth ball by adding sufficient egg to combine the ingredients.
3. Knead lightly on a lightly cornfloured board and use as required.

Note: Instant mashed potatoes can be substituted for freshly cooked mashed potatoes.

Sausage Rolls

Pastry
1 quantity short pastry
egg and milk for glazing

Filling
500 g beef mince
pepper
1 onion
good pinch herbs or chopped fresh herbs
⅓ cup water
1–2 tablespoons flour blended with a little water

1. Place mince, pepper, chopped onion, herbs and water in saucepan.
2. Place on heat and cook until brown, stirring well.
3. Add blended flour and cook until thickened, stirring constantly. Allow to cool.
4. Make short pastry.
5. Knead lightly and roll out thinly; cut into strips 7.5 × 6 cm.
6. Place spoonfuls of meat at ends of strips, brush the other end with water and roll up.
7. Place on a greased tray and mark tops with a knife. Brush over with egg and milk.
8. Bake in a moderate to hot oven for 15 to 20 minutes.
9. Serve hot garnished with parsley.

Mini Meat Pies

The ingredients are the same as for the sausage rolls — only the shape is different

1. Roll pastry out thinly.
2. Cut out with a round cutter and line patty tins.
3. Fill with meat. Wet edge of pastry and cover with smaller rounds of pastry.
4. Make a small hole in the middle of each.
5. Brush over with egg and milk.
6. Bake in a moderate to hot oven for 15–20 minutes.
7. Serve hot, garnished with parsley.

Meat and Vegetable Pasties

Pastry
1 quantity short pastry
egg and milk for glazing

Filling
200 g lean beef mince
1 small potato, diced
1 small onion, diced
½ carrot, diced
½ turnip, diced (optional)
freshly ground pepper
1 tablespoon fresh chopped parsley

1. Place mince, potato, onion, carrot, turnip, pepper and parsley in a bowl and mix well.
2. Divide into four or six portions.
3. Make short pastry.
4. Place pastry on a floured board, knead lightly and roll out until pastry is about 5 cm thick.
5. Use a small saucepan lid and cut out four to six circles.
6. Place one portion of filling on each circle of pastry.
7. Moisten the edge of half the circle then fold over to meet the other half.
8. Pinch edges together, making a shell-like pattern by twisting the pastry slightly with the thumb and index finger forming a crest or ridge over top of pastry.
9. Prick well then brush over with egg and milk.
10. Place on a greased tin in a moderate to hot oven and bake for 20 to 25 minutes.
11. Serve hot with green vegetables or as a luncheon snack.

(Serves 4–6)

Variation

- Substitute 1 cup red kidney beans or combination of ½ cup peas and ½ cup corn for the mince and add ½ cup grated cheese.
- Add 2 tablespoons chutney for added flavour.
- For traditional English pasties substitute cubed beef (e.g. skirt, round). Stew and cool and add to vegetable mix.

Savoury Mince Pie

Pastry

1 quantity short pastry *or*

2 sheets frozen short pastry

egg and milk for glazing

Filling

oil

1 large onion, diced

1 carrot, diced

500 g lean beef mince

1 teaspoon Worcestershire sauce

1 tablespoon tomato paste

freshly ground pepper

1 beef stock cube

⅓ cup water

1–2 tablespoons flour

2 tomatoes (optional)

1. Brush or spray pan with oil, heat and sauté onion and carrot until onion is transparent.
2. Add mince, sauce, tomato paste, seasoning and water and allow to cook slowly until meat is thoroughly cooked.
3. Thicken with blended flour. Allow to cool.
4. Cut pastry into two pieces, one a little larger than the other.
5. Roll out larger piece to line a larger plate or 20 cm sandwich tin.
6. Fill with cooked mince and moisten edges of pastry with water.
7. Cover with slices of tomato.
8. Roll out remaining pastry and cover mince, first moistening edges with water.
9. Press edges together firmly.
10. Decorate with leftover pastry and make a small hole in the centre.
11. Brush over with milk or milk and egg.
12. Bake in a moderate to hot oven for about 30 minutes.
13. Serve hot with vegetables.

(Serves 6–8)

Bacon and Egg Tart

Pastry

1 quantity short pastry *or*

2 sheets frozen short pastry

egg and milk for glazing

Filling

8 bacon rashers

5–6 eggs

chopped fresh parsley

freshly ground pepper

1. Make short pastry and line a deep pie dish or 20 cm sandwich tin with half the mixture. Moisten edges with water.
2. Trim bacon rashers and cut each into three or four pieces.
3. Partly cook in a hot pan and drain on absorbent paper.
4. Arrange rashers on the pastry.
5. Carefully drop in whole eggs and season with pepper and parsley.
6. Roll out remaining pastry and cover tart.
7. Press edges together, and brush over the top with egg and milk.
8. Bake in a moderate to hot oven for about 30 minutes.
9. Serve hot or cold cut into wedges.

Note: This tart is suitable for picnics or for luncheons.

(Serves 6–8)

Salmon Quiche

Pastry

½ **quantity short pastry** *or*

1 sheet frozen short pastry

Filling

oil

1 onion, diced

2 bacon rashers, trimmed and diced

1 220 g can red or pink salmon

3 eggs

1 cup milk

freshly ground pepper

1 tablespoon chopped fresh parsley

½ **cup cheese, grated**

1. Make pastry and line a 22 cm quiche dish.
2. Brush with egg white and set aside to dry while preparing filling.
3. Brush or spray pan with oil, heat and sauté onion and bacon until onion is transparent.
4. Drain salmon. Reserve the liquid.
5. Whisk eggs and milk together. Add salmon liquid, pepper and chopped parsley.
6. Spread flaked salmon over the pastry. Sprinkle onion and bacon and half the cheese over the top.
7. Carefully pour in egg mixture over the back of a spoon. Sprinkle with remainder of the cheese.
8. Stand dish on a baking tray and bake in a hot oven (200°C) for 10 minutes then reduce heat to 160°C for a further 35 minutes or until set.
9. Serve hot or warm garnished with parsley.

Note: ½ cup cream may be added for richer filling in place of ½ the milk.

(*Serves 6–8*)

Variations

Asparagus Quiche

Omit salmon and add a 300 g can of asparagus cuts, well drained.

Seafood Quiche

Omit salmon and add 125 g cooked prawns and crab.

Corn Quiche

Omit salmon and add 300 g cream corn and 1 teaspoon curry powder. Increase the cheese to ¾ cup.

Vegetable Quiche

Omit salmon and add

1 onion, diced

1 small carrot, diced

1 zucchini, quartered and sliced

½ small capsicum, diced

½ cup corn kernels, drained

Sauté onion, carrot, zucchini and capsicum for 2 to 3 minutes. Add corn. Place over the pastry keeping back a little of the vegetable until custard has been added. Add remainder if there is room for it. Cheese content may be increased to ¾ cup.

Note: 4 chopped mushrooms and ½ cup broccoli sprigs may be added.

Quiche Lorraine (France)

Pastry

½ **quantity short pastry**

Filling

150 g bacon

2 eggs

2 egg yolks

150 mL cream

150 mL milk

freshly ground pepper

50 g tasty cheese, grated

1. Make pastry and line a 20 to 22 cm quiche dish. Brush with egg white and set aside to dry while filling is prepared.
2. Remove rind from the bacon and chop. Fry gently until golden brown. Arrange bacon over the pastry.
3. Beat the whole eggs, egg yolks and cream together lightly in a bowl. Add the milk and pepper.
4. Pour into pastry case. The custard should almost fill the case.
5. Sprinkle the top with grated cheese.
6. Bake in a fairly hot oven (190°C) for about 10 minutes then reduce heat to 160°C and bake for a further 20 to 25 minutes or until set.
7. Remove from oven and allow to stand for 10 minutes before serving. Garnish with parsley and serve with tossed salad.

(Serves 6–8)

Pumpkin Pie (U.S.A.)

Pastry

½ **quantity short pastry**

Filling

2 eggs

¾ **cup milk**

1¼ **cups cooked pumpkin**

½ **cup cream**

1 teaspoon cinnamon

¼ **teaspoon nutmeg**

¾ **cup sugar**

1. Make pastry and line a 20 cm deep pie dish. Decorate the edge.
2. Beat eggs, add the milk, sieved pumpkin, cream, cinnamon, nutmeg and sugar.
3. Whisk until well mixed.
4. Stand pie dish on baking tray and pour filling into the shell.
5. Place in a hot oven (200°C) and bake for about 20 minutes. Reduce heat to moderate and cook for a further 20 to 30 minutes or until set.
6. When cold top with whipped cream and sprinkle lightly with cinnamon.
7. Alternatively serve warm, accompanied with a bowl of whipped cream.

(Serves 6–8)

Baked Jam Roll

Pastry

1 quantity short pastry

Filling

¾ **cup jam**

½ **cup sultanas**

Syrup

½ **cup sugar**

¾ **cup water**

1 tablespoon butter

1. Make short pastry.
2. Knead on a lightly floured board.
3. Roll out into a rectangular shape until pastry is approximately 6 mm in thickness.
4. Spread jam and sprinkle with sultanas to within 12 mm of the edges.
5. Roll up and place in a greased pie dish or deep tray.
6. Dissolve sugar in hot water. Add butter and when melted pour over roll.
7. Bake in a moderate to hot oven for about 30 minutes, basting with syrup halfway through cooking time.
8. Serve hot with boiled custard.

Note: If more convenient make two small rolls and place side by side in pie dish.

Variation

Apple and Dried Fruit Filling

2 cooking apples, thinly sliced

½ cup currants or sultanas

1 to 2 tablespoons sugar

¼ teaspoon mixed spice

¼ teaspoon cinnamon

Mix all filling ingredients together and allow to stand while pastry is being made. Stir occasionally. Sprinkle on rolled-out pastry and roll up. Proceed as for jam roll.

(Serves 6–8)

Sweet Short Pastry

1 cup plain flour (125 g)

1 cup self-raising flour (125 g)

125 g shortening

2 tablespoons caster sugar

1 egg yolk

¼ **cup cold water or milk (approx.)**

1. Sift flours into a bowl.
2. Rub shortening through the flour with the fingertips.
3. Add sugar and mix well.
4. Mix into a dry dough with egg yolk and milk beaten together.
5. Turn onto a lightly floured board and knead until smooth.
6. Use as required.

✕ Sweet Short Pastry

Use gluten-free Short Pastry (page 203) and add 2 tablespoons caster sugar.

Apple Pie

Pastry

1 quantity sweet short pastry

Filling

6–8 cooking apples

1–2 tablespoons sugar

¼–½ cup water

1. Make sweet short pastry.
2. Turn onto a lightly floured board and knead until smooth.
3. Cut dough into two pieces.
4. Roll out one piece to line a tart plate.
5. Fill with cooked apples. Moisten edge of pastry.
6. Roll out other piece of pastry and cover filling.
7. Press edges down firmly. Make a hole in the centre.
8. Decorate with leftover pastry then brush over with milk.
9. Bake in moderate to hot oven for 30 to 40 minutes.
10. Sprinkle top with icing sugar.

Filling

11. Peel and core apples and slice into a saucepan.
12. Add water and sugar and cook gently until tender.
13. Drain off any surplus juice before using.

(Serves 6–8)

Orange Tartlets

Pastry

½ quantity sweet short pastry *or*

1 quantity biscuit pastry

Filling

3 oranges, juiced

1 lemon, juiced

water to make liquid up to 2 cups

½ cup sugar

1 tablespoon butter or margarine

3 tablespoons cornflour

2 tablespoons custard powder

1. Make sweet short or biscuit pastry.
2. Turn out on a floured board and knead until smooth.
3. Roll out thinly and cut with fluted cutter.
4. Line patty tins, prick well and brush lightly with egg and milk.
5. Bake in a moderate oven until golden brown.
6. Place strained juices, water, sugar and butter in a saucepan and heat.
7. Blend cornflour and custard powder with sufficient cold water to make a smooth paste and when orange mixture is boiling, stir thickening in quickly.
8. Allow to cook for 2 minutes, stirring all the time.
9. Cool a little before filling tart shells.
10. When set, top each tartlet with whipped cream.

Pineapple Tart

Pastry

½ **quantity sweet short pastry**

Filling

1 450 g can crushed pineapple

2 tablespoons cornflour *or* **custard powder**

1. Blend cornflour with a little of the pineapple juice to make a smooth paste.
2. Place undrained pineapple in a saucepan and heat.
3. Remove from heat and add blended cornflour, stirring continuously.
4. Return to heat. Bring to boil and simmer 1 to 2 minutes until thick and clear. Allow to cool.
5. Make sweet short pastry.
6. Turn out on a floured board and knead until smooth.
7. Take about two-thirds of the pastry and roll out to line a small tart plate.
8. Pour prepared and cooled filling into shell.
9. Roll out remaining piece of pastry into a rectangle.
10. Cut into strips about 12 mm wide.
11. Twist strips and make latticework on top of filling.
12. Brush pastry carefully with egg and milk.
13. Bake in a moderate to hot oven for about 20 minutes.
14. Serve hot or cold with boiled custard.

(Serves 6–8)

Apfelkuchen (Germany)

(Apple Pie)

Pastry
125 g butter or margarine
1 tablespoon caster sugar
1½ cups plain flour

Filling
rolled oats
4 cooking apples
1½ tablespoons flour
¼ cup caster sugar
1 tablespoon cream
2 eggs
60 g butter
50 g flaked almonds

1. Beat butter and sugar until creamy. Stir in the flour gradually to form a firm dough.
2. Knead lightly then roll out on greasproof paper.
3. Line a 30 cm pie dish and trim the edge.
4. Sprinkle a thin layer of rolled oats on the bottom to absorb juice.
5. Peel and slice apples thinly and arrange in the pie dish.
6. Mix together the flour, sugar, cream and egg yolks. Add the melted butter and beat well to combine. Add half the almonds. Lastly add beaten egg whites.
7. Pour evenly over the apples and sprinkle with remaining almonds.
8. Bake in a hot oven (200°C) for 35 to 40 minutes or until filling is cooked and brown. Reduce heat towards the end if top is browning too quickly.
9. Serve hot or cold with cream or boiled custard.

Note: Apples vary and some may be dry. If so, simmer apple slices in a little water for 2 to 3 minutes then dry and proceed as described.

(Serves 6–8)

Christmas Mince Pies (England)

Rich short crust pastry
2 cups plain flour
180 g butter
1 egg yolk
1½ tablespoons water

Filling
1 jar fruit mince
egg for glazing
icing sugar

1. Sift flour and rub in the butter. Add egg yolk and water to make a stiff dough.
2. Chill for 1 hour before rolling the pastry out thinly.
3. Cut into rounds and line patty tins. Cut smaller rounds for the lids. (Makes about 12 to 18.)
4. Fill with mincemeat, moisten edges with water then cover with lids. Press edges together.
5. Glaze with a little beaten egg mixed with water. Make a small slit in the tops.
6. Bake in a moderate oven (190°C) for about 25 minutes or until golden brown.
7. Serve warm or cold dusted with icing sugar.

Puff Pastry

250 g butter
2 cups plain flour
1 teaspoon lemon juice
½ cup (approx.) iced water
egg for glazing

1. Form butter into a 10 cm square pat.
2. Sift flour. Mix lemon juice with the water.
3. Mix water into flour to make a soft but not sticky dough.
4. Turn onto a floured board and knead well.
5. Roll out into a strip 30 cm long and a little wider than the butter pat.
6. Place butter in the centre and fold in three.
7. Turn pastry around so that the open ends are at the top and bottom.
8. Secure ends and press butter in with rolling pin.
9. Roll out, keeping the piece of even width and taking care not to roll over ends of pastry.
10. Fold in three, turn, close ends, press butter in and roll out.
11. Place in refrigerator for 30 minutes.
12. Roll twice more in the same way. Cool for 30 minutes.
13. Repeat rollings twice more making 6 in all. Cool again.
14. When required for use roll out and cut into shapes.
15. Glaze with white of egg.
16. Bake in a very hot oven (250°C). Do not open oven door for the first 10 minutes.

Vol au Vents

1 quantity puff pastry

**small tin of asparagus cuts,
2 dozen oysters, small tin
of corn kernels *or* ¼ cup
grated cheese and
2 slices ham finely
chopped.**

300 mL white sauce

egg and milk for glazing

1. Roll pastry to 6 mm thickness.
2. Cut out with a round cutter approx. 3 cm diameter.
3. Gather up remaining pastry and roll out very thinly.
4. Cut with the same cutter as previously.
5. Brush over pastry rounds with a little water then lay other pastry rounds carefully on top (to keep vol au vents straight while rising). Take care not to finger edges of patties.
6. Brush over with beaten egg and milk.
7. Cut an inner ring to about half the depth of the vol au vent with a small cutter dipped in hot water.
8. Place vol au vents on a cold wet tray.
9. Bake in a hot oven (230°C) for 20 to 25 minutes without opening the oven door.
10. Gently lift tops off without breaking them.
11. Scoop out soft inside and fill with savoury mixture.
12. Place tops on carefully.

Filling

13. Make the white sauce.
14. Remove from heat and add chosen fillings.
15. Season to taste with pepper.
16. Heat through but do not boil.

Steak and Kidney Pie (England)

1 kg blade or round steak
2 sheep's kidneys
flour
oil
2 onions, chopped
2 cups stock
pepper
1 bay leaf
flour for thickening
a little chopped parsley
375 g pkt puff pastry
egg yolk for glazing

1. Cut steak into 2 cm cubes. Skin, core and dice kidneys. Toss in flour.
2. Brush or spray pan with oil, heat and sauté onions until transparent. Add steak and kidneys and brown well.
3. Add stock, pepper and bay leaf.
4. Cover and simmer for 1 to 1½ hours or until almost cooked. Adjust seasonings and add a little thickening.
5. Pour meat into a pie dish. Sprinkle with parsley and cool.
6. Roll out pastry into a rectangle a little larger than the dish.
7. Cut thin strips from the ends of pastry rectangle and fit around edge of dish. Brush with water then place remaining pastry on top of pie. Press edges together then trim off surplus with a sharp knife.
8. Make a small hole in the centre of the pie.
9. Decorate with leftover pastry. Glaze with a little egg yolk and water.
10. Stand pie dish on baking tray and bake in a hot oven (220°C) for 20 minutes, then reduce to 180°C and bake for a further 25 to 30 minutes or until well browned.

(*Serves 6–8*)

Variation

Chicken Filling
1 kg chicken, cooked and chopped
4 to 5 bacon rashers, trimmed and diced
1 440 g can of cream of chicken *or* mushroom soup
½ cup cream *or* milk
1 onion, chopped *or* 3–4 shallots
pepper

1. Brush or spray pan with oil, heat and sauté onion and bacon until onion is transparent.
2. Place soup and cream in a large bowl, mix and add chicken, bacon and onion. Add more seasoning if required and water to dilute if too thick.
3. Pour chicken into a pie dish and cover with pastry as above.

Ham and Cheese Puffs

Pastry

375 g puff pastry

Filling

½ cup chopped shallots
¼ cup chopped parsley
2 large slices ham, diced
1 cup grated Swiss cheese
pepper
milk for glazing

1. Place shallots, parsley, ham, cheese and pepper in a bowl and mix well.
2. Roll pastry out thinly and cut out eight rounds with a small saucepan lid.
3. Divide filling evenly between the pastry rounds, placing it on one half of the circle. Pack as much as possible.
4. Brush edge of round with milk or water, fold in half and seal edges.
5. Place on greased trays, brush with milk and make two slits in the top of puffs.
6. Bake in a very hot oven (230°C) for 10 to 15 minutes.
7. Serve hot.

(Serves 8)

Apple Strudel (Austria)

4 or 5 sheets filo pastry
50 g butter or margarine melted

Filling

4–6 apples
½ cup sultanas or raisins
½ cup brown sugar
½ teaspoon ground ginger
½ teaspoon cinnamon
1 teaspoon grated lemon rind
1 tablespoon lemon juice
½ cup soft breadcrumbs
2 tablespoons flaked almonds (optional)

1. Peel and slice apples. Combine with sultanas, sugar, spices, lemon rind and juice, breadcrumbs and flaked almonds.
2. Place one sheet of pastry on a board and brush with melted butter.
3. Place second sheet on top and brush with butter. Repeat until all the sheets are in place but do not brush the last one with butter.
4. Place the apple mixture about 4 cm from the long edge of pastry allowing about the same distance at each end for turning under. Pack the filling as tightly as possible.
5. Fold in ends and roll up.
6. Place roll on a well-greased baking tray or use baking paper and make a horseshoe shape if too long for the tray.
7. Brush over with butter and bake in a moderate oven for 35 minutes or until golden brown.
8. Sift icing sugar over the roll and sprinkle with flaked almonds.
9. Serve warm with whipped cream.

Note: To reduce fat content substitute butter with skim milk.

(Serves 4–6)

Biscuit Pastry (1)

60 g butter
¼ cup caster sugar (50 g)
1 small egg
½ cup plain flour
¾ cup self-raising flour } **(155 g)**
2 tablespoons cornflour or rice flour

1. Beat butter and sugar to a cream.
2. Add the egg and beat well.
3. Sift flours and cornflour together and add gradually to the wet mixture to make a stiff paste.
4. Knead well on a lightly floured board. Wrap in plastic wrap and chill for 30 minutes.
5. Roll out on grease proof or baking paper. Use as required.
6. Bake in a moderate oven until golden brown.

Note: This recipe will make one pastry shell and eight or nine tartlet cases.

Biscuit Pastry (2)

60 g butter
60 g margarine } **(120 g)**
⅓ cup sugar (70 g)
3 tablespoons milk
1½–2 cups self-raising flour (190–250 g)

1. Beat butter and sugar to a cream.
2. Sift dry ingredients.
3. Gradually add to mixture with milk and make into a stiff paste.
4. Knead well on a lightly floured board.
5. Roll out and use as required.
6. Bake in a moderate oven until golden brown.

Note: This recipe is sufficient for two shells or one covered tart.

Biscuit Pastry

90 g butter
⅓ cup caster sugar
1 egg
½ cup rice flour
½ cup maize cornflour (gluten free)
½ cup soy flour
½ teaspoon gluten-free baking powder

1. Cream butter and sugar, add egg and mix well.
2. Sift dry ingredients well and add to butter mixture and combine well.
3. Turn onto a lightly cornfloured board and knead until smooth.
4. Wrap in plastic wrap and chill for an hour.
5. Use as required.

Lemon Meringue Tart

1 23 cm pastry shell

1½ cups water

4–5 tablespoons cornflour

2 egg yolks

½ cup lemon juice

2 strips lemon rind

¾ cup white sugar

1 tablespoon butter or margarine

Meringue

2 egg whites

⅓ cup caster sugar

1. Blend cornflour with the water.
2. Add egg yolks, strained lemon juice, rind, sugar and butter.
3. Stir over the heat until the mixture thickens. Cook for 2 minutes.
4. Remove rind and allow to cool a little.
5. Pour into cooked tart shell.
6. Whisk egg whites until stiff peaks form.
7. Gradually add sugar and beat until all sugar has dissolved.
8. Pile on top of filling. Brown lightly in a slow oven.

(Serves 8–9)

Quick Version Lemon Meringue Tart

Base

180 g plain biscuits, crushed

90 g butter or margarine, melted

Filling

1 400 g tin condensed milk

½ cup lemon juice

2 egg yolks

Meringue

2 egg whites

½ cup caster sugar

1. Combine biscuits and butter and press into a 23 cm pie dish. Chill.
2. Place condensed milk in a bowl, add lemon juice and lightly beaten egg yolks and combine well.
3. Spoon filling into the crumb crust and spread evenly.
4. Whisk egg whites until stiff peaks form and gradually add sugar and beat until sugar has dissolved.
5. Spoon on top of filling and bake in a moderate oven (180°C) for 15 minutes until golden.

(Serves 8)

Lemon Cheese Tartlets

Pastry

60 g butter

¼ cup caster sugar

1 small egg yolk

½ cup plain flour

½ cup self-raising flour

2 tablespoons cornflour

Lemon Cheese

¾ cup sugar

3 tablespoons butter or margarine

2 eggs

2 lemons

1. Beat butter and sugar to a cream.
2. Add egg yolk and beat well.
3. Sift dry ingredients together and gradually add to mixture.
4. Knead well on a floured board then roll out thinly.
5. Cut out with a scone cutter and line greased patty tins.
6. Prick well then bake in a moderate oven until golden.
7. Allow to stand for a few minutes before removing from tins.
8. Place sugar, butter, beaten eggs and juice of lemons in a double saucepan.
9. Add 2 strips of lemon rind.
10. Cook gently until mixture is thick and no egg taste remains.
11. Allow to cool. Remove pieces of rind.
12. Fill pastry cases with lemon cheese.
13. Tartlets may be decorated with cream if desired.

Note: This recipe will make eight or nine tartlets.

Passionfruit Mallow Tart

1 23 cm biscuit tart shell

Filling

60 g butter or margarine

⅓ cup sugar

200 mL water

3 tablespoons lemon juice

2 tablespoons cornflour

4–6 passionfruit

1 egg yolk

Marshmallow

2 teaspoons gelatine

½ cup hot water

1 teaspoon lemon juice

1 egg white

⅓ cup caster sugar

extra passionfruit pulp

Filling

1. Place butter, sugar, water and cornflour blended with lemon juice in a saucepan.
2. Stir over low heat until mixture boils. Cook for 2 minutes.
3. Add passionfruit pulp and mix well.
4. Add egg yolk gradually, stirring continuously.
5. Cool slightly then pour in pastry case.

Marshmallow

6. Dissolve gelatine in hot water.
7. Allow to cool. Add lemon juice.
8. Beat egg white until stiff then gradually add dissolved gelatine, then sugar, beating constantly until thick.
9. Pile on top of filling. Trickle extra passionfruit on top.
10. Chill well.

(Serves 8–9)

Apricot Cream Tart

**1 23 cm biscuit pastry tart
shell**

Cream Filling

½ cup sugar

**3 tablespoons custard
powder**

¾ cup evaporated milk

¾ cup apricot nectar

3 egg yolks

1 teaspoon vanilla

½ cup coconut

3 egg whites

¼ cup caster sugar

**1 large can apricots,
drained**

Glaze

¾ cup apricot nectar

1 tablespoon gelatine

**2–3 drops almond essence
(optional)**

1. Combine sugar and custard powder in a saucepan, add milk and juice and cook, stirring continuously, until thick.
2. Pour a little onto the beaten egg yolks, beat well then return to the saucepan. Cook for a few minutes longer, stirring constantly and do not allow to boil.
3. Add vanilla and coconut. Allow to cool.
4. Whisk egg whites until stiff then gradually add sugar. Fold into the custard.
5. Pour into cooked pastry shell and refrigerate until set.
6. Decorate top of the tart with drained apricot halves, cut side down.

Glaze

7. Mix gelatine with nectar and heat until dissolved. Add essence and colouring.
8. Chill until beginning to set. Spoon over apricots and chill.
9. Decorate with whipped cream if desired.

(Serves 8–9)

Caramel Meringue Tart

**1 23 cm biscuit pastry tart
shell**

**½ cup brown sugar (firmly
packed)**

3 tablespoons flour

1 cup milk

2 egg yolks

60 g butter or margarine

3 tablespoons hot water

vanilla

Meringue

2 egg whites

⅓ cup caster sugar

1. Place sugar and flour in a saucepan and mix.
2. Add the milk and mix until smooth.
3. Add egg yolks, butter and hot water.
4. Stir over the heat until mixture thickens. Allow to boil for 2 minutes.
5. Cool slightly, flavour with vanilla and pour into pastry shell.
6. Make meringue and pile on top of filling.
7. Brown lightly in a slow oven.
8. Serve with whipped cream.

(Serves 8–9)

Pineapple Meringue Tart

1 23 cm biscuit pastry tart shell

1 450 g can crushed pineapple

¼ cup sugar (optional)

2 egg yolks

2 tablespoons cornflour

Meringue

2 egg whites

⅓ cup sugar

1. Place pineapple and sugar in a saucepan and bring to boiling point. Simmer gently for 5 minutes.
2. Add egg yolks and cornflour blended with a little water.
3. Allow to cook well.
4. Cool then pour into cooked pastry shell.
5. Make meringue and pile on top of filling.
6. Brown lightly in a slow oven.

(Serves 8–9)

Fruit Flan

Pastry

1 sweet short pastry or biscuit pastry tart shell

Custard Filling

600 mL milk

3 heaped tablespoons custard powder

2 tablespoons sugar

vanilla

Fruit Topping

Variety of fruit, drained well (must be canned for syrup or juice content)

½ cup fruit syrup or juice and 3 teaspoons gelatine OR ¼ cup apricot jam heated with 1 tablespoon water

Custard

1. Blend custard powder with a little of the milk.
2. Pour remainder of milk into a saucepan, add sugar and heat until near boiling point.
3. Remove from heat and gradually add custard powder mixture, stirring continuously.
4. Return to heat, stir constantly and bring to boil. Simmer for 1 to 2 minutes.
5. Remove from heat and add vanilla. Cool. To prevent skin forming, cover with plastic wrap ensuring that it is touching the custard surface.

Topping

6. Place syrup and gelatine in a small saucepan and stir over low heat until gelatine has dissolved.
7. Refrigerate until the liquid is the consistency of unbeaten egg white.

To assemble:

8. Pour cooled custard into the tart shell and spread evenly.
9. Arrange fruit on top of custard.
10. Spoon gelatine liquid evenly over the fruit.
11. Refrigerate until set.

Variation

For a special occasion, the cooled tart shell can be brushed with melted chocolate prior to assembly.

Choux Pastry

60 g butter
1 cup water
1 cup plain flour
3 large eggs

1. Place butter and water in a saucepan and bring to boil. Remove from the heat, stir in flour all at once and beat until smooth.
2. Return to heat and beat well until the mixture leaves the sides of the saucepan. Cool slightly.
3. Add the eggs one at a time, beating well after each one has been added.
4. The mixture should be thick, smooth and glossy.
5. Use as required.

✗ Choux Pastry

1 cup water
⅓ cup butter
1¼ cups maize cornflour (gluten free)
½ teaspoon salt
4 eggs

1. Place water and butter in a saucepan and bring to boil.
2. Stir in cornflour and salt and cook until the mixture is very thick and leaves the sides of the pan. Cool slightly.
3. Add the eggs one at a time, beating well after each.
4. Pipe or spoon mixture onto greased trays and bake at 230°C for 10 minutes. Do not open oven door during this time.
5. Reduce heat to 190°C and continue to cook for 15 to 20 minutes until golden.
6. Use as required.

Chocolate Eclairs

1 quantity choux pastry
¾ cup chocolate icing
cream
vanilla
icing sugar

1. Using a bag or plastic storage bag with the corner cut off press out into 6 to 8 cm lengths on a greased tray.
2. Bake in a moderate oven for 30 to 40 minutes, gradually reducing heat.
3. Do not open oven door for first 20 minutes.
4. When cool split lengthwise and fill with sweetened, flavoured, whipped cream.
5. Coat with chocolate icing.

Cream Puffs

1 quantity choux pastry (page 221)

Custard for Puffs

1½ tablespoons butter or margarine

3 tablespoons flour

3 tablespoons sugar

300 mL milk

2 egg yolks

vanilla

1. Put dessertspoons of Choux Pastry mixture on greased and floured trays and sprinkle trays lightly with water.
2. Bake in a moderately hot oven (200°C) for 20 minutes. Reduce heat to 180°C for a further 20 minutes. Do not open the door for the first 20 minutes.
3. When cooked, remove from oven and make small slit in puffs to allow steam to escape. Return to oven for a few minutes to dry out.
4. When cold, open the puffs and remove the soft centres.
5. Fill with flavoured cream or custard.
6. Sprinkle heavily with icing sugar.

Custard

7. Melt butter in a small saucepan. Remove from heat.
8. Add flour and mix well.
9. Add milk gradually, return to heat and stir until boiling. Cook for 1 minute.
10. Remove from heat and add yolks of eggs beaten with a little milk.
11. Add sugar to taste.
12. Return to heat and cook without boiling for 1 minute.
13. Add vanilla and allow to cool.

Note: Puffs can be made into savoury puffs by filling with thick white sauce which has cheese, chives, ham or asparagus added.

Profiteroles

Make puffs as for Cream Puffs and when cold fill with Creme Patissiere and drizzle over chocolate sauce (see page 222)

Serving size — 2 to 3 puffs per serve

Creme Patissiere (Pastry Custard)

3 egg yolks

¼ cup caster sugar

2 tablespoons cornflour

½ cup milk, warmed

1 teaspoon vanilla

Variation

Fill with Chantilly Cream (whipped cream sweetened with icing sugar and flavoured with vanilla).

1. Place yolks, sugar and flour in a bowl and whisk until pale and creamy.
2. Add milk gradually to the egg mixture and whisk well.
3. Place in saucepan and cook over medium heat until the mixture boils and thickens, stirring constantly.
4. Remove from heat and stir in vanilla. Cool and use as desired.

Plain Cake (1)

125 g butter or margarine
²/₃ cup caster sugar (140 g)
2 large eggs
vanilla
⅓ cup milk
**1½ cups self-raising flour
  (190 g)**

Plain Cake (2)

125 g butter or margarine
²/₃ cup caster sugar (140 g)
2 large eggs
vanilla
½ cup milk
2 cups self-raising flour (250 g)

1. Beat butter and sugar to a cream.
2. Add the eggs one at a time and beat well. Add vanilla.
3. Sift flour and add to mixture alternately with milk.
4. Make into a soft dough.
5. Pour into a greased and floured block tin.
6. Bake in a moderate oven for approximately 40 minutes.
7. Turn out and stand on a wire frame to cool.

Variations to Plain Cake (2)

Sultana or Cherry Bar

Add ½ cup sultanas or cherries and bake in a bar tin for approximately 40 minutes.

Chocolate Block Cake

Add: 3 tablespoons cocoa

2 teaspoons honey

Increase milk to ¾ cup

Bake in a block tin approximately 25 × 14 cm or two small bar tins for approximately 30 minutes.

Orange Ring Cake

Add: grated rind of 1 orange

1 tablespoon orange juice

Reduce milk by 1 tablespoon

Bake in a ring tin for approximately 30 to 40 minutes.

Marble Cake

When mixed, divide cake mixture into three portions. Colour one pink, one chocolate (use 1 tablespoon cocoa blended with a little hot milk) and leave the third portion plain. Spoon alternately into a block tin and bake for 40 to 45 minutes.

Plain Cake

125 g butter or margarine
½ cup caster sugar
2 eggs
¼ cup milk
1½ cups maize cornflour (gluten free)
1½ teaspoons gluten-free baking powder
½ teaspoon vanilla

Follow method as for plain cake on opposite page but substitute cornflour and gluten-free baking powder for self-raising flour.

Note: This recipe can be used to make small cakes. Bake small cakes at 200°C for 15 to 20 minutes (makes 18).

Butter Icing

1 cup pure icing sugar
1–2 tablespoons butter or margarine
1–2 tablespoons water or milk
vanilla

1. Place icing sugar into a bowl and work in softened butter with a wooden spoon.
2. Add sufficient water to make a smooth spreading consistency.
3. Add vanilla and beat well.

Variations

Fruit

Add strained fruit juice and 1 teaspoon lemon juice instead of water. Use less butter for fruit icings.

Chocolate

Mix 1 to 2 tablespoons cocoa with a little boiling water and add.

Coffee

Add 1 tablespoon coffee essence to icing sugar and butter. Add water as required.

Mocha

Add 2 teaspoons coffee essence and 2 teaspoons cocoa blended with 1½ tablespoons hot water and milk.

Strawberry

Add strawberry essence and a little pink colouring.

Marble Icing

plain butter or fruit icing
cochineal
1 teaspoon cocoa

1. Make icing a little thinner than usual.
2. Divide icing into three portions.
3. Colour one portion pink.
4. Blend cocoa with a small quantity of boiling water and add to second portion.
5. Leave the third portion white.
6. Spread in horizontal bars about 12 mm wide across the surface of the cake.
7. With a skewer dipped in hot water draw up and down the length of the cake about 12 mm apart. The colours will be drawn into each other.

✳ Vanilla Frosting

80 g butter or margarine,
  softened
1½ teaspoons vanilla
3 cups icing sugar
¼ cup milk
½ cup chopped nuts
  (optional)

1. Using an electric mixer, beat butter and vanilla until light and fluffy.
2. Add the icing sugar and beat until smooth.
3. Place milk in a cup and microwave for 30 to 45 seconds until very warm.
4. Add milk to frosting, 1 tablespoon at a time.
5. Beat until frosting is of required consistency.
6. Use as required and decorate with chopped nuts.

Variation

Fruit Frosting

For fruit frosting, omit vanilla and add instead 2 tablespoons of instant fruit-flavoured drink mix and 2 teaspoons lemon juice.

(Fills and frosts two 23 cm layers)

✳ Chocolate Frosting

120 g butter or margarine, softened
1 teaspoon vanilla
3½ cups icing sugar
¼ cup cocoa
¼ cup milk

1. Using an electric mixer, beat butter and vanilla until light and fluffy.
2. Beat in icing sugar and cocoa at high speed until smooth.
3. Place milk in a cup and microwave for 30 to 45 seconds until very warm.
4. Gradually add to mixture a tablespoon at a time. Beat until the required consistency.

Variation

Mocha Frosting

For mocha frosting, mix 1 tablespoon of instant coffee with 3 tablespoons of milk and beat until smooth. Add the remaining milk if required.

(Fills and frosts two 23 cm layers, or coats a ring cake)

Cream Cheese Frosting

30 g cream cheese
1½ tablespoons butter
1 teaspoon lemon juice
1 cup icing sugar

1. Beat cream cheese, butter and lemon juice in a small bowl with an electric beater.
2. When light and fluffy add sifted icing sugar and beat until smooth.
3. Use as required for topping ring, banana, nut and mixed fruit cakes.

Note: If sides of cake are to be covered as well as the top, double the quantities.

Small Cakes

60 g butter or margarine
⅓ cup caster sugar
vanilla
1 large egg
1 cup self-raising flour
⅓ cup milk

1. Beat butter and sugar to a cream. Add the vanilla.
2. Add egg and beat well.
3. Add flour and milk alternately and mix lightly into a soft dough.
4. Spoon into paper containers.
5. Bake in a good moderate oven (190°C) for 10 to 12 minutes.

Variation

Quick Mix Small Cakes

Place all ingredients in a bowl and beat for 3 minutes. Continue as in step 4 above.

(Makes 12 cakes)

Butterflies

1 batch small cakes
¼ cup red jam
**mock cream or freshly
   whipped cream**
icing sugar

1. Using a knife with a sharp point, carefully remove a small portion from the top of each cake.
2. Place a little jam in each cake.
3. Fill with a little mock cream.
4. Cut top of cakes in half and arrange as if butterfly wings on top of cream.
5. Sift icing sugar lightly over tops of cakes.

Friands — French Small Cakes

½ cup plain flour
**1½ cups icing sugar
   mixture**
1 cup almond meal
6 egg whites
**185 g butter or margarine,
   melted**

1. Sift flour and icing sugar into a bowl. Stir in almond meal.
2. Lightly whisk egg whites until frothy but not firm and fold into almond mixture.
3. Add melted butter and stir until combined.
4. Spoon mixture into a greased, 12-hole muffin pan until ¾ full.
5. Top with one of the variations if desired and bake in a moderate oven for 25 to 30 minutes or until golden.
6. Allow to stand in the pan for 5 minutes before placing on a rack to cool.
7. Serve dusted with icing sugar.

Variations

Apple, Apricot or Peach

Place drained, stewed or canned fruit slices on top of the mixture in the pans.

Berry

Scatter blueberries or raspberries over the top of the mixture in the pans.

Passionfruit

Drizzle passionfruit pulp over the mixture in the pans.

Chocolate

Sprinkle 50 g chopped milk chocolate over the mixture before baking.

Or, if desired, melt ¼ cup marmalade over a gentle heat and brush tops of cooked, warm friands before cooling.

Note: For gluten-free friands, substitute pure icing sugar in place of icing mixture and rice flour for plain flour.

Kentish Cake

125 g butter or margarine

2/3 cup caster sugar

2 large eggs

vanilla

2 tablespoons cocoa

2 tablespoons boiling water

1½ cups self-raising flour

2 tablespoons coconut

3 tablespoons sultanas, cherries and nuts

¼ cup milk

1. Beat butter and sugar to a cream.
2. Add eggs one at a time and beat well. Add vanilla.
3. Blend cocoa with hot water and then add when cool.
4. Sift flour. Add coconut and fruit and nuts.
5. Add to mixture alternately with milk.
6. Mix into a soft dough.
7. Pour into a greased and floured block tin.
8. Bake in a moderate oven for 30 to 40 minutes.
9. When quite cold ice with chocolate icing.
10. Decorate with chopped nuts and cherries or coconut.

Madeira Cake

125 g butter or margarine

½ cup sugar

2 large eggs

1½ cups self-raising flour

a little finely grated lemon rind

lemon essence

¼ cup milk

1. Beat butter and sugar to a cream.
2. Add eggs one at a time and beat well.
3. Sift flour and add grated rind.
4. Add flour and milk alternately and mix lightly into a soft dough.
5. Lastly add lemon essence.
6. Pour into a greased bar tin.
7. Bake in a moderate oven for 35 to 40 minutes or until cooked.
8. When cake is set place pieces of lemon peel on top of cake.

Mock Cream

2 tablespoons butter

4 tablespoons caster sugar

6 tablespoons milk

vanilla

1. Soften butter and beat to a cream with the sugar.
2. Very gradually add the milk and beat until no sugar grains remain.
3. Flavour with vanilla.

Note: Milk should be at room temperature. If the milk is not readily absorbed add a teaspoon of hot water.

Banana Cake

60 g butter or margarine

90 g caster sugar

1 egg, lightly beaten

2 bananas, mashed

¼ teaspoon bicarbonate of soda

2 tablespoons warm milk

1 cup self-raising flour

1. Cream butter and sugar and add egg, mashed bananas and bicarbonate of soda. Mix well.
2. Gradually fold in milk and flour alternately.
3. Pour mixture into a well-greased loaf tin and cook in a moderate oven for 30 minutes.
4. Serve sliced or, if desired, ice with lemon-butter icing.

Banana Cake — Low fat

1¼ cups self-raising flour

1 teaspoon cinnamon

1 tablespoon margarine, low fat

½ cup brown sugar

1 egg, lightly beaten

¼ cup low-fat milk

½ cup mashed banana

1. Sift flour and cinnamon into a large bowl and rub in margarine.
2. Add sugar, egg, milk and banana and stir in lightly.
3. Pour the mixture into a greased loaf tin and bake in a moderate oven for approximately 30 minutes or until cooked when tested.
4. Serve sliced.

Carrot Cake

1⅓ cups self-raising flour

1 teaspoon bicarbonate of soda

1 teaspoon cinnamon

½ teaspoon nutmeg

2 cups grated carrot

1 cup chopped walnuts

⅔ cup vegetable oil

1 cup sugar

1 teaspoon vanilla

3 eggs, lightly beaten

Lemon Frosting

50 g cream cheese

2 tablespoons butter, softened

2 teaspoons lemon juice

1 teaspoon finely grated lemon rind

2 cups icing sugar mixture

1. Sift flour, bicarbonate of soda and spices into a bowl.
2. Add carrots, walnuts, oil, sugar, vanilla and eggs and mix lightly.
3. Place in a greased and papered 28 × 20 cm lamington tin and bake in a moderate oven (180°C) for 35 to 45 minutes or until cooked when tested with a skewer.
4. Stand for a few minutes before turning out carefully to cool.
5. Ice with lemon frosting and serve cut into squares and, if desired, top with fresh passionfruit.

6. Combine all ingredients and beat well until smooth and creamy.

Carrot Cake

125 g butter or margarine

1 tablespoon honey

½ cup caster sugar

1 teaspoon vanilla

2 eggs

½ cup soy flour

½ cup maize cornflour (gluten free)

1 teaspoon gluten-free baking powder

½ teaspoon bicarbonate of soda

1 teaspoon mixed spice

1 cup finely grated carrot

½ cup walnuts or pecans, chopped

1. Cream butter, honey and sugar until light and fluffy and add vanilla.
2. Add eggs one at a time, beating well after each.
3. Sift dry ingredients and stir into egg mixture until combined.
4. Add carrot and walnuts and stir in gently.
5. Pour into a greased loaf tin and bake in a moderate oven for 40 to 45 minutes.
6. When cold, ice with lemon and/or cream cheese frosting

Cream Cheese Icing (or see Cream Cheese Frosting on page 227)

30 g butter or margarine, softened

60 g cream cheese

1 teaspoon finely grated lemon rind

1½ cups pure icing sugar

1. Place butter and cream cheese in a bowl and beat well.
2. Add lemon rind and sifted icing sugar and continue to beat until smooth.

Hummingbird Cake

1 cup plain flour

½ cup self-raising flour

½ teaspoon bicarbonate of soda

½ teaspoon cinnamon

1 cup caster sugar

½ cup desiccated coconut

2 eggs, lightly beaten

¾ cup oil

1 cup mashed banana

450 g can crushed pineapple, drained

½ cup chopped pecans

½ teaspoon vanilla

Cream Cheese Frosting

100 g cream cheese

¾ cup icing sugar mixture

1–2 teaspoons lemon juice or passionfruit pulp

1. Combine sifted flours, soda and cinnamon in a large bowl and mix in sugar and coconut.
2. Add eggs, oil, banana, pineapple, nuts and vanilla and stir until combined.
3. Place mixture into a greased, deep cake tin, 20 cm in diameter and bake in a moderate oven for approximately 1 hour.
4. Allow cake to stand in pan for 10 minutes before turning out.
5. Top with cream cheese frosting.

Cream Cheese Frosting

6. Beat cream cheese until smooth.
7. Gradually add icing sugar and juice or pulp and beat until mixture is light and creamy.

Peaches

2 dozen small cakes

¾ cup soft vanilla butter icing

1 rasberry or strawberry jelly

2 cups coconut

1. When cakes are cool, split open and spread with a little icing.
2. Make jelly with a little less water (1 to 1¼ cups only) than usual and allow to stand in refrigerator until beginning to set.
3. Dip cakes in jelly one at a time then roll in coconut.
4. Allow to set firmly in refrigerator but do not store there as cakes become hard

Note: Peaches are best made during the cooler months of the year.

Variation

Omit the icing and when ready to serve partly split cakes and pipe with sweetened whipped cream.

Lamingtons

125 g butter or margarine
²/₃ cup caster sugar
vanilla
2 large eggs
½ cup milk
2 cups self-raising flour

1. Beat butter and sugar to a cream. Add the vanilla.
2. Add eggs one at a time and beat well. Sift flour.
3. Add flour and milk alternately and mix lightly into a soft dough.
4. Turn into a greased and floured lamington tin.
5. Bake in a moderate oven for about 30 minutes.
6. When quite cold cut into squares of uniform size.
7. Dip each cake in icing then roll in coconut. Set aside to become firm.

Icing
1½ cups icing sugar
1½–2 tablespoons cocoa
boiling water
vanilla

8. Sift icing sugar into a bowl.
9. Blend cocoa with a little boiling water.
10. Work into icing sugar, adding more water if necessary. Add vanilla.

Quick Mix Plain Cake

1½ cups self-raising flour
½ teaspoon baking powder
125 g butter, softened or margarine
²/₃ cup caster sugar
2 eggs
vanilla
⅓ cup milk

1. Place flour and baking powder into an electric mixer bowl. Add the other ingredients.
2. Beat at medium speed then increase very gradually to top speed beating altogether 2 minutes from starting time.
3. Pour into a greased and floured block tin and bake in a moderate oven for approximately 30 minutes.
4. When cold ice with vanilla butter icing.
5. Cut into squares.

Variations

Coffee Cake

Add 1 tablespoon of coffee powder. Ice with coffee butter icing and sprinkle with chopped pecans or walnuts.

Orange Cake

Add grated rind of 1 orange. Replace 1 tablespoon of milk with 1 tablespoon of orange juice. Ice with orange butter icing.

✷ One Bowl Orange Cake — Low fat

60 g margarine, fat reduced

1 cup caster sugar

1 teaspoon vanilla

2 eggs

4 egg whites

200 g vanilla yoghurt
low fat and gluten free

1 cup polenta

½ cup desiccated coconut

4 teaspoons grated orange
rind

⅓ cup orange juice

1. Cream margarine, sugar and vanilla.
2. Gradually add eggs and egg whites and beat well after each addition.
3. Add yoghurt, polenta, coconut, rind and juice and beat for 2 minutes.
4. Pour into a greased ring pan and bake in a moderate oven for 40 to 50 minutes until golden.

Quick Mix Chocolate Cake

2 cups self-raising flour

1 teaspoon baking soda

3 tablespoons cocoa

1 cup caster sugar

1 large egg

vanilla

90 g butter or margarine

1 cup milk

1. Place dry ingredients into a bowl.
2. Add egg, vanilla, butter and about three-quarters of the milk.
3. Beat approximately 3 minutes with an electric mixer. Add remainder of milk if necessary.
4. Pour into two 20 cm sandwich tins.
5. Bake in a moderate oven for about 20 minutes.
6. Finish with chocolate icing.

Chocolate Glaze Icing

2–3 tablespoons cocoa

3 tablespoons water

1¼ cups icing sugar

1. Place cocoa and water into a small saucepan and allow to boil.
2. Turn into a bowl and add some of the sugar.
3. Stand bowl over a saucepan of hot water to warm contents slightly. Do not allow to become too hot.
4. Gradually add remainder of sugar.
5. Add more water or sugar to obtain correct consistency. It should cling to the back of a spoon.
6. Pour onto centre of cake and allow to run down the sides.
7. Fill gaps with icing using a warm knife.

✴ Quick Mix Chocolate Cake — Low fat

60 g margarine, reduced fat

1 cup boiling water

¾ cup cocoa

1½ cups caster sugar

1 cup rice flour

½ cup maize cornflour (gluten free)

½ cup potato flour

2 teaspoons gluten-free baking powder

1 teaspoon xanthan gum (optional)

1 teaspoon bicarbonate of soda

200 g vanilla yoghurt, low fat and gluten free

2 eggs

vanilla

1. Place margarine, boiling water, cocoa and sugar in a saucepan and heat until margarine is melted and sugar dissolved. (This step can be done in the microwave.)
2. Allow mixture to cool.
3. Place sifted flours, baking powder, xanthan gum and bicarbonate of soda in a large bowl.
4. Mix yoghurt, eggs and vanilla and add to cooled cocoa mixture and combine well.
5. Add cocoa and yoghurt mixture to the sifted flours and beat well for 2 to 3 minutes or until mixture is smooth and free of lumps.
6. Pour into a greased 20 cm springform tin and bake in a moderate oven for 40 to 50 minutes or until a skewer comes out clean.

Chocolate Cream Filling

300 mL whipping cream

2 tablespoons caster sugar or pure icing sugar

2 tablespoons cocoa

1. Place cream, sugar and cocoa in a bowl and beat until stiff peaks form.
2. Use as a filling to join two layer cakes.

Coconut Meringue

Cake

70 g butter or margarine

½ cup caster sugar

3 egg yolks

vanilla

1 cup self-raising flour

¼ to ⅓ cup milk

Topping

3 egg whites

¾ cup icing sugar, sifted

1 cup coconut

1. Beat butter and sugar until creamy.
2. Add egg yolks, one by one and beat well. Add vanilla.
3. Add sifted flour alternately with milk to make a soft mixture.
4. Turn into a greased, paper-lined 20 cm square cake tin.
5. Beat egg whites until stiff then fold in icing sugar and coconut.
6. Spoon carefully over the cake mixture.
7. Bake in a moderate oven for about 40 minutes.
8. Allow to stand for a few moments before lifting the cake out onto a cooler.

Chocolate Mud Cake

250 g butter, chopped
180 g milk chocolate, chopped
1½ cups caster sugar
¾ cup milk
1¼ cups plain flour
¾ cup self-raising flour
1 teaspoon vanilla
2 eggs, lightly beaten

Chocolate Icing

200 g milk chocolate, chopped
⅓ cup cream

1. Place butter, chocolate, sugar and milk into a saucepan and stir over low heat until chocolate and butter are melted and sugar is dissolved.
2. Remove from heat, pour into a large bowl and cool for 15 to 20 minutes.
3. Add sifted flours, vanilla and eggs and pour into a deep, greased and paper-lined 22 cm round tin. Make sure that the paper at the sides extends 5 cm above the edge of the tin.
4. Bake in a moderately slow oven (160°C) for approximately 1½ hours.
5. Cool the cake in the tin and, when cold, remove from tin.
6. Spread cake with chocolate icing and chill until needed.
7. Serve in wedges with whipped cream and decorate with white chocolate shavings.

Chocolate Icing

8. Combine chocolate and cream in a heatproof bowl over simmering water until the chocolate is melted.
9. Remove the bowl from the heat and cool until thickened and of a spreading consistency.

Note: White chocolate can be substituted for milk chocolate to make a White Chocolate Mud Cake.

(Serves 10–12)

Chocolate Mud Cake

⅓ cup cocoa
⅓ cup hot water
150 g dark chocolate, chopped and melted
150 g butter or margarine, melted
1⅓ cups brown sugar, firmly packed
1 cup ground almonds
4 eggs, separated

1. Combine cocoa and water and stir until smooth.
2. Stir in chocolate, butter, sugar and almonds until well combined.
3. Stir in yolks one at a time.
4. Beat egg whites until stiff and fold into the chocolate mixture.
5. Pour mixture into a greased and paper-lined tin.
6. Bake in a moderate oven for about 1¼ hours or until firm.
7. Cool in the pan.
8. Serve dusted with icing sugar.

(Serves 6–8)

Christmas Cake (1)

250 g butter

1⅓ cups brown sugar (packed)

5 large eggs

3 teaspoons mixed spice

1 teaspoon grated nutmeg

1 teaspoon cinnamon

1½ cups seeded raisins

2 cups sultanas

¾ cup currants

1½ cups plain flour

1 cup self-raising flour

⅓ cup mixed peel

⅓ cup cherries

½ cup almonds

3 tablespoons rum or brandy

juice and rind 1 orange

½ teaspoon coffee powder

1 tablespoon caramel essence

1. Prepare fruit. Cut raisins and cherries in halves.
2. Blanch almonds and cut into fine strips.
3. Mix all fruits and almonds together and mix with a little flour.
4. Sift flours and spices.
5. Beat butter and sugar to a cream.
6. Beat all the eggs in a separate bowl and add to mixture gradually.
7. Add caramel, coffee and grated orange rind.
8. Gradually add dry ingredients.
9. Add fruit, juice and rum and mix well.
10. Spoon onto a paper-lined 20 cm tin. Hollow centre out a little.
11. Smooth top over with a wet palm of the hand.
12. Place in a moderate oven. After 10 minutes drop temperature to 150°C. After 1 hour drop temperature to 125°C and if becoming too brown, cover with baking paper.
13. Continue baking until cake is cooked. Test with a skewer.
14. Allow to cool in the tin.

Christmas Cake (2)

250 g butter

1⅓ cups brown sugar (packed)

4 large eggs

3 tablespoons rum or sherry

2 cups plain flour

½ teapoon nutmeg

1 teaspoon mixed spice

⅓ cup mixed peel

1½ cups currants

1½ cups sultanas

1½ cups raisins

⅓ cup cherries

½ cup almonds

orange juice

1. Prepare fruit. Cut raisins and cherries in halves.
2. Blanch almonds and cut into fine strips.
3. Mix all fruits and almonds together.
4. Sift flour and spices
5. Beat butter and sugar to a cream.
6. Beat the eggs and add mixture gradually.
7. Gradually add dry ingredients.
8. Add prepared fruit and rum and juice if necessary.
9. Mix well together then spoon into a lined 20 cm cake tin. Hollow centre out.
10. Place in a moderate oven. After 10 minutes drop temperature to 150°C. After 1 hour drop temperature to 125°C.
11. Continue baking until cake is cooked. Test with a skewer.
12. Allow to cool in the tin.

Royal Icing
(for piping)

1 egg white
100 g pure icing sugar
½ teaspoon lemon juice or
a few drops of acetic acid

1. Beat egg white a little but do not make frothy.
2. Gradually add sifted icing sugar.
3. Add lemon juice and beat well.
4. Test by placing finger on surface of icing and drawing it up to a peak. If the peak falls the icing is not stiff enough.
5. Keep covered with a damp cloth.

Fondant Icing
(for covering fruit cakes)

8 cups pure icing sugar
½ cup liquid glucose
2 egg whites
1 tablespoon lemon juice

1. Sift the icing sugar into a bowl.
2. Make a well in the centre and add softened glucose, egg whites and flavouring.
3. Beat, gradually working icing sugar into the mixture.
4. When a stiff paste is formed turn onto a board lightly dusted with icing sugar and knead until smooth and free from stickiness.
5. If several colours are required divide paste and knead colouring into paste.
6. Roll out and use as required.

Boiled Fondant Icing
(for covering fruit cakes)

1 cup sugar
170 g glucose
½ cup water
1 teaspoon gelatine
1 tablespoon cold water
8–12 cups icing sugar

1. Place sugar, glucose and water in a saucepan.
2. Stir over low heat until dissolved then allow to boil.
3. Brush sides of pan to remove sugar.
4. Boil until syrup reaches 112°C.
5. Remove from heat and add soaked gelatine.
6. Stir until dissolved then add 2 cups icing sugar and mix.
7. Pour into a well in icing sugar in a bowl.
8. Cover and stand until cool enough to handle.
9. Knead first in the bowl then on a board until stiff paste has formed. It should be free from stickiness.
10. Roll out and use as required.

Almond Paste
(for covering fruit cakes)

4 cups sifted icing sugar

250 g ground almonds

2 egg yolks

1 teaspoon lemon juice

2 tablespoons sherry

1. Sift icing sugar into a bowl. Add the ground almonds.
2. Beat the egg yolks then add lemon juice and sherry.
3. Stir into icing sugar and almonds and mix into a rather dry paste.
4. Turn onto a board lightly dusted with icing sugar.
5. Knead until smooth then roll and use as required.

Dundee Cake (Scotland)

250 g butter

1 cup caster sugar

grated rind 1 lemon

4 large eggs

2 cups plain flour

1 cup self-raising flour

⅓–½ cup milk

1½ cups sultanas

1½ cups currants

½ cup mixed peel

½ cup almonds

2 teaspoons golden syrup

1. Beat butter, sugar and lemon rind until soft and light.
2. Beat eggs well then add to mixture a little at a time.
3. Sift flour and add one-third of it to the mixture.
4. Add the prepared fruit and golden syrup.
5. Fold in remaining flour with the milk and mix well.
6. Turn into a prepared 20 cm round tin.
7. Cover the top with the prepared almonds.
8. Brush top with milk and bake in a very moderate oven for about 2¼ hours.

Boiled Fruit Cake

2½–3 cups mixed fruit

1 cup sugar

1 cup water

2 teaspoons mixed spice

160 g butter or margarine

2 eggs

1 cup self-raising flour

1¼ cups plain flour

1 teaspoon baking soda

2 teaspoons hot water

¼ cup rum

1. Place mixed fruit, sugar, water, spice and butter in a saucepan.
2. Boil for 10 minutes.
3. Allow to cool.
4. Beat eggs and add to the mixture.
5. Fold in sifted flours, dissolved soda and rum.
6. Mix well together then pour into a prepared 20 cm round tin.
7. Bake in a slow to moderate oven for 1½ hours.

American Fruit Cake (U.S.A.)

(Stained Glass Window Cake)

1 cup dates

1 cup glacé pineapple

½ cup glacé apricots

½ cup green glacé cherries

½ cup red glacé cherries

1 cup brazil nuts

2 eggs

½ cup brown sugar, lightly
    packed

1 teaspoon vanilla

1 tablespoon rum

90 g butter

½ cup plain flour

½ teaspoon baking powder

1–2 tablespoons rum or
    brandy, extra

1. Chop dates, pineapple and apricots into fairly large pieces. Leave other fruit and nuts whole. Mix together.
2. Beat eggs until light and fluffy, add sugar, vanilla, rum and softened butter.
3. Continue beating until well blended then add sifted flour and baking powder and prepared fruit and nuts. Mix well.
4. Spoon into a greased and lined loaf tin approximately 23 × 12 cm.
5. Bake in a slow oven for about 1½ hours or until quite firm when tested with a skewer.
6. Cake may appear greasy but the butter will be absorbed as the cake cools.
7. Remove from oven and pour extra spirits over the surface. Cool on a wire rack.
8. Serve cut into small squares with after-dinner coffee.
9. Store, well wrapped, in the refrigerator.

✻ Fruit Cake

1 kg mixed dried fruits,
    chopped

2 tablespoons orange juice

125 g butter or margarine

220 g brown sugar

3 eggs

1 cup white rice flour

1 cup soy flour

1 teaspoon mixed spice

1 teaspoon gluten-free
    baking powder

1 teaspoon xanthan gum

125 g walnuts, almonds or
    pecans

1. Soak dried fruit in orange juice overnight.
2. Cream butter and sugar and add eggs one at a time beating well after each.
3. Combine rice flour, soy flour, spices, baking powder and xanthan gum in a bowl and add to egg mixture.
4. Add the dried fruit mixture and nuts and combine well.
5. Pour into a greased and lined 20 cm square tin and bake in a 150°C oven for approximately 2 hours or until cake is quite firm when tested with a skewer.
6. Cover and cool until completely cold. Remove from tin and wrap in foil and refrigerate until used.

Note: Best served at room temperature.

Plain Sponge

3 large eggs

²/₃ cup caster sugar

1 tablespoon cornflour in a measuring cup and fill remainder of cup with sifted plain flour

½ teaspoon cream of tartar

¼ teaspoon baking soda

2 teaspoons butter or margarine

3 tablespoons milk

1. Separate whites from yolks of eggs.
2. Whisk whites until soft peaks form, then gradually add sugar and yolks alternately.
3. Whisk until sugar has dissolved.
4. Sift dry ingredients together 3 times and fold into the mixture.
5. Lastly add warmed milk and butter.
6. Pour into two well-greased and lightly-floured 18 cm sandwich tins.
7. Bake in a moderate oven (180°C) for 15–20 minutes.
8. Turn onto a wire frame and allow to cool.
9. Fill with whipped cream.

Sponge Variations

Coffee Sponge

Add 2 teaspoons of instant coffee in 2½ tablespoons milk.

Finish with coffee cream or coffee flavoured icing.

Chocolate Sponge

Sift 1 tablespoon of cocoa with dry ingredients.

Add 2 teaspoons golden syrup.

Finish with cream or chocolate icing.

Sponge Roll

Omit butter and cornflour and use 3 tablespoons cold water instead of milk. Sugar may be reduced slightly. Bake in a swiss roll pan for approximately 10 minutes in a moderate oven (180°C).

Turn out onto a clean tea towel sprinkled with caster sugar. Trim edges if necessary, roll up quickly and allow to cool slightly. Unroll carefully, remove tea towel and spread with jam and roll up.

Decorate with extra caster sugar if desired.

Plain Sponge

4 eggs, separated
pinch salt
½ cup caster sugar
½ teaspoon vanilla
1 cup maize cornflour
(gluten free)
2 teaspoons gluten-free
baking powder
1 tablespoon water
1 tablespoon butter or
margarine

1. Place egg whites in a warm, dry bowl with salt and beat until stiff.
2. Add sugar gradually, beating well after each addition and beat until thick and glossy.
3. Add egg yolks one at a time and beat well after each. Add vanilla.
4. Sift cornflour and baking powder three times.
5. Place water and butter in saucepan and heat until butter is melted.
6. Fold in flour mixture and add butter and water mixture.
7. Pour into two, well-greased, 18 cm sandwich tins and bake in a moderate oven for 20 to 25 minutes.
8. Turn onto wire frame and allow to cool.

Honey Sponge Roll

3 large eggs
½ cup caster sugar
1 tablespoon melted honey
½ cup arrowroot
1 tablespoon plain flour
1 teaspoon cinnamon
1 teaspoon cream of tartar
½ teaspoon bicarbonate of
soda

1. Separate whites from yolks of eggs.
2. Whisk whites until fluffy then add egg yolks.
3. Gradually add sugar and beat for about 10 minutes.
4. Add melted honey.
5. Fold in dry ingredients which have been sifted together three times.
6. Pour into a sponge roll tin which has been lined with baking paper.
7. Bake in a moderate oven for about 10 to 15 minutes.
8. Turn out onto a clean tea towel, lightly sprinkled with caster sugar, remove paper, cut off crusts and roll up quickly and carefully.
9. When cold unroll and fill with cream.
10. Re-roll and sprinkle with icing sugar.

Cinnamon Tea Cake

60 g butter or margarine

⅓ cup caster sugar

vanilla

1 egg

½ cup milk

1¼ cups self-raising flour

Topping

1 teaspoon butter or margarine

2 teaspoons sugar

1 teaspoon cinnamon

1. Beat butter and sugar to a cream. Add vanilla.
2. Add the egg and beat well.
3. Sift flour and add to mixture alternately with milk.
4. Mix into a soft dough.
5. Pour into a greased and floured 18 cm sponge sandwich tin.
6. Bake in a moderate oven for about 20 minutes.
7. Turn onto a cooler, brush top with butter and sprinkle with a mixture of cinnamon and sugar.

Variations

Belgian Tea Cake

On top of the mixture in the tin arrange thin slices of apple. Apple is improved by part stewing before use. Sprinkle with some of the cinnamon and sugar. Bake as for the plain tea cake and sprinkle with the remainder of the cinnamon and sugar or spread with warmed apricot jam.

Pineapple Tea Cake

Spread top of the mixture with 1 tablespoon butter and 2 tablespoons honey creamed together. Sprinkle about half a can of crushed pineapple, well drained, on top. Lastly sprinkle ¼ cup coconut evenly over the pineapple. Bake as above. (Use a 20 cm tin.)

Date and Banana Tea Cake

Filling

½ cup dates

1 banana

2 teaspoons lemon juice

Place chopped dates, mashed banana and lemon juice in a saucepan. Stir over low heat until softened and smooth. Pour half the cake mixture into a well-greased and floured 18 cm sandwich tin. Spread date mixture over, then cover with remainder of cake mixture. Sprinkle with cinnamon and sugar. Bake in a moderate oven for 20 to 25 minutes.

Spiced Apple Tea Cake

Filling

1 large or two small cooking apples

2 tablespoons sugar

2 tablespoons water

½ teaspoon mixed spice

½ teaspoon cinnamon

Cook sliced apple with sugar and water and cool. Pour half the cake mixture into a greased and floured 18 cm sponge sandwich tin. Carefully arrange apple slices on top and sprinkle with spice and cinnamon. Spread remainder of cake mixture evenly over the top. Sprinkle with cinnamon and sugar. Bake for 20–25 minutes in a moderate oven.

Powder Puffs

2 large eggs
½ cup caster sugar
½ cup self-raising flour
½ cup cornflour

1. Break eggs into a bowl and beat until frothy.
2. Gradually add sugar, beat well for about 10 minutes.
3. Sift flour and cornflour together three times.
4. Fold dry ingredients into mixture lightly.
5. Place in teaspoonfuls on warmed, greased trays.
6. Bake in a moderate oven for 5 or 6 minutes.
7. Join in pairs with sweetened whipped cream.
8. Allow to stand in refrigerator for 2 hours before serving. Dust with icing sugar.

Passionfruit Cheese

125 g butter
½ cup sugar
½ lemon
4 egg yolks
4 passionfruit

1. Place butter, sugar and beaten egg yolks into a double saucepan.
2. Add the strained juice of passionfruit and lemon.
3. Cook over low heat until mixture thickens.
4. If necessary add more juice.
5. Use to fill sponge cakes.

Biscuits and Slices

Foundation Biscuit Mixture

125 g butter or margarine
½ cup caster sugar
1 egg
vanilla
1¾ cups self-raising flour

1. Beat butter and sugar to a cream.
2. Add the egg and beat well. Add vanilla.
3. Gradually add sifted flour.
4. Mix into a stiff paste.
5. Take small pieces of mixture and roll into balls.
6. Place on greased trays. Press out lightly with a floured fork.
7. Bake in a moderate oven until golden brown.

Variations

Jam Drops

Roll mixture into balls and place on greased trays. Make a hollow in each with the floured end of a wooden spoon. Place a little jam in each biscuit. Bake in a moderate oven until golden brown.

Pusher Biscuits

Place mixture into a biscuit pusher and force out onto a greased tray. Bake in a moderate oven until golden brown. Cut into lengths while still soft. Alternatively press out dough to 3 to 5 mm thickness and cut out shapes with cutters.

Coconut Biscuits

Add 2 to 3 tablespoons of coconut to the basic mixture. Drop small pieces off a spoon onto greased trays. Place a small piece of cherry on each biscuit. Bake in a moderate oven until golden brown.

Spice and Nut Biscuits

Add 1 teaspoon mixed spice and ½ cup chopped walnuts. Roll mixture into balls and place on greased trays. Press down with a fork. Bake in a moderate oven until brown.

Ginger Biscuits

Add ½ cup chopped crystallised ginger. Roll mixture into balls and place on greased trays. Press down with a fork. Bake in a moderate oven until brown.

Crunchy Sultana Biscuits

Add ½ cup sultanas and ¾ cup crushed cornflakes to the mixture. Take small pieces of mixture and place on trays. Bake in a moderate oven until golden brown. Half a cup of chocolate chips could also be added to the mixture.

Peanut Butter Biscuits

125 g butter or margarine
½ cup peanut butter
½ cup white sugar
½ cup brown sugar
1 egg
1½ cups self-raising flour

1. Beat butter, peanut butter, white and brown sugar together.
2. Add the egg and beat well.
3. Sift the flour and add gradually to the mixture.
4. Take small pieces of mixture and place on trays. Press out with a fork.
5. Bake in a moderate oven until brown.

Macadamia Crunchies

125 g butter or margarine
½ cup caster sugar
1 small egg
1 cup self-raising flour
½ cup chopped macadamia nuts
1 cup crushed cornflakes
glacé cherries

1. Beat butter and sugar to a cream. Add the egg and beat well.
2. Add the flour and mix well.
3. Add chopped macadamia nuts and crushed cornflakes.
4. Drop small teaspoonfuls on greased trays.
5. Place a small piece of cherry on top of each.
6. Bake in a moderately hot oven for 10 minutes or until golden brown.

Chocolate Chip Cookies

125 g butter or margarine
½ cup sugar
½ cup brown sugar, lightly packed
½ teaspoon vanilla
1 egg
1¾ cups self-raising flour
125 g chocolate chips
60 g pecan or walnut pieces (optional)

1. Cream butter, sugars and vanilla.
2. Gradually add lightly beaten egg, beating well after each addition.
3. Mix in sifted flour.
4. Add chocolate chips and nuts and mix well.
5. Shape mixture into small balls, place on lightly greased trays, and press out lightly with a fork, allowing room for spreading.
6. Bake in a moderate oven for 10 to 12 minutes.

Chocolate Chip Cookies

1 cup maize cornflour
(gluten free)

1 cup buckwheat flour

¼ teaspoon bicarbonate of
soda

½ teaspoon cream of tartar

Sift all ingredients together, substitute for the self-raising flour in the previous Chocolate Chip Cookie recipe and proceed as for Chocolate Chip Cookies.

Gingernuts

2 cups plain flour

½ teaspoon baking soda

1 teaspoon cinnamon

2 teaspoons ginger

125 g butter

1 cup sugar

1 egg

2 teaspoons golden syrup

extra sugar for rolling

1. Sift the dry ingredients into a bowl.
2. Rub in the butter until mixture is of a fine crumbly consistency. Add sugar.
3. Beat egg and golden syrup together and add.
4. Work into a firm dough with the hands.
5. Roll into small balls and dip in sugar.
6. Place on greased trays, sugar side up, about 5 cm apart.
7. Bake in a moderate oven for about 15 minutes.

Anzacs

1 cup plain flour

1 cup rolled oats

¾ cup coconut

¾ cup sugar

140 g butter

3 teaspoons golden syrup

3 tablespoons boiling water

1 teaspoon baking soda

1. Sift flour into a bowl.
2. Add rolled oats, coconut and sugar.
3. Melt butter in a saucepan, add syrup and water.
4. Add baking soda, allow to foam and pour immediately into dry ingredients.
5. Mix well then take small pieces of mixture and press out thinly on greased trays, allowing space between each for spreading.
6. Bake in a slow oven, as they burn easily.

Quick-Mix Anzac Slice

1½ cups rolled oats

1 cup plain flour

½ cup self-raising flour

1½ cups caster sugar

1¼ cups desiccated coconut

175 g butter or margarine, melted

2 tablespoons golden syrup

¼ cup water

½ cup flaked coconut (optional)

1. Place rolled oats, flour, sugar and desiccated coconut in a large bowl.
2. Add butter, syrup and water and mix well.
3. Press mixture into a 20 × 30 cm biscuit tray lined with baking paper. Press on flaked coconut.
4. Bake in a moderate oven (180°C) for 40 minutes or until golden and firm. Cool in pan before cutting.

Shortbread (Scotland)

100 g butter

¼ cup caster sugar (50 g)

1–1¼ cups plain flour (150–200 g)

1. Cream butter and sugar together until white.
2. Add sifted flour to form a stiff dough.
3. Turn out onto a lightly floured board, knead and place on bottom of upturned sponge tins.
4. Press each into circles of 18 mm thickness, pinch edges, mark into sections and prick well.
5. Bake in a slow oven for approximately 45 minutes.

Variation

Press out dough. Cut into fingers or rounds.

✗ Shortbread

2⅓ cups maize cornflour (gluten free)

⅓ cup soy flour

¼ cup rice flour (finely ground)

1 cup pure icing sugar

250 g butter

1. Sift dry ingredients into a bowl, add butter and rub into flour until mixture comes together.
2. Roll the dough between two sheets of baking paper until approximately 1.25 cm thick.
3. Remove top layer of baking paper and cut the dough into rectangles (approximately 7 × 2 cm) and place onto a lightly greased baking tray.
4. Bake in a slow oven (150°C) for approximately 45 minutes or until a faint golden colour.

Butterscotch Biscuits

125 g butter or margarine
1 cup brown sugar
1 egg
½ teaspoon vanilla
2 cups self-raising flour
½ Mars Bar

1. Beat butter and sugar until creamy.
2. Add the egg and vanilla and beat well.
3. Sift flour, add gradually and mix into a paste.
4. Grate Mars Bar which has been hardened in the refrigerator. Stir into the mixture.
5. Shape into balls and place on a greased tray. Press out with a floured fork.
6. Bake in a moderate to hot oven for 8 to 10 minutes.

Custard Creams

185 g butter
½ cup icing sugar
1¼ cups self-raising flour
  or **½ self-raising and ½ plain flour**
⅓ cup custard powder

1. Beat butter and sugar to a cream.
2. Sift flour and custard powder together.
3. Gradually add the butter and sugar and mix into a stiff paste.
4. Roll into small balls and place on a greased tray.
5. Press each biscuit down slightly with a floured fork.
6. Bake in a slow to moderate oven until a pale golden colour.
7. Join in pairs with lemon icing.

Crunchy Health Biscuits

1 tablespoon honey
1 tablespoon treacle or golden syrup
1 tablespoon water
125 g margarine
½ teaspoon bicarbonate of soda
1¼ cups rolled oats
½ cup coconut
½ cup raw sugar
¼ cup wheat germ
¼ cup bran

1. Place honey, treacle, water and margarine in a saucepan and bring to the boil. Add soda and stir.
2. Combine dry ingredients in a bowl.
3. Add honey mixture and mix well.
4. Drop small pieces off a spoon onto greased trays.
5. Bake in a moderate oven for 12 to 15 minutes.

Macaroon Fingers

2 egg whites
½ teaspoon vanilla
½ cup icing sugar
¼ cup plain flour
1 cup coconut
60 g chocolate

1. Beat egg whites until stiff. Add vanilla.
2. Gradually beat in sifted icing sugar. Beat until stiff and glossy.
3. Fold in flour and coconut.
4. Using a piping bag with plain tube, pipe 5 cm lengths onto greased trays (about 3 dozen) or, alternatively, drop spoonfuls onto trays.
5. Bake in a slow to moderate oven (180°C) for 15 to 20 minutes or until barely coloured.
6. Stand for a minute then loosen with a knife. Allow to cool.
7. Melt chocolate over hot water.
8. Dip each finger lengthwise in the chocolate and stand until set.

Melting Moments

125 g butter
2 tablespoons icing sugar
¾ cup plain flour
2 tablespoons cornflour

1. Beat butter and icing sugar until creamy.
2. Sift flour and cornflour together and add gradually.
3. Mix well then place in a biscuit pusher or an icing bag with large star pipe.
4. Pipe large stars onto a greased baking tray.
5. Bake for about 20 to 30 minutes in a slow oven.
6. Serve with cold sweets or coffee.

Variation

Roll mixture into balls and place on greased trays. Mark with a fork dipped in flour and cook in slow oven for 30 minutes. Join in pairs with orange or passionfruit butter icing once cooked.

Muesli Biscuits

⅛ cup honey
90 g shortening
¼ teaspoon bicarbonate of soda
1 cup untoasted muesli
½ cup plain flour
½ cup coconut
¼ cup sugar

1. Place honey and shortening in a small saucepan and melt over low heat. Add soda and stir.
2. Place remainder of ingredients into a bowl and mix together.
3. Add liquid ingredients and combine thoroughly.
4. Take small pieces of the mixture and place on trays.
5. Press out fairly thinly and top with small a piece of glacé cherry or ginger or chocolate melt.
6. Bake in a moderate oven until brown.

Lincoln Crisps

1 cup chopped raw peanuts
1 cup coconut
4 cups cornflakes
3 small or 2 large egg whites
1 cup caster sugar
1 teaspoon vanilla
2 tablespoons butter or margarine melted

1. Place peanuts, coconut and cornflakes in a bowl.
2. Whisk egg whites to a stiff froth and gradually beat in sugar. Flavour with vanilla.
3. Add the dry mixture and lastly melted butter.
4. Mix well then place in small heaps on a well-greased tray.
5. Bake in a moderate oven until lightly browned.
6. Allow to stand until firm but not completely cold, then remove carefully with a knife.

Caramel Fingers

125 g butter or margarine
½ cup brown sugar (firmly packed)
vanilla
1 egg
1 tablespoon water
1¼ cups self-raising flour
½ cup chopped dates, sultanas or mixed fruit

1. Beat butter and sugar to a cream. Add vanilla.
2. Add egg and beat well.
3. Add water and mix thoroughly.
4. Sift flour onto a plate. Add fruit and nuts and mix together.
5. Add to mixture in bowl and mix lightly.
6. Spread out on a greased and floured tray, about 28 × 18 cm.
7. Bake in a moderate oven for 20 to 25 minutes.
8. Cut into fingers while still warm.

Chocolate Slice

1¼ cups self-raising flour
2 tablespoons cocoa
¾ cup coconut
½ cup caster sugar
125 g butter or margarine
1 egg

1. Mix dry ingredients together.
2. Melt butter, beat egg well. Add both to dry ingredients.
3. Mix well then press into a biscuit tray about 28 × 18 cm.
4. Bake 10 to 15 minutes in moderate oven.
5. Cut into squares.
6. When cool pour chocolate icing over top and leave to set. Divide squares.
7. Ice while warm.

Chocolate Icing

1½ cups icing sugar
1 tablespoon butter or margarine
1 tablespoon cocoa
hot water
vanilla

1. Sift icing sugar into a bowl, add butter and cut through.
2. Blend cocoa with a little hot water.
3. Add to icing sugar with enough water to make a spreadable consistency.
4. Flavour with vanilla.

Brownies

125 g butter
100 g dark cooking chocolate, chopped
½ cup brown sugar, firmly packed
2 eggs, lightly beaten
¾ cup plain flour
¼ cup cocoa

1. Combine butter and chocolate in a saucepan and stir over low heat until smooth. Remove from heat.
2. Stir in sugar and eggs and then add sifted flour and cocoa.
3. Pour into a greased, lined 20 cm cake tin and spread evenly.
4. Bake in a moderate oven for approximately 20 minutes or until a skewer comes out clean when inserted into the centre of the slice. Leave in tin to cool.
5. When cold, ice with chocolate icing if desired, or dust with icing sugar and cut into small squares.

Variation

Add ½ cup chopped walnuts or pecans at the end of step 2.

Health Slice

125 g margarine
½ cup raw sugar
1 egg
1 teaspoon cinnamon
½ cup toasted sesame seeds
½ cup sultanas
1 cup wholemeal self-raising flour

1. To toast sesame seeds place in a heavy based saucepan and shake over medium heat until lightly browned.
2. Beat margarine and sugar to a cream. Add the egg and beat well.
3. Add the remainder of the ingredients and mix well.
4. Spread mixture on the base of a baking tray approximately 28 × 18 cm.
5. Bake in a moderate oven for 20 minutes.
6. Cut into squares or fingers.

Quick Mix Slice

1 cup self-raising flour
1 cup coconut
3 weetbix
¾ cup brown sugar
125 g butter or margarine

1. Sift flour into a bowl.
2. Add coconut, crumbled weetbix and sugar and mix.
3. Add the melted butter and mix well.
4. Press into a lamington tin approximately 28 × 18 cm.
5. Bake in a moderate oven for about 20 minutes.
6. Cool slightly before cutting into fingers.
7. Ice if required.

Caramel Marshmallow Slice

Biscuit Base

½ cup plain flour

½ cup self-raising flour

1 cup desiccated coconut

½ cup brown sugar, firmly packed

100 g butter or margarine, melted

Caramel

1 400 g can condensed milk

30 g butter or margarine

2 tablespoons golden syrup

Marshmallow

1 cup caster sugar

1 cup water

1 tablespoon gelatine

1 teaspoon vanilla

Biscuit Base

1. Combine flour, coconut, sugar and butter in a bowl and press into a greased, foil-lined 30 × 20 cm lamington tin.
2. Bake in a moderate oven for 15 minutes or until lightly browned. Cool.

Caramel

3. Combine condensed milk, butter and syrup in a saucepan and whisk over heat until simmering. Simmer until mixture is golden brown and thickened, approximately 8 minutes.
4. Pour over biscuit base and spread evenly.

Marshmallow

5. Combine sugar, water and gelatine in a saucepan and stir over low heat until gelatine dissolves. Do not boil.
6. Simmer and continue to stir for 5 minutes.
7. Pour into a bowl, cool.
8. Add vanilla and beat until thick.
9. Pour marshmallow over caramel, spread evenly and sprinkle with coconut.
10. Refrigerate until set and cut into squares.

Variation

Quick Mix Slice (page 252) can be used as a base for this slice.

Choc–Caramel Slice

For biscuit base and caramel, proceed as for Caramel Marshmallow Slice.

Chocolate Topping

125 g milk chocolate melts

1 tablespoon vegetable oil

1. Place chocolate and oil in a heat-proof bowl. Stand over a pot of simmering water and stir until chocolate has melted and the mixture is smooth.
2. Spread chocolate mixture over caramel and allow to set. Cut into squares.
3. Refrigerate until firm.

Raspberry Coconut Slice

Pastry

60 g butter or margarine
¼ cup caster sugar
1 small egg
vanilla
1¼ cups self-raising flour

Topping

½ cup raspberry jam
1 large egg
1 cup coconut
¾ cup sugar

Pastry

1. Beat butter and sugar to a cream.
2. Add the egg and beat well. Add vanilla.
3. Sift flour and add to mixture gradually.
4. Work into a stiff paste.
5. Press out evenly in a greased tin approximately 28 × 18 cm.
6. Spread thinly with raspberry jam.

Topping

7. Beat egg then add coconut and sugar and mix well.
8. Spread coconut mixture lightly over the surface.
9. Bake in moderate oven until golden brown.
10. Cool slightly before cutting into squares.

Almond Fingers

Biscuit Base

140 g butter or margarine
⅓ cup caster sugar
1½ cups plain flour

Filling

½ cup cream, whipped
⅓ cup brown sugar
1 egg yolk
½ cup ground almonds
1 teaspoon cinnamon

Icing

½ cup icing sugar
lemon juice

Pastry

1. Cream butter and sugar until light and fluffy. Stir in flour, mix well.
2. Press into a greased lamington tin and bake in a moderate oven for about 20 minutes. Allow to cool.

Filling

3. Mix together the cream, sugar, egg yolk, ground almonds and cinnamon.
4. Spread over biscuit base and bake in a slow to moderate oven for a further 40 minutes.
5. Allow to become quite cold.

Icing

6. Sift icing sugar into a bowl and add enough lemon juice to make a spreading consistency. Beat until smooth then spread over filling.
7. Refrigerate until icing is firm then cut into fingers.

Chinese Squares

1¼ cups self-raising flour

⅔ cup light brown sugar (firmly packed)

¾ cup chopped dates or mixed fruit

½ cup walnuts or pecans

125 g butter or margarine

1 egg

1. Place all dry ingredients in a bowl and mix well.
2. Melt butter, beat egg well then add both to dry ingredients.
3. Mix well together then press into a greased swiss roll tin.
4. Bake in a moderate oven.
5. Cut into squares when cool.

Variation

Cover slice with melted chocolate when warm and decorate with chopped pecans or walnuts.

Fruit Slice

Pastry

125 g butter or margarine

⅓ cup caster sugar

1 egg

2–2⅓ cups self-raising flour

a little milk

Filling

500 g mixed fruit

¼ cup water

juice ½ lemon

1 tablespoon golden syrup

1 tablespoon cornflour

1. Place fruit, water, lemon juice and syrup in a saucepan. Allow to simmer until fruit is soft.
2. Thicken with cornflour blended with a little cold water. Cool before using.
3. Cream the margarine and sugar. Add egg and beat well.
4. Gradually add the sifted flour and a little milk, if necessary, to make a stiff paste.
5. Knead well on a floured board. Roll out half the mixture on grease-proof or baking paper and line a tray approximately 30 × 20 cm. Pastry should extend up the sides of the tray about 2 cm.
6. Spread filling over pastry.
7. Roll out remainder of pastry until large enough to cover filling. Moisten edges of pastry in the tray.
8. Cover with pastry and press edges together.
9. Prick top with a fork, brush with milk and bake in a moderate oven for about 30 minutes.
10. Stand for a few minutes then turn out and trim edges.
11. When cold, ice with lemon icing, sprinkle with coconut and cut into 24 pieces.

Peanut Slice

1 cup cornflakes

1 cup desiccated coconut

1 cup self-raising flour

¾ cup brown sugar

2 tablespoons peanut butter

150 g butter or margarine

1. Place cornflakes, coconut and flour in a bowl and mix well.
2. Place sugar, peanut butter and butter in a saucepan, heat until butter is melted, stirring continuously.
3. Add butter mixture to dry ingredients and mix well.
4. Press into a greased biscuit tin and bake in a moderate oven (180°C) for 12 to 15 minutes.
5. Cool, top with chocolate icing and cut in squares.

Tropical Fruit Slice

250 g packet Morning Coffee biscuits

440 g can condensed milk

1 tablespoon lemon juice

470 g can crushed pineapple, drained

3 tablespoons passionfruit pulp

125 g copha

1. Line the base of a greased and papered 20 × 28 cm biscuit tin with biscuits.
2. Place condensed milk, lemon juice, pineapple and passionfruit in a bowl and mix well.
3. Melt copha, add to pineapple mixture and combine well and pour over biscuit base.
4. Top with another layer of biscuits and spread with fruit icing.
5. Refrigerate until set and cut into squares.

Cherry Ripe Slice

400 g can condensed milk

250 g plain biscuits, e.g. Marie, Milk Coffee or Arrowroot, crushed

100 g glacé cherries, finely chopped

2⅔ cups desiccated coconut

125 g copha

Topping

1 cup drinking chocolate, sifted

125 g copha

Slice

1. Place condensed milk, biscuits, cherries and coconut in a large bowl and mix well.
2. Melt copha, add to dry ingredients and combine well.
3. Press into a greased biscuit tin.

Topping

4. Place drinking chocolate in a bowl.
5. Melt copha and add to drinking chocolate and stir well until smooth.
6. Pour over base and spread smoothly.
7. Place in refrigerator until set and cut into squares.

Fruit and Nut Squares

¾ cup sultanas
1 cup coconut
⅓ cup chopped walnuts
½ cup crushed cornflakes
⅓ cup drinking chocolate
⅓ cup crushed sweet biscuits
⅔ cup condensed milk
1 tablespoon sherry
120 g dark chocolate

1. Combine sultanas, coconut, walnuts, cornflakes, drinking chocolate and crushed biscuits.
2. Add condensed milk and sherry.
3. Mix well to a stiff spreading consistency.
4. Spread over the base of a greased, lined lamington tin.
5. Refrigerate until firm.
6. Break up chocolate and melt in a bowl over hot water.
7. Spread quickly over surface of the mixture and allow to set.
8. Cut into squares or fingers.

Meringues

2 egg whites
2 pinches cream of tartar
½ cup caster sugar
vanilla

1. Whisk egg whites and cream of tartar until very stiff.
2. Add caster sugar gradually, beating until mixture is very thick.
3. Flavour with vanilla.
4. Line a tin tray with baking paper.
5. Pipe or pile small spoonfuls onto paper.
6. Bake in a very slow oven until quite firm and meringues will separate from the paper easily.
7. Serve as is or joined in pairs with sweetened, flavoured whipped cream.

Note: Small single meringues make an attractive topping for trifles, cheesecakes and sweet pies.

Variation
Before baking, meringues may be sprinkled with hundreds and thousands.

Almond Bread

3 egg whites, large
½ cup caster sugar
1 cup plain flour
1 cup almonds (unblanched)

1. Beat egg whites until stiff.
2. Gradually add sugar and beat until dissolved.
3. Fold in sifted flour and whole almonds.
4. Pour into a lightly greased 19 × 9 cm loaf tin.
5. Bake in a moderate oven for 30 to 40 minutes.
6. Stand in tin until cold.
7. Turn out, wrap in aluminium foil and put aside for two days.
8. With a very sharp knife cut into wafer-thin slices.
9. Place on baking tray and allow to dry out in a slow oven.
10. Store in an air-tight jar.
11. Serve with coffee or with ice-cream.

Christmas Slice

185 g glacé cherries, chopped
185 g sultanas
1 tablespoon brandy
125 g copha, chopped
315 g dark chocolate, chopped
1 teaspoon instant coffee
¾ cup toasted coconut
185 g toasted, unsalted cashews, chopped

1. Place cherries and sultanas in a small bowl, sprinkle with brandy and allow to stand overnight.
2. Place copha and chocolate in a small saucepan, melt over a gentle heat and stir in coffee.
3. Pour half the chocolate mixture over a greased and paper-lined biscuit tin, sprinkle with coconut, cashews, cherries and sultanas and press down lightly.
4. Pour remaining chocolate mixture over, chill until set and cut into small squares.
5. Store in a sealed container in the refrigerator.

White Christmas

2 cups rice bubbles
1 cup mixed fruit
¾ cup icing sugar
1 cup coconut
1 cup powdered milk
250 g copha
vanilla

1. Mix all dry ingredients together.
2. Melt copha, add vanilla and pour over mixture.
3. Mix together well.
4. Press into a greased flat tin.
5. Set in refrigerator then cut into squares or fingers.
6. Store in refrigerator.

Rum Balls

single sponge
½ cup almond meal
1 tablespoon cocoa
1–2 tablespoons rum
¼ cup apricot jam
¼ cup coconut

1. Make cake crumbs in a processor then place in a bowl.
2. Add almond meal, cocoa, rum and sufficient apricot jam to bind the mixture.
3. Shape into small balls (about 20) and roll in coconut.
4. Place on baking paper and stand until firm. Store in refrigerator.

Note: This is a basic recipe. Finely chopped glacé fruits, raisins or nuts may be added.

Variation

8 weetbix
1 tin condensed milk
2 tablespoons cocoa
1 cup coconut
1 cup mixed fruit
2 tablespoons rum
Mix and continue from step 3 above.

Apricot Balls

250 g dried apricots
½ tin condensed milk
½ cup brown sugar (optional)
½ cup coconut
1–2 tablespoons sherry (optional)
grated rind 1 orange
extra coconut

1. Mince apricots and place in a bowl.
2. Add other ingredients and mix well.
3. Form into balls and roll in coconut.
4. Store in refrigerator.

Chocolate Crackles

1⅓ cups icing sugar
½ cup cocoa
1 cup coconut
3½ cups rice bubbles
230 g copha
vanilla

1. Combine icing sugar, cocoa, coconut and rice bubbles in a bowl.
2. Melt copha and add vanilla. Pour over dry ingredients and mix.
3. Spoon into paper containers.
4. Allow to set in refrigerator.
5. Store in refrigerator.

Cream Cheese Slice

Base

1 packet lattice biscuits

Filling

3 teaspoons gelatine dissolved in ¼ cup water
250 g cream cheese
125 g butter or margarine
½ cup caster sugar
1 tablespoon lemon juice

Base

1. Arrange lattice biscuits, shiny side up, in the base of a biscuit tray.

Filling

2. Dissolve gelatine in water.
3. Beat cream cheese, butter and sugar until smooth.
4. Add gelatine and lemon juice and beat well to combine.
5. Spread evenly on top of biscuits and arrange another layer of biscuits on top of filling.
6. Refrigerate until set and slice into fingers.

Fruity Chews — 'Cook' in Fridge

180 g dried apricots
½ cup sultanas
½ cup raisins
¼ cup dates
½ cup rolled oats
2 tablespoons sesame seeds, toasted
¼ cup coconut
½ cup skim milk powder
2 tablespoons honey
¼ cup orange juice

1. Chop dried fruits finely and mix together. Add sesame seeds, coconut and milk powder.
2. Mix honey with the orange juice and mix well.
3. Press into a foil-lined lamington tray.
4. Refrigerate for several hours before cutting into fingers.

Scones, Loaves and Muffins

Plain Scones

2 cups self-raising flour (250 g)
2 tablespoons butter or margarine
¾–1 cup milk
extra flour for rolling

1. Sift flour into a bowl.
2. Rub butter into flour with fingertips.
3. Make a well in the centre.
4. Pour milk in all at once. Using a knife mix quickly and lightly until a moist dough is formed.
5. Turn out onto a floured board. Knead lightly and press out to 2.5 cm thickness.
6. Cut out with a scone cutter. Place close together on a floured tray.
7. Brush over with beaten yolk of egg and milk.
8. Bake in a hot oven 12 to 15 minutes.
9. Wrap in a cloth until cold.
10. Serve hot or warm with butter or with jam and whipped cream.

Note: For lighter scones use ½ water and ½ milk; wholemeal self-raising flour may be used.

Scones

1¾ cups white rice flour
½ cup potato flour
¼ cup arrowroot
pinch salt (optional)
¼ cup pure icing sugar
2 teaspoons xanthan gum
2 teaspoons gluten-free baking powder
1 teaspoon bicarbonate of soda
30 g butter or margarine
1 egg, lightly beaten
1⅓ cups buttermilk

1. Sift flours, salt, sugar, gum, baking powder and bicarbonate of soda into a bowl.
2. Rub in butter until the mixture resembles fine breadcrumbs.
3. Make a well in the centre and stir in egg and enough milk to make a soft dough.
4. Place on a floured board and knead lightly and press out to 2.5 cm thickness.
5. Continue as for step 6 for Plain Scones.

Cheese Scones

2 cups self-raising flour
2 tablespoons butter
½ cup grated cheese
2 pinches cayenne pepper
¾–1 cup milk
1 egg yolk (optional)

1. Sift flour into a bowl.
2. Rub in butter with fingertips.
3. Add grated cheese and cayenne pepper.
4. Beat egg and add to milk.
5. Make a well in centre of dry ingredients and stir in egg and milk.
6. Mix into a moist dough.
7. Turn onto a floured board, knead and press out with the hand.
8. Cut into scones and place close together on a floured tray.
9. Brush over with egg and milk.
10. Bake in a hot oven for 10 to 15 minutes.
11. Wrap in a towel to cool.
12. Serve hot or warm with butter or cream cheese.

Date or Sultana Scones

2 cups self-raising flour
2 tablespoons butter or margarine
½ cup chopped dates or sultanas
2 tablespoons caster sugar
¾–1 cup milk
1 egg

1. Sift flour into a bowl.
2. Rub in butter with fingertips.
3. Add the sultanas and sugar and mix well.
4. Whisk egg and milk together.
5. Make a well in the dry ingredients and stir in liquid.
6. Mix into a moist dough.
7. Turn onto a floured board, knead and press out with the hand.
8. Cut into scones and place on a floured tray.
9. Brush over with egg and milk.
10. Bake in a hot oven for about 12 to 15 minutes.
11. Roll in a towel to cool.
12. Serve hot or warm with butter or margarine.

Sweet Potato Scones

2 tablespoons butter or margarine

¾ cup brown sugar, lightly packed

1 egg

1 cup mashed sweet potato (golden variety)

2 cups wholemeal self-raising flour

milk if required

1. Cream butter and sugar, add egg and beat well.
2. Add cooked, mashed potato which has been rubbed through a sieve.
3. Add the flour and enough milk to mix into a soft scone dough. The quantity of milk will depend on the moisture content of the potato.
4. Turn onto a floured board and press out with the hand to about 2.5 cm thickness.
5. Cut into scones and place close together on a greased and floured tray. Brush with a little egg and milk.
6. Bake in a hot oven (220°C) for 10 to 15 minutes.
7. Serve warm or cold with butter, margarine or cream cheese with chopped parsley.

Savoury Cheese Ring

Scone Mixture

2 cups self-raising flour

3 tablespoons butter or margarine

½ cup grated cheese

pinch cayenne pepper

1 egg

1 cup milk (approx.)

Filling

250 g luncheon beef knob, diced bacon, salami or ham

2 or 3 gherkins

2 teaspoons melted butter or margarine

2 teaspoons chopped parsley

1 small onion

¼ cup grated cheese

1 tablespoon tomato sauce

1. To prepare filling, dice meat and gherkins finely. Grate the onion and chop parsley.
2. Combine all ingredients and mix well.
3. Sift flour and cayenne pepper into a bowl.
4. Rub butter through with the fingertips.
5. Add the grated cheese.
6. Add beaten egg and milk to make a moist scone dough.
7. Turn onto a floured board and knead lightly. Roll out into a rectangle approximately 30 × 20 cm.
8. Spread with filling to within 2.5 cm of edge and roll.
9. Place on greased tray, twist into a ring, moisten ends and join.
10. Cut two-thirds of the way through the ring with scissors or a sharp knife, at 2.5 cm intervals.
11. Turn each section on its side.
12. Brush well with egg and milk.
13. Bake in a moderate oven for 30 to 35 minutes.
14. Slice and serve warm.

Fruit and Nut Ring

Scone Mixture

2 cups self-raising flour

3 tablespoons butter or margarine

1 egg

2 tablespoons caster sugar

1 cup milk (approx.)

Filling

½ cup dates

½ cup mixed fruit

few drops lemon juice

½ cup water

¼ cup chopped nuts

1. Chop dates and place in saucepan with fruit, lemon juice and water.
2. Cook until mixture is of spreading consistency. Allow to cool.
3. Sift flour into a bowl.
4. Rub butter into flour with fingertips.
5. Beat egg and sugar together then add milk.
6. Stir into dry ingredients and mix into a moist dough.
7. Turn onto a floured board and knead lightly. Roll out into a rectangle approximately 30 × 20 cm.
8. Spread with fruit mixture to within 2.5 cm of edge.
9. Roll up, place on a greased tray, twist into a ring, moisten ends and join.
10. Cut two-thirds through the ring at 2.5 cm intervals and turn each section on its side.
11. Brush with milk and sprinkle with chopped nuts.
12. Bake in a moderate oven for 30 to 35 minutes.
13. Brush with glaze made by dissolving 1 tablespoon of sugar in 1 tablespoon of hot water.
14. Serve warm or cold spread lightly with butter or margarine.

Variation

Banana and Caramel Ring

Mash 2 bananas and spread over rolled out dough, sprinkle with ½ cup lightly packed brown sugar. Roll up and cut into 8 slices. Place slices in a greased 20 cm round cake tin and bake as per instructions.

Damper

4 cups plain flour

2 teaspoons baking powder or 2 cups self-raising flour

2 cups water (approx.)

1. Place flour and rising into a bowl.
2. Make a well in the centre and stir in the water. Mix lightly.
3. Turn onto a floured board and knead lightly until smooth.
4. Press into a round shape about 20 cm in diameter on a greased tray.
5. Bake in a moderate oven for approximately 25 minutes or until damper sounds hollow when tapped with the fingers.
6. Serve hot or cold with butter, margarine or jam.

Bread Knots

2 cups self-raising flour

1 35 g packet French onion soup mix

¼ cup finely grated cheddar cheese

1 tablespoon finely chopped parsley

¾ to 1 cup buttermilk

sesame seeds

1. Sift flour into a large bowl and add soup mix. Mix well.
2. Add in cheese and parsley and stir.
3. Make a well in the centre and add sufficient buttermilk to make a firm dough.
4. Turn onto a floured board and knead lightly for 1 minute.
5. Divide dough into 8 pieces and roll each piece into a long log shape.
6. Twist each length of dough into a knot and place onto a greased tray.
7. Brush with milk and sprinkle with sesame seeds and bake in a hot oven (200°C) for 20 to 25 minutes or until browned.
8. Serve warm with a little butter or margarine.

Roti — Flat, Unleavened Indian Bread

450 g wholemeal flour

lukewarm water

1. Place flour in a bowl and add water gradually working it into the flour with fingertips until the dough comes together.
2. Place the dough on a floured board and knead until well combined.
3. Return to bowl, leave 10 to 15 minutes and then knead again for 1 to 2 minutes.
4. Divide the dough into 4 pieces and shape each piece into a ball. On a floured board, roll each ball into a thin disc approx. 15 cm in diameter.
5. Heat a flat, non-stick pan on medium and when hot, place one roti in pan at a time and dry fry for about 1 minute until browned, pressing it down as it cooks.
6. Turn it over and cook the other side.
7. Repeat with other roti and serve promptly.

Naan Bread — Leavened Indian Bread

450 g white flour (use bread flour)

1 tablespoon baking powder

1 tablespoon sugar

2 tablespoon plain yoghurt

1 teaspoon salt

2 teaspoons sesame seeds or poppy seeds

lukewarm water

20 g ghee, melted

1. Place all ingredients, except ghee, in a large bowl.
2. Add water gradually and work it into the flour with the fingertips until the dough comes together.
3. Remove from bowl, place on a floured board and knead until well combined.
4. Return to bowl and leave in a warm place for 1 to 2 hours to prove until double in size.
5. Place on a floured board and knead again and divide into 4 pieces.
6. Shape each piece in a ball and then on a floured board, roll into a disc approx. 15 cm in diameter and 5 mm thick.
7. Preheat grill to medium, cover grill rack with foil and place naan on the foil and grill it until it develops brown patches.
8. Remove from grill, turn over and brush the uncooked side with ghee.
9. Return to grill and cook until sizzling. Serve immediately.

Pizza Base — Without Yeast

Scone Dough

1¼ cups self-raising flour

1½ tablespoons butter or margarine

milk to mix

1. Sift flour into a bowl and rub in the butter with fingertips.
2. Mix into a moist dough with milk.
3. Turn onto a floured board, knead lightly then roll out and line a pizza tin. If possible make the edge a little thicker.
4. Fill as for the yeast dough pizza. (See Yeast Cookery section, page 284.)

Note: This makes one pizza only.

Pumpkin Scones

2 tablespoons butter or
  margarine
$\frac{1}{3}$ cup sugar
1 egg
$\frac{1}{2}$ cup cold mashed
  pumpkin
2 cups self-raising flour
$\frac{1}{4}$–$\frac{1}{3}$ cup milk

1. Beat butter and sugar to a cream.
2. Add the egg and beat well.
3. Add well-mashed pumpkin.
4. Sift flour twice.
5. Add milk and flour alternately and mix into a moist dough.
6. Turn onto a floured board and knead lightly.
7. Press out with palm of hand until about 2.5 cm thickness.
8. Cut into scones and place close together on a greased and floured tray.
9. Brush tops of scones with milk.
10. Bake in a hot oven until well browned.
11. Roll in a towel to cool.
12. Serve hot or cold with butter, margarine or jam.

Note: One cup of pumpkin may be used, in which case little or no milk will be required.

Zucchini Bread

3 eggs
1$\frac{1}{4}$ cups sugar
3 teaspoons vanilla
$\frac{1}{4}$ cup oil
2 cups grated zucchini
$\frac{1}{2}$ cup chopped dates
  (optional)
1 cup plain flour
1 cup self-raising flour
1 cup bran flakes soaked in
  $\frac{1}{4}$ cup hot water
$\frac{1}{2}$ teaspoon bicarbonate of
  soda
3 teaspoons cinnamon
1 cup chopped walnuts

1. Beat eggs until light and foamy.
2. Add the sugar, vanilla and oil and beat well.
3. Stir in the zucchini and dates.
4. Add the sifted flours, bran, soda and cinnamon.
5. Lastly add the walnuts.
6. Turn into a paper-lined and greased block tin.
7. Bake in a moderate oven for 1 to 1$\frac{1}{2}$ hours.
8. Serve in slices, spread with butter or margarine.

Gingerbread

1¾ cups plain flour

3 teaspoons ginger

2 teaspoons mixed spice

125 g butter

½ cup caster sugar

⅓ cup golden syrup

2 large eggs

3 tablespoons milk

1 teaspoon baking soda

1. Sift flour and spices into a bowl.
2. Heat butter, sugar and syrup, stirring until the mixture is smooth.
3. Beat eggs well.
4. Warm the milk and stir in the baking soda.
5. Mix all liquid ingredients. Stir into dry ingredients and mix until smooth.
6. Pour into a greased and paper-lined tin.
7. Bake in a slow to moderate oven for 50 to 60 minutes.
8. Serve sliced and lightly spread with butter or margarine.

Quick Apricot Loaf

1 cup wholemeal flour

1 cup milk

1 cup desiccated coconut

¾ cup sugar

1 cup dried apricots, diced

1. Combine all dry ingredients in a bowl and stir in milk to combine well.
2. Pour into a greased loaf tin and bake in a moderate oven (180°C) for 35 to 45 minutes.
3. Serve sliced.

Date and Banana Loaf

120 g butter or margarine

½ cup brown sugar, firmly packed

1 egg

½ teaspoon lemon essence

¾ cup mashed bananas

½ cup rolled oats

1½ cups wholemeal self-raising flour

½ teaspoon baking powder

½ cup milk

¾ cup chopped dates

1. Cream the butter and sugar. Add the egg and beat well.
2. Add well-mashed bananas and lemon essence.
3. Mix together rolled oats, flour and baking powder. Add to the mixture alternately with milk.
4. Lastly add the dates. Add more milk if necessary.
5. Turn into a well-greased loaf tin and bake in a moderate oven for 50 to 60 minutes.
6. Serve cut in slices as is or lightly spread with butter or margarine.

Date Loaf

1 cup dates

½ cup brown sugar, firmly packed

2 tablespoons butter or margarine

1 teaspoon baking soda

1 cup boiling water

1 egg

¾ cup self-raising flour

¾ cup plain flour

1. Chop dates and place in a mixing bowl.
2. Add sugar, butter and baking soda.
3. Pour boiling water over and mix well together.
4. Allow to stand until almost cold.
5. Add the beaten egg.
6. Sift the dry ingredients together and add gradually. Mix well.
7. Pour into a greased and floured loaf tin.
8. Bake in a slow to moderate oven for 40 to 45 minutes.
9. Serve sliced as is or lightly spread with butter, margarine or cream cheese.

Note: To vary the flavour add 2 tablespoons chopped crystallised ginger.

Bran Loaf

1 cup bran

1 cup milk

1 cup dried fruits (apricots, raisins, sultanas, nuts)

¾ cup brown sugar

1 banana, mashed

1 cup wholemeal self-raising flour

1. Place all the ingredients, except the flour, into a bowl.
2. Mix well then allow to stand for 1 hour.
3. Add the flour and mix well.
4. Turn into a greased loaf tin.
5. Bake in a moderate oven for approximately 50 minutes.
6. Serve sliced as is or lightly spread with butter or margarine.

Note: This is a moist, rather heavy loaf.

Nut Bread

½ cup caster sugar

45 g butter or margarine

1 egg

grated lemon rind

½ cup milk

1½ cups self-raising flour

1 teaspoon mixed spice

½ cup chopped pecans or walnuts

1. Beat butter and sugar. Add egg and lemon rind and beat well.
2. Add milk and sifted flour and spice alternately. Add the nuts and mix well. The consistency will be fairly thin.
3. Spoon into a well-greased nut loaf tin and cover with the lid.
4. Bake in a moderate oven (190°C) for approximately 50 minutes.
5. Allow to stand for 10 minutes before turning out. Slice and serve as is or lightly spread with butter or margarine.

Note: This loaf cuts better on the second day.

Sultana and Apricot Loaf

¾ **cup raw sugar**
1 cup sultanas
1 cup All-Bran
200 g dried apricots, chopped
1½ cups milk
1½ cups self-raising flour

1. Place sugar, sultanas, All-Bran and apricots in a bowl.
2. Add the milk and allow to stand for 2 hours.
3. Add sifted flour and mix well.
4. Spoon into a loaf pan, approximately 22 × 11 cm, which has been well greased and lined on the base with baking paper.
5. Bake in a moderate oven (180°C) for approximately 1 hour.
6. Serve in slices as is or lightly spread with butter or margarine.

✴ Sultana and Apricot Loaf

1 cup milk
1 cup chopped, dried apricots
1 cup sultanas
1 cup brown sugar, lightly packed
2 cups soy flour
½ cup maize cornflour (gluten free)
1 teaspoon bicarbonate of soda

1. Combine milk, apricots, sultanas and brown sugar and place in a bowl in the refrigerator overnight.
2. Mix together soy flour, cornflour and bicarbonate of soda, add milk mixture and stir until just combined.
3. Pour mixture into a greased loaf tin and bake in a moderate oven for approximately 30 minutes or until a skewer comes out clean.
4. Serve sliced as is, or lightly spread with butter or margarine.

Doughnuts

2 cups self-raising flour
60 g butter
1½ tablespoons sugar
1 egg
¾ **cup milk (approx.)**
oil for frying
2 teaspoons cinnamon
3 tablespoons caster sugar

1. Sift flour into a bowl.
2. Rub in butter with the fingers. Add the sugar.
3. Mix in beaten egg and enough milk to make a smooth soft dough.
4. Turn onto a floured board, knead lightly and roll out to approximately 2 cm thickness.
5. Cut into rounds with a 7.5 cm cutter and remove centres with a 2.5 cm cutter.
6. Deep fry for about 3 minutes until golden brown.
7. Mix cinnamon and sugar together and shake warm doughnuts in it.
8. Serve hot.

Plain Muffins (U.S.A.)

2 cups self-raising flour _or_
  1 cup self-raising flour
  and 1 cup wholemeal
  self-raising flour
1 teaspoon baking powder
2 tablespoons sugar
1 egg, lightly beaten
1 cup milk
4 tablespoons butter or
  margarine, melted

1. Sift together flour and baking powder. Add sugar.
2. Combine beaten egg, milk and melted butter.
3. Add all at once to the flour mixture stirring quickly until just mixed. (The mixture should be a little lumpy.)
4. Fill greased muffin pans two-thirds full and bake in a hot oven (220°C) for 18 to 20 minutes.
5. Serve warm.

(Makes 12 muffins)

Variations

Cheese Muffins

Add 1 cup grated cheese.

Fruit Muffins — Banana and Apple

Add one large mashed banana or one cooking apple peeled and diced with 1 teaspoon cinnamon.

Dried Fruit Muffins

Add ½ cup chopped apricots, dates, raisins or sultanas.

Orange Muffins

Add grated orange rind and ¼ cup orange juice. Reduce milk to ¾ cup.

Carrot and Sultana Muffins

Add one cup grated carrot, ¼ cup sultanas and ¼ cup chopped pecans or walnuts.

Nut Muffins

Add ½ cup chopped macadamias or pecans.

Plain Muffins

2 cups rice flour
¾ teaspoon salt
½ cup sugar
2 teaspoons gluten-free
  baking powder
1 tablespoon xanthan gum
1¼ cups milk
1 egg
3 tablespoons oil or melted
  butter
vanilla

1. Combine flour, salt, sugar, baking powder and xanthan gum in a bowl.
2. Add milk, egg, oil and vanilla and stir quickly until just mixed.
3. Spoon into greased muffin pans and bake in a moderate oven until golden and firm to the touch.

Variation

As for Plain Muffins.

(Makes 12 muffins)

Oat Bran Muffins

1 cup self-raising flour
2 teaspoons baking powder
1 cup oat bran
½ cup sugar
½ cup sultanas
2 eggs
¾ teaspoon finely grated orange rind
½–¾ cup orange juice
¼ cup oil

1. Sift flour and baking powder into a bowl.
2. Stir in bran, sugar and sultanas.
3. Beat eggs then add rind, juice and oil.
4. Mix well then pour into a well in the centre of dry ingredients. Stir with a fork until just mixed. Do not beat.
5. Three-quarters fill muffin pans which have been oiled (about 12).
6. Bake in a hot oven (200°C) for 18 to 20 minutes or until well risen and golden.
7. Serve warm.

Blueberry Muffins

90 g butter or margarine
⅔ cup sugar
1 egg, lightly beaten
2 cups self-raising flour
¾–1 cup milk
1 425 g can blueberries, well drained or use frozen berries

Note: Other well-drained fruit may be used instead of blueberries.

1. In a small bowl cream butter and sugar until light and fluffy.
2. Add the egg and beat well.
3. Into a large bowl sift flour.
4. Make a well in the centre and fold in butter mixture alternately with milk. Stir until just combined. Do not beat.
5. Spoon a small amount of mixture into each of 12 muffin pans.
6. On each place a teaspoon of blueberries.
7. Top with a tablespoon of mixture.
8. Bake in a hot oven (200°C) for 18 to 20 minutes or until golden brown. Serve warm.

Blueberry Muffins — Low fat

1 cup blueberries (canned or frozen)

4 teaspoons brown sugar

1 cup white self-raising flour

1 cup wholemeal self-raising flour

1 teaspoon baking powder

1 egg

½ cup low-fat yoghurt (strawberry, blueberry, raspberry)

1 cup low-fat milk

1. Place blueberries in a saucepan with sugar, heat gently to dissolve sugar. Remove from heat.
2. Place flour and baking powder in a bowl, make a well in the centre and add beaten egg, yoghurt, milk and blueberries. Stir until just combined. Do not heat.
3. Spoon mixture into greased muffin pans and bake in a hot oven (200°C) for 15 to 20 minutes or until golden.

Savoury Muffins

4 bacon rashers, chopped

2 shallots, chopped

2 cups self-raising flour

1 teaspoon baking powder

½ cup grated cheese

1 cup corn kernels

1 egg, lightly beaten

1½ tablespoons margarine, melted

1 cup milk

1. Place bacon and shallots in a small pan.
2. Cook over medium heat until bacon is cooked but not hard. Allow to cool.
3. Sift flour into a bowl.
4. Add bacon, cheese and corn and mix.
5. Make a well in the centre and pour in egg, margarine and milk and mix well.
6. Spoon mixture into 12 well-greased muffin pans, filling them two-thirds full.
7. Bake in a hot oven (200 to 220°C) for approximately 20 minutes.
8. Serve warm.

BREAD

This must be fresh. A variety of breads can be used, e.g. white, wholemeal, rye or grain. They should not be cut too thinly.

BUTTER, MARGARINE AND SPREADS

If using butter, it needs to be at room temperature for several hours. If necessary, cream butter in a warm bowl until of good spreading consistency or soften in microwave on defrost mode, until of spreading consistency.

Spread each slice of bread with butter or margarine as this helps to prevent filling from soaking into the bread.

Cream cheese, light cream-cheese spread, mashed avocado, hummus, pesto or mayonnaise can be substituted for butter or margarine.

FILLINGS

These may be savoury or sweet or a combination of the two. Fillings should be moist, well flavoured and applied liberally.

EGGS

- Mashed hard-boiled eggs, moistened with mayonnaise and flavoured with curry powder, onion, bacon or chives
- Mashed hard-boiled eggs, moistened with cream and mixed with grated carrot and shredded lettuce

MEATS

- Thinly sliced cold meats or shaved meats with chutney sauce, pickles or mayonnaise. Meats could include: chicken, turkey, ham, corned beef, roast meats, or sausage meats e.g. windsor.

CHEESE

- Sliced or grated cheese or creamed, cottage or ricotta cheese spreads can be combined with chopped celery, gherkins, capsicum, apple, nuts or salad vegetables.
- Cheese with sliced tomato.

FISH

- Salmon, tuna, sardines or crab mashed and moistened with mayonnaise. Add finely chopped onion or shallots for added flavour.

VEGETABLES

- Sliced tomato, cucumber or sprouts with meats and pastes
- Sliced tomato with mint or basil leaves
- Mashed avocado with lemon juice
- Shredded lettuce, grated carrot, chopped celery in combination with meat, fish or cheese
- Asparagus with cream cheese
- Sun-dried tomatoes and char-grilled capsicums

FRUIT AND NUTS

- Sliced pineapple with mint
- Chopped raisins and grated apple
- Chopped dates and peanut paste
- Nuts, chopped and combined with celery, cheese, apple
- Bind together with cream or mayonnaise

PREPARED FILLINGS

- Vegemite and Marmite
- Meat and fish pastes combined with cheese and chopped vegetables
- Peanut paste and honey or dried fruits
- Spaghetti or baked beans with cheese, bacon or Tabasco sauce
- Sweet corn with bacon or ham
- Hommus and other prepared dips

Plain Sandwiches

brown or white bread

softened butter or
margarine

fillings

pepper

garnish

1. Slice bread thinly and arrange slices in pairs.
2. Spread butter evenly on all slices.
3. Spread filling liberally over one slice of each pair.
4. Cover with second slice and press together firmly.
5. Place three pairs together and trim off crusts if required.
6. Cut into four diagonally.
7. Arrange on a plate and garnish with shredded lettuce or parsley sprigs. Serve as soon as possible.
8. If not being served immediately, wrap in plastic wrap.

TOASTED SANDWICHES

Prepare sandwiches and use savoury fillings such as ham, chicken, crab, salmon, cheese, tomato or asparagus or combinations as previously suggested. Do not cut. Place under a preheated griller and brown both sides or cook in toasted sandwich maker.

Cut into four to serve.

If using an electric frypan butter the outside of the sandwich instead of the inside.

Preheat frypan to 190° to 210°C, brush surface with butter and place sandwiches in pan. Brown both sides. Use an egg-lifter to press sandwiches flat while cooking. Cut into four and serve immediately.

Ham Club Sandwich

3 slices toast

butter or margarine

1 slice ham

2 teaspoons mustard
pickles

1 small tomato

2 teaspoons salad dressing

2 lettuce leaves

2 olives

1. Butter hot toast on one side if desired.
2. Place slice of ham on one piece and spread with finely chopped pickles.
3. Place another slice of toast on top and cover with sliced tomato and mayonnaise. Sprinkle with pepper.
4. Cover with third slice of toast, buttered side down.
5. Place in oven and heat through.
6. Arrange lettuce on a plate and place sandwich, cut in half diagonally, in the leaves.
7. Garnish with sprouts or parsley.

Variations

Ham or grilled bacon with asparagus

Salmon or chicken with tomato

Cooked sliced sausages with tomato

Asparagus Rolls

thinly sliced fresh bread
butter or margarine
asparagus spears
pepper

1. Drain asparagus tips and sprinkle liberally with pepper.
2. Spread butter on bread if desired. Remove crusts.
3. Place asparagus tips diagonally on slices of bread.
4. Roll up cornerwise and press lightly.
5. Pack closely together, cover and chill.
6. Serve garnished with shredded lettuce, parsley, or celery leaves.

Note: Combine a little lemon juice or mustard with the butter to give additional flavour.

Open Sandwich

1 slice wholemeal rye or grain bread
1 teaspoon butter or margarine
1 lettuce cup
2 tablespoons red or pink salmon
1 thick slice of tomato
1 teaspoon mayonnaise
1 gherkin
parsley
alfalfa sprouts

1. Spread bread with butter and place on a plate.
2. Arrange lettuce cup on bread and in it place the salmon.
3. On top place a thick slice of tomato with mayonnaise in the centre.
4. Garnish with parsley and sprouts.

Variations

Cold meat or ham, tomato, cheese

Tomato and hard boiled eggs

Avocado, sprouts and salad

Chopped chicken and mango sauce

Grilled Open Sandwich

Toast bread and top with

- ham and cheese
- pineapple, ham and cheese
- asparagus and cheese
- chicken, cranberry sauce and cheese

and place under the grill until the cheese is melted and lightly browned.

Pinwheels

30 g cream cheese
2 gherkins, chopped finely,
  or parsley, or chives
pepper
1 small tin fish paste
a little lemon juice
2 slices brown bread
2 slices white bread
1 tablespoon butter
parsley

1. Mix cream cheese with gherkins, parsley or chives. Add pepper to taste.
2. To the fish paste add a few drops of lemon juice and pepper.
3. Butter the bread and remove crusts.
4. Spread cheese mixture on the brown bread and fish paste on the white bread.
5. Roll up each slice and wrap in plastic wrap. Chill, then remove wrap.
6. Cut into 6 mm slices.
7. Serve garnished with parsley.

Savoury Loaf

1 loaf unsliced bread
  (white, wholemeal or
  multigrain)
1 bunch spinach or 1
  small–medium lettuce
180 g ham or turkey slices
180 g cheese, thinly sliced
2 tomatoes, thinly sliced
90 g marinated capsicum,
  thinly sliced
1 avocado, thinly sliced
2–3 shallots, finely sliced
¼ cup finely chopped
  parsley

1. Cut top from loaf lengthwise and hollow out bread leaving a 2 cm thickness. Reserve top.
2. If using spinach, microwave or steam until tender and drain well. Place spinach or lettuce leaves on the base of the hollowed out loaf and add layers of the other ingredients in the order given. Repeat the layers.
3. Place top on loaf and press down well. Wrap securely in plastic wrap and place weight on top, e.g. a bag of rice.
4. Refrigerate for at least an hour, slice and serve garnished with sprouts.

Note: A thin spread of chutney, cranberry sauce or mustard can be added after meat layer for extra flavour.

(Makes approximately 20 slices)

Ribbon Sandwiches

2 slices brown bread
2 slices white bread
1 tablespoon butter
1 hard boiled egg
1 tablespoon mayonnaise
3 asparagus spears
1 tablespoon cheese
  spread
pepper

1. Mash hard boiled egg and combine with mayonnaise. Season with pepper.
2. Chop asparagus and season with pepper.
3. Spread two slices of bread with butter and make a sandwich with egg filling.
4. Butter top of sandwich and cover with a layer of cheese.
5. Butter another slice of bread and place over cheese.
6. Butter top of sandwich and cover with asparagus.
7. Butter fourth slice and cover asparagus with buttered side downwards.
8. Press firmly, trim off crusts and cut into four then into eight rectangles.
9. Arrange on a plate with cut side upwards.
10. Garnish with a little shredded lettuce, parsley or sprouts.

This is but one suggestion. Any combination is acceptable providing the flavours blend. Make use of the commercial products readily available. Some of the spreads given in the Appetisers section could also be used.

Fillings should always be reasonably moist so the slices of bread hold together thus making cutting easier. Made-up fillings are preferable to sliced tomatoes and cucumber which tend to slip.

If preferred, use only three slices of bread — two brown and one white or two white and one brown. It will be easier to select two fillings which blend.

Variations

Ham, pickles and cream cheese with flavourings e.g. chives
Chicken, mayonnaise and lettuce
Avocado and mayonnaise

White Bread

50 g compressed yeast (or 2 × 7 g sachets dry yeast)
1¾ cups water (variable)
6 cups plain flour
1½ teaspoons salt
2 teaspoons butter or margarine
1 teaspoon sugar
1 50 mg ascorbic acid tablet

1. Crumble yeast in ¾ cup lukewarm water. Stir gently with a fork until yeast has dispersed.
2. Place flour and salt in a large bowl, rub in the butter, add sugar and crushed ascorbic acid tablet. Mix thoroughly.
3. Make a well in the centre, add yeast mixture and remaining water. Mix to a soft dough with a knife. The dough should be soft but not sticky. If too dry add more water. If too wet, knead a little extra flour into mixture while still in the bowl.
4. Turn onto a lightly floured board and knead thoroughly until dough is smooth and satin-like, approximately 10 minutes. If mixture is still sticky, knead in more flour gradually until dough is easy to handle. Dough will spring back when pressed with the finger if kneaded sufficiently. Cover with a clean cloth and rest for 5 minutes.
5. Divide dough in half. Roll each piece with a rolling pin to a rectangle 20 × 30 cm (or as wide as the length of the tin). Roll up each piece as for jam roll starting with the 20 cm side. Do not roll too tightly.
6. Place in two, well-oiled loaf pans 20 × 10 × 8 cm with sealed edges of loaves underneath.
7. Cover with a sheet of plastic and clean cloth and stand in a warm place approximately 30 minutes, until loaves have doubled in bulk and mixture has risen about 2 cm above tops of the tins. Press gently with fingers — a slight indentation shows loaves are ready to bake.
8. Bake for 25 to 30 minutes in a hot oven (230°C). To test, tap loaf lightly. The loaf should sound hollow when done. Bake a few minutes more if necessary. Remove from tins immediately and cool on a wire rack.

Note: Bread flour will give a better result.

Variations

Brown Bread

Use 3 cups plain white flour and 3 cups 100 per cent wholemeal, finely ground.

Wholemeal Bread

Use 6 cups 100 per cent wholemeal, finely ground.

Bread Rolls

Cut dough into 20 to 22 even-sized pieces. Shape into rolls and place on an oiled tray, leaving room for the dough to expand. Stand in a warm place covered with a piece of plastic and a clean cloth until rolls have doubled in bulk.

Bake for 15 to 20 minutes in a hot oven (230°C). Rolls may be brushed with water and sprinkled with sesame or poppy seeds before baking.

✗ Bread

1½ teaspoons dry yeast

2 cups white rice flour

1½ teaspoons xanthan gum

1 teaspoon salt

⅓ cup milk powder

2 tablespoons sugar

2 eggs

3 tablespoons oil

250 mL water

1 teaspoon vinegar

1. Place yeast, flour, xanthan gum, salt, milk powder and sugar in a large bowl and mix thoroughly.
2. Place eggs, oil, water and vinegar in a bowl and whisk together.
3. Add egg mixture to dry ingredients to mix to a soft dough, adding a little more water if necessary.
4. Knead on a floured board for 10 minutes.
5. Place in an oiled loaf pan, cover with plastic and leave to rise for one hour.
6. Bake in a moderate oven for approximately 45 minutes. To test, tap loaf lightly and the loaf should sound hollow when done.

Whole-wheat Bread or Health Bread

4 cups whole-wheat flour

30 g wheat germ (optional)

1 teaspoon salt

½ cup warm water

2 teaspoons dried yeast

2 teaspoons sugar

½ cup hot water

3 teaspoons molasses

1. Place flour, wheat germ and salt in a bowl.
2. Mix together the warm water, yeast and sugar and stir until yeast has dispersed.
3. Mix together the hot water and molasses.
4. When yeast mixture is frothy mix all the ingredients together. If dough is too moist add more flour.
5. Knead lightly on a floured board. Dough will spring back when pressed with a finger if kneaded sufficiently.
6. Divide into three sections and knead each into a long roll. Place in three oiled bar tins.
7. Cover and stand in a warm place until loaves have doubled in bulk.
8. Bake in a hot oven (230°C) for approximately 1 hour.

Note: Two teaspoons of safflower oil may be added to this recipe.

Turkish Pide Bread

½ cup warm water

pinch sugar

3 teaspoons dry yeast

3 cups plain flour

½ teaspoon salt

2 tablespoons olive oil

¾ cup warm water, extra

1 egg, lightly beaten

sesame seeds

1. Place water, sugar and yeast into a large bowl and leave in a warm place for 5 minutes until frothy.
2. Add flour, salt, oil and extra water and mix to a soft dough.
3. Turn onto a floured board and knead for 10 minutes.
4. Place dough in an oiled bowl, cover with plastic wrap and leave until doubled in size.
5. Divide dough in half, make into a ball and, using the palm of the hand, flatten the dough into a piece approximately 18 to 20 cm in diameter. Place on a greased baking tray.
6. Brush with egg and sprinkle with sesame seeds and bake at 220°C for approximately 8 minutes or until puffy and golden.
7. Serve immediately while hot.

Sweet Dough

2 7 g sachets dried yeast
140 mL lukewarm water
4 cups plain flour
1 teaspoon salt
½ 50 mg ascorbic acid tablet
60 g butter or margarine
¼ cup sugar
½ cup evaporated milk (undiluted)

1. Crumble yeast into a small bowl. Add ¼ cup of the water and stir well to disperse yeast. Sift flour and salt. Add crushed ascorbic acid tablet then rub in the butter or margarine. Add sugar.
2. Make a well in the centre and pour in evaporated milk, yeast and remaining water. Mix well with a knife to form a soft dough (add more lukewarm water if required).
3. Turn onto a floured board and knead thoroughly for 10 minutes (dough should be smooth and satiny and spring back when pressed). Cover with a clean cloth and stand in a warm place for 5 minutes.
4. Shape dough as required, place in tins and stand in a warm place until mixture almost doubles in bulk (30 to 45 minutes). Bake as directed in the recipe.

Variations

Buns

Soak ½ cup sultanas or mixed dried fruit in warm water for 15 minutes. Drain and dry on paper towel. Knead fruit into dough before proving. Divide into 16 to 18 pieces and shape into buns. Place on an oiled oven tray or lamington tin 2 cm apart. Prove as directed in basic recipe.

Bake at 200°C for 15 to 20 minutes. Remove from trays and glaze while hot with sugar syrup, or ice when cool.

Glaze for Buns

Boil together ¼ cup water and 1 tablespoon sugar. Remove from heat, cool slightly then stir in ½ teaspoon gelatine and a few drops of lemon essence. Brush on top of buns.

Swedish Tea Ring

½ **quantity of sweet dough**

2 **teaspoons butter or margarine**

½ **teaspoon cinnamon**

¼ **cup caster sugar**

¼ **cup raisins, chopped**

1. Roll the dough out to an oblong 23 × 13 cm.
2. Spread with softened butter then sprinkle with caster sugar, chopped raisins and cinnamon.
3. Roll the dough up tightly, beginning at the wide side and seal by pinching the edges together.
4. Place roll on an oiled tray forming it into a ring. Join the ends.
5. Cut two-thirds through the ring at 2.5 cm intervals and turn each section on its side.
6. Cover with a cloth and prove for 30 to 40 minutes. Bake until golden brown in a moderate to hot oven (200°C) for 25 to 30 minutes.
7. While still warm spread with soft icing and decorate with nuts and cherries.

Pizza

Crust

1 **7 g sachet dry yeast, or 25 g compressed yeast**

1 **teaspoon sugar**

150 **mL water (½ boiling, ½ cold)**

2 **cups plain flour**

pinch salt

2 **teaspoons oil or melted margarine**

Sauce

1 **110 g can tomato paste**

pepper

Toppings

sliced tomatoes, onions, mushrooms, stuffed olives, strips of bacon, pepperoni, capsicum, pineapple, anchovies, ham, grated cheese (mozzarella)

1 **teaspoon oregano**

1. Dissolve yeast and sugar in warm water.
2. Sift flour and salt and warm.
3. Add warm water to flour and mix to a dough.
4. Turn dough onto a floured board and knead for 3–4 minutes until smooth.
5. Oil mixing bowl and return dough. Rest in a warm place. Cover and allow to prove.
6. Prepare topping.
7. Oil tray. Press dough onto tray.
8. Spread tomato paste over dough. Sprinkle pepper on.
9. Arrange topping over tomato paste.
10. Top with grated cheese and sprinkle with oregano.
11. Bake in a hot oven (200°C) for 30 minutes.

Jams and Jellies

FRUIT

Very fresh fruit is essential to good flavour and setting. It should be just ripe and of good colour. Freshly picked fruit is ideal. If fruit is freshly picked discard seeds; if not, put the seeds in a cup and barely cover with water. This strained water may be added to the pulp with the sugar to give extra pectin.

Apricot Jam

1 kg prepared fresh apricots

4 cups sugar

juice of 1 lemon

1 tablespoon blanched almonds

1. Wash apricots and remove any blemishes.
2. Cut in halves and remove stones.
3. Place apricots and half the sugar in layers in a bowl.
4. Stand overnight.
5. Place fruit, syrup, lemon juice and remainder of sugar in a pan.
6. Cook slowly until apricots are soft and transparent.
7. Add almonds.
8. Cool slightly then bottle and seal.

Dried Apricot Jam

250 g dried apricots (light colour)

4 cups water

3½ cups sugar

1 tablespoon blanched almonds

1. Soak apricots in water overnight.
2. Place in a large saucepan and cook for 15 minutes or until soft.
3. Add sugar and stir until dissolved.
4. Boil for half an hour.
5. Add almonds.
6. Bottle and seal.

Pineapple Jam

1 kg pineapple
juice 1 large lemon
1 cup water
4 cups sugar

1. Cut pineapple in half lengthways and scrape pulp out with a spoon or grate pineapple on the coarse section of grater.
2. Weigh fruit and place in a saucepan. Add lemon juice and water.
3. Allow to boil until pulp is tender.
4. Add sugar and boil for 30 minutes.
5. Bottle and seal.

Plum Jam

1 kg plums
½ cup water
juice of 1 lemon
4 cups sugar

1. Grease the bottom of a preserving pan lightly with butter.
2. Wash plums, cut in halves, remove stones.
3. Place in preserving pan, add water and juice.
4. Allow fruit to soften a little over low heat.
5. Add sugar and stir until dissolved.
6. Boil quickly until a little will set on a saucer.
7. Bottle and seal.

Rosella Jam

rosellas
1 cup sugar to each cup of pulp
lemon juice
water

1. Cut the ends off the fruit and extract the seeds.
2. Put seeds and cuttings into a saucepan and cover with water.
3. Boil for 1 hour or until liquid is syrupy.
4. Strain into a preserving pan. Discard seeds.
5. Add rosella husks and cook for 20 to 30 minutes or until soft.
6. Measure and add one cup of sugar to each cup of pulp.
7. Add juice of 1 lemon for every 2 cups of pulp.
8. Boil rapidly for about 20 minutes, stirring continuously.
9. Bottle and seal.

Strawberry Jam

1 kg strawberries, preferably small
1 kg sugar
1 or 2 lemons

1. Choose clean, ripe strawberries. If possible do not wash them. If washing is necessary allow to dry on absorbent paper.
2. Place strawberries in a large saucepan with the sugar and lemon juice.
3. Bring slowly to boiling point to dissolve sugar. Stir occasionally.
4. Boil rapidly for 20 minutes, stirring occasionally.
5. Bottle and seal.

Note: If possible put strawberries and sugar in layers in a dish and stand overnight. This helps to keep strawberries whole.

For a smoother jam mash strawberries while boiling.

* Strawberry Jam

2 punnets of strawberries, cut in half
1 cup white sugar
juice of 1 lemon

1. Place all ingredients in a large microwave-proof dish and cook on HIGH for 20 to 25 minutes or until it jellies. Stir occasionally until sugar dissolves.
2. Skim off any foam and cool.
3. Pour into clean, dry and warmed bottles.
4. Seal when cold.

Apple Jelly

12 firm green cooking apples
cold water to cover
1 cup sugar to each cup of juice
1 teaspoon lemon juice to each cup juice

1. Wash apples and cut each into 10 or 12 pieces.
2. Place fruit in a large saucepan or preserving pan.
3. Barely cover with cold water.
4. Boil until fruit is soft and pulpy.
5. Strain carefully through a flannel strainer and allow to drip overnight.
6. Measure juice into a clean saucepan, add sugar and lemon juice.
7. Boil rapidly until a small quantity jellies on a cold plate.
8. Bottle and seal.

Lemon Jelly

5 large lemons

6 cups water

1 cup sugar to each cup juice

1. Wash lemons thoroughly.
2. Cut each lemon into 6 or 8 pieces.
3. Cover with water and boil until water is reduced to half quantity.
4. Allow to stand overnight.
5. Strain through a flannel strainer and measure.
6. Add sugar and stir until dissolved.
7. Boil quickly until a small quantity jellies on a cold plate.
8. Bottle and seal.

Three Fruits Marmalade

1 grapefruit

1 orange

1 lemon

water

sugar

1. Wash fruit well then slice thinly.
2. To every ½ kilogram of sliced fruit add 4 cups of water and stand overnight.
3. Place in a preserving pan and boil until skins are soft.
4. Measure pulp and add 1 cup of sugar to each cup of pulp.
5. Boil rapidly for 30 to 45 minutes or until a small amount will set on a saucer.
6. Cool slightly, bottle and seal.

Grapefruit Marmalade

½ kg grapefruit

juice of 1 or 2 lemons

4 cups water

6 cups sugar

1. Wash fruit thoroughly.
2. Slice fruit finely with a very sharp knife.
3. Place in a bowl, add water and stand overnight.
4. Put pips in a small bowl with some of the water, stand overnight.
5. Place fruit, lemon juice and water in a preserving pan. Add liquid from pips.
6. Boil gently until rind is quite tender.
7. Add sugar and boil rapidly until a little will jelly on a saucer. This should take from 30 to 45 minutes.
8. Cool slightly then bottle and seal.

Sweet Orange Marmalade

½ kg oranges
juice 2 lemons
4 cups water
4 cups sugar

1. Wash oranges well then slice thinly.
2. Place in an earthenware bowl and cover with water.
3. Allow to stand overnight.
4. Place in a preserving pan with lemon juice and heat until boiling.
5. Cook gently until the peel is soft and water is reduced by half.
6. Add sugar and boil rapidly for about 30 minutes or until a little will set on a chilled saucer.
7. Cool slightly then bottle and seal.

Lemon Marmalade

6 large lemons
5 cups water
8 cups sugar

1. Wash lemons thoroughly.
2. Slice very thinly.
3. Place in an earthenware bowl and cover with water.
4. Allow to stand overnight.
5. Place in a preserving pan and boil until tender.
6. Add sugar and boil quickly for 30 to 45 minutes or until it jellies when placed on a chilled saucer.
7. Cool slightly, bottle and seal.

Cumquat Marmalade

2 cups cumquats
2½–3½ cups water
3 cups sugar

1. Slice fruit finely, removing pips.
2. Place fruit in a bowl and pips in a small basin.
3. Pour a little water on the pips and the rest on the sliced fruit.
4. Allow to stand overnight.
5. Strain water off pips and add to fruit.
6. Place in a preserving pan and cook slowly until peel is soft.
7. Add sugar and boil rapidly for 20 to 30 minutes.
8. Cool slightly, bottle and seal.

Apple Chutney

1 kg apples
3–4 onions
1 clove garlic
½ cup sugar
¼ cup dates
¼ teaspoon cayenne pepper
1 teaspoon salt
2 teaspoons ginger
1 teaspoon mustard
600 mL vinegar
1 teaspoon mixed spice

1. Peel and core apples and cut into quarters.
2. Mince apples, onions and garlic.
3. Place in a preserving pan with other ingredients.
4. Simmer gently for about 1 hour.
5. Bottle and seal.

Mango Chutney

2 cups sugar
1½ litres vinegar
3–4 onions
4–5 apples
2–3 tomatoes
6 small chillies
1¼ cups sultanas or raisins
2 cloves garlic
½ cup preserved ginger
piece green ginger
1½ kg firm mango pulp
¼ teaspoon cayenne pepper
1 tablespoon salt

1. Boil sugar with half the vinegar to make a syrup.
2. Peel and finely cut the onions, apples, tomatoes, chillies, raisins, garlic and ginger. Add mango pulp.
3. Place in syrup in preserving pan.
4. Add cayenne pepper and salt.
5. Add remainder of vinegar as required.
6. Boil for about 2 hours or until mixture is of good consistency.
7. Bottle and seal.

Papaw Chutney

1 kg firm papaw
4–5 firm tomatoes
3 onions
1½ cups sultanas
1 chilli
piece green ginger
2 cloves garlic
750 mL vinegar
2 lemons
2 cups sugar
1 tablespoon salt
2 teaspoons mustard

1. Peel papaw, tomatoes and onions.
2. Chop finely or mince papaw, tomatoes, onions, sultanas, chilli, ginger and garlic.
3. Place in a preserving pan, add 200 mL vinegar and lemon juice and simmer for 20 minutes or until soft.
4. Add sugar, salt and mustard mixed with the remaining vinegar.
5. Boil for a further 5 to 10 minutes.
6. Bottle and seal.

Choko Chutney

5 chokoes (large)
1½ cups sultanas
1½ cups raisins
2 cups dates
½ cup preserved ginger
1 large green cooking apple
1 onion
1½ cups sugar
1 tablespoon salt
½ teaspoon cayenne pepper
2½ cups vinegar

1. Prepare chokoes and cut into small pieces.
2. Add chopped fruits and ginger, chopped onion and apple.
3. Add sugar, salt, cayenne pepper and vinegar.
4. Cook gently uncovered for approximately 2 hours until ingredients are tender and of good chutney consistency.
5. Bottle and seal.

Mixed Pickles

1 medium sized cauliflower
1 cucumber
500 g small pickling onions
250 g French beans
1 bright red chilli for each bottle
1.5 litres white vinegar
1 tablespoon peppercorns
20 g whole ginger
2 blades mace
1 teaspoon allspice
2 tablespoons sugar

1. Divide cauliflower into flowerets.
2. Slice unpeeled cucumbers, peel onions and cut beans into 2.5 cm strips.
3. Soak all vegetables overnight in strong brine solution made with ½ cup of salt to one litre of water.
4. Drain, cover vegetables with boiling water and stand until cold.
5. Pack in jars.
6. Boil vinegar with flavourings, strain, cover vegetables.
7. Seal immediately.

Mustard Pickles

1 cauliflower
250 g beans
2 cucumbers
½ kg small onions
salt
1 litre white vinegar
½ cup sugar
2 teaspoons mustard
1 teaspoon turmeric
1 teaspoon curry powder
2 tablespoons flour

1. Wash cauliflower and divide into flowerets.
2. Peel and slice beans and cucumbers and peel onions.
3. Place together in a large bowl and sprinkle liberally with salt.
4. Allow to stand for 24 hours then wash vegetables in cold water. Place in a large pan and scald with boiling vinegar and sugar.
5. Mix mustard, turmeric, curry powder and flour with a little vinegar and add to mixture.
6. Boil for about 10 minutes.
7. Bottle and seal.

Tomato Relish

1½ kg tomatoes
500 g onions
¼ cup salt
2 cups sugar
1 cup white vinegar
2 tablespoons cornflour
2 teaspoons curry powder

1. Skin tomatoes and chop roughly.
2. Peel onions and chop finely.
3. Place both in an earthenware or glass (not plastic) bowl and sprinkle with salt. Allow to stand overnight.
4. Pour off almost all the liquid, add sugar and vinegar and boil until tender.
5. Blend cornflour and curry powder with a little vinegar and add.
6. Cook until mixture has thickened.
7. Bottle and seal.

Note: Mixture is fairly thin but will thicken on standing. Because of the small vinegar content relishes do not keep indefinitely and should be stored in the refrigerator.

Pickled Onions

4 kg pickling onions, peeled
white sugar
white vinegar

1. Place 1 teaspoon of sugar in the bottom of each bottle and fill the bottles with peeled onions.
2. Fill the jars with vinegar and seal.
3. Stand for 4 weeks before using.

Corn and Tomato Relish

1½ kg ripe tomatoes
2 large onions
2 sticks celery
1 440 g can corn kernels
1 440 g can crushed
  pineapple
1½ cups sugar
2 cups white vinegar
1 tablespoon salt
1½ tablespoons medium
  curry powder
1 tablespoon mustard
  powder
1–2 tablespoons cornflour

1. Skin and chop tomatoes.
2. Peel and chop onions.
3. Cut celery finely.
4. Place all ingredients in a large saucepan and boil for
   1 hour.
5. Thicken with cornflour blended with a little vinegar.
6. Bottle and seal.

Spiced Vinegar

2 litres white vinegar
1 teaspoon whole cloves
1 teaspoon mustard seeds
1 tablespoon finely
  chopped fresh ginger
1 tablespoon peppercorns
1 large clove garlic,
  crushed
1 stick cinnamon
1 cup sugar
2 bay leaves
1 teaspoon salt

1. Place all ingredients in a saucepan, bring to boil and
   simmer for 15 minutes.
2. Remove from heat, cover and allow to infuse until cold.
3. Bottle as is, or strain if desired and seal.

Plain Toffee

2 cups sugar
¾ cup water
1 tablespoon vinegar

1. Place all ingredients in a saucepan, stir over a gentle heat until sugar has dissolved.
2. Brush sides of the saucepan with a little water to remove undissolved sugar.
3. Bring to the boil and boil without stirring until the syrup is a pale amber colour.
4. Remove from heat and allow bubbles to subside.
5. Pour into patty papers or into a flat, greased pan and mark into squares. Allow to cool and harden.

Peanut Toffee

2 cups white sugar
¾ cup water
⅛ teaspoon cream of tartar or 1 tablespoon white vinegar
lemon essence
½ cup raw peanuts, skinned

1. Place sugar, water and cream of tartar in a saucepan.
2. Stir over heat until the sugar has dissolved.
3. Brush sides of saucepan with water.
4. Boil without stirring until toffee is a pale amber colour and continue to brush sides of saucepan while boiling.
5. Remove from heat and allow bubbles to settle. Add essence and swirl through.
6. Pour into greased moulds or patty papers.
7. Sprinkle with peanuts.
8. Allow to harden.
9. Store in an airtight jar.

Variation

Add peanuts to toffee mixture and stir to combine evenly.

Russian Caramels

3 tablespoons butter
2 tablespoons golden syrup
½ cup sugar
½ can condensed milk
vanilla

1. Place butter, syrup, sugar and milk into a saucepan.
2. Stir over heat until mixture boils.
3. Continue to cook, stirring well, for about 15 minutes or test for 'chewiness' on a cold saucer.
4. Add vanilla and turn onto a buttered plate or greased surface. Mark into squares.
5. Cut when cool and wrap in cellophane.

French Jellies

2 tablespoons gelatine
1 cup water
2 cups sugar
colouring
flavouring
1 cup icing sugar
¼ cup cornflour

1. Soak gelatine in ½ cup cold water.
2. Dissolve sugar in ½ cup water in a saucepan.
3. Add gelatine to syrup and boil for 5 minutes.
4. Remove from heat, colour and flavour.
5. Pour into wet moulds.
6. Stand overnight. Cut into squares and roll in a mixture of icing sugar and cornflour.

Note: Mixture will boil over if saucepan is not large enough.

Butterscotch

2 cups sugar
¾ cup water
2 tablespoons glucose or ⅛ teaspoon cream of tartar
3 tablespoons butter

1. Place sugar, water and glucose in a saucepan.
2. Stir over heat until the sugar has dissolved.
3. Brush sides of saucepan with water.
4. Boil without stirring until mixture is an amber colour.
5. Continue to brush sides of saucepan while boiling.
6. Remove from heat and add butter.
7. Stir until all butter is absorbed.
8. Pour into a buttered plate or tin.
9. When partly set mark into squares.
10. When set break and store in an airtight jar.

Marshmallows

1½ tablespoons gelatine
100 mL cold water
1¼ cups sugar
140 mL hot water
colouring
flavouring
toasted coconut

1. Place gelatine and cold water in a mixing bowl.
2. Place sugar and hot water in a saucepan and bring to boiling point.
3. Pour over gelatine and stir until gelatine has dissolved.
4. Beat until thick and white.
5. Add colouring and flavouring.
6. Pour into a buttered tray.
7. Stand until set.
8. Cut into squares and toss in toasted coconut.

Coconut Ice

1½ cups sugar
2 tablespoons glucose *or*
  ⅛ teaspoon cream of
  tartar
½ cup water
vanilla
¾ cup coconut
cochineal

1. Place sugar, glucose and water in a saucepan.
2. Stir over heat until sugar has dissolved.
3. Brush sides of saucepan to remove grains of sugar.
4. Boil without stirring until mixture reaches 113°C.
5. Remove from heat and cool a little.
6. Add vanilla and coconut and beat until thick and creamy.
7. Pour onto a buttered dish or greased surface.
8. Make another batch of mixture as before and colour pale pink.
9. Pour on top of white layer.
10. Do not turn out until quite cold and firm.
11. Cut into squares.

Coconut Ice (Uncooked)

500 g icing sugar
250 g desiccated coconut
1 teaspoon vanilla
30 g copha
1 egg white
½ cup condensed milk
pink food colouring

1. Sift icing sugar into a bowl.
2. Add coconut and vanilla and mix.
3. Melt copha over low heat.
4. Add to icing sugar with egg white and condensed milk and mix well.
5. Divide mixture in half, colour one half with pink colouring.
6. Press white half into a greased, paper-lined 20 cm square tin.
7. Press pink half onto white layer.
8. When cold remove from the tin and cut into squares. Store in refrigerator.

Peanut Brittle

2 cups sugar
¾ cup water
⅛ teaspoon cream of tartar
1 teaspoon bicarbonate of soda
1 cup peanuts, unsalted

1. Place sugar, water and cream of tartar in a saucepan.
2. Stir over heat until sugar has dissolved.
3. Boil without stirring until toffee is a pale amber colour. Brush sides of pan with water.
4. Remove from heat, add soda free from lumps and peanuts cut into three or four pieces.
5. Stir lightly then pour at once onto a greased marble slab or cold surface.
6. Spread thinly with a large buttered knife.
7. When set break into irregular pieces.
8. Store in an airtight jar.

Vanilla Fudge

2 cups sugar
¾ cup milk
⅛ teaspoon cream of tartar or 2 tablespoons glucose
1½ tablespoons butter
vanilla

1. Place sugar, milk, cream of tartar and butter in a saucepan.
2. Stir over low heat until dissolved.
3. Allow to boil to 115°C or until a soft ball can be formed when a little of the mixture is placed in cold water.
4. Remove from heat and cool a little.
5. Add vanilla and beat until thick and creamy.
6. Pour into a buttered tin.
7. When partly set, mark into squares.
8. Allow to harden before removing from tin.

Chocolate Fudge

2 cups sugar
¾ cup milk
1½ tablespoons butter
2 tablespoons cocoa
⅛ teaspoon cream of tartar or 2 tablespoons glucose
vanilla

1. Place sugar, milk, butter, cocoa and cream of tartar in a saucepan.
2. Stir over low heat until dissolved.
3. Allow to boil to 115°C or until a soft ball can be formed when a little of the mixture is placed in cold water.
4. Remove from heat and allow to cool a little.
5. Add vanilla and beat until thick and creamy.
6. Pour into a buttered tin.
7. When partly set mark into squares.
8. Allow to harden before removing from tin.

Ginger Fudge

Wash and dry ½ cup crystallised ginger, chop finely and add to Vanilla Fudge.

✳ Fudge

125 g butter

⅔ cup evaporated milk

1½ cups caster sugar

100 g white marshmallows

1 teaspoon vanilla

185 g chocolate (white for caramel fudge, dark for chocolate fudge)

1. Place butter, milk, sugar and marshmallows in a large microwave-safe dish with a lid.
2. Microwave on MEDIUM for 5 minutes, stirring every 1½ minutes.
3. Microwave on MEDIUM HIGH for 8 minutes, without stirring.
4. Add vanilla and broken up chocolate and beat with electric mixer for 5 minutes on high speed.
5. Pour into a greased biscuit tray and refrigerate until set.
6. Cut into squares.

Chocolate Spiders

1 large block cooking chocolate

2 tablespoons peanut butter

2 packets cooked crunchy egg noodles

1. Melt cooking chocolate, remove from heat and stir in peanut butter until smooth and well mixed.
2. Add noodles and stir until noodles are well covered with chocolate.
3. Put spoonfuls on a paper-lined tray or spread mixture evenly over a paper-lined tray and break into pieces when set.
4. Place in refrigerator to set.

Variation

½ cup finely chopped crystallised cherries, sultanas or nuts can be added to the chocolate mixture.

Mocha Roughs

250 g cooking chocolate
60 g copha
2 teaspoons instant coffee
120 g desiccated coconut

1. Chop the chocolate and copha roughly, add the coffee and melt over hot water, stirring occasionally.
2. Remove from the heat and stir in the coconut.
3. Place teaspoonfuls of mixture (about 50) on trays covered with waxed paper. Chill until firm.
4. Store in refrigerator.

Coconut Roughs (Uncooked)

$1/3$ cup hot mashed potato
30 g butter, melted
$1 2/3$ cups icing sugar
$1 1/2$ tablespoons cocoa
$1 3/4$ cups coconut
1 teaspoon vanilla

1. Add butter to hot potato and beat well. Gradually beat in the sifted icing sugar and cocoa.
2. Add coconut and vanilla and mix well.
3. Place teaspoonfuls onto greased paper.
4. Refrigerate until firm.

Rocky Road

$1/4$ cup desiccated coconut
1 100 g packet pink marshmallows, halved and 1 100 g white marshmallows, halved OR make marshmallows (see recipe on page 296)
$1/2$ cup chopped mixed nuts, unsalted
$1/2$ cup chopped glacé cherries, optional
375 g milk chocolate melts

1. Line base and sides of shallow 27 × 18 cm tin with foil.
2. Sprinkle half coconut over the base of the tin.
3. Place marshmallows in tin in alternating colours, leaving space between pieces.
4. Sprinkle remaining coconut, nuts and cherries between marshmallows and around the sides of the tin.
5. Place chocolate in a heatproof bowl. Stand over a pan of simmering water and stir until chocolate has melted and is smooth. Cool slightly.
6. Pour chocolate over and through the marshmallow mixture.
7. Allow to set, then cut into pieces.

Variation

White-chocolate melts can be substituted for milk-chocolate melts.

Beverages

Iced Coffee

1 tablespoon instant coffee
300 mL water
300 mL milk
2 teaspoons sugar
ice-cream

1. Dissolve coffee in a little hot water then add to cold water.
2. Add sugar and milk and stir until sugar has dissolved.
3. Pour into glasses. Add ice cubes made with black coffee.
4. Top with ice-cream and a slight sprinkling of drinking chocolate powder.

Iced Tea

6 teaspoons tea
½ cup sugar
¾ cup lemon juice
ice cubes

1. Pour 3 cups boiling water over the tea, allow to infuse, add sugar and allow to cool.
2. Add 3 cups cold water and lemon juice and stir well.
3. Refrigerate and serve with ice cubes.

Vanilla Milkshake

1 cup cold milk
vanilla to taste
1 tablespoon ice-cream

1. Place ingredients in a blender and blend for 20 seconds.
2. Pour into a chilled glass and sprinkle with nutmeg.

Variations

Banana Milkshake

Add half a banana and process in a blender.

Chocolate Milkshake

Add 1–2 teaspoons drinking chocolate and process in blender.

Malted Milks

Add 1–2 teaspoons malted milk powder to any of the above.

Fruit Smoothie

1 banana or any other fruit e.g. strawberries, peaches, frozen berries or canned fruit

1 cup milk

1 tablespoon honey

1 tablespoon vanilla ice-cream, natural yoghurt or fruit yoghurt

1. Peel and chop fruit.
2. Blend ingredients until smooth.
3. Serve immediately.

Hi-Fibre Smoothie

1 banana, peeled and chopped

1 tablespoon wheat germ

1 tablespoon oat bran

3 tablespoons natural yoghurt

1 cup milk

3 teaspoons honey

1. Blend all ingredients until smooth.
2. Serve immediately.

Egg Flip

1 egg

1 teaspoon sugar

1 cup cold milk

few drops of vanilla

nutmeg

1. Beat egg and sugar until frothy.
2. Add milk and vanilla and stir well.
3. Strain into a glass.
4. Sprinkle a little nutmeg on top.

Beef Tea

250 g lean steak

¼ teaspoon salt

1 cup water

a few drops lemon juice

1 slice toast

1. Remove any fat from the steak then shred finely.
2. Place in a heatproof jug with salt, water and lemon juice.
3. Cover with greased paper.
4. Allow to stand for 30 minutes.
5. Place jug in a saucepan of water.
6. Allow to simmer for 1 to 2 hours or as long as possible, stirring occasionally.
7. Strain and serve in a cup with sippets of toast in the saucer.

Lemon Barley Water

2 tablespoons barley

600 mL boiling water

finely grated lemon rind
    and juice of one lemon

2 teaspoons sugar *or*
    1 tablespoon honey

1. Wash barley and place in a saucepan.
2. Add water and lemon rind.
3. Simmer for 30 minutes.
4. Strain, add lemon juice and sugar.
5. Chill before serving.

Fruit Cup

2 bottles lemon cordial

1 bottle orange cordial

2 bottles water

1 can crushed pineapple

4 large bottles lemonade

3 large bottles dry ginger
    ale

1 dozen passionfruit

3 bananas

finely chopped mint

1. Mix together lemon and orange cordial, water and
    pineapple and chill well.
2. Just before serving, add lemonade, ginger ale,
    passionfruit, chopped bananas and mint.

Fruit Punch

2 cups sugar, or less

300 mL water

300 mL freshly made tea

600 mL fruit cordial (fruit
    cup)

300 mL lemon juice

600 mL orange juice

600 mL pineapple juice

3 litres iced water

3 bottles soda water

glacé cherries

mint, banana, orange,
    lemon, apple

1. Boil sugar and 300 mL of water for 5 minutes.
2. Add tea, cordial and juices.
3. When required add iced water and soda water. Pour into
    punch bowl.
4. Garnish with fruit and mint.

Fresh Fruit Punch

1½ cups fruit cup cordial

1 punnet strawberries, hulled and chopped

juice 1 orange

juice 1 lemon

2 bananas sliced

2 peaches, peeled and chopped

1 lemon, thickly sliced

1.25 litres lemonade

1.25 litres ginger ale

750 mL spumante or sparkling wine

ice cubes

1. Place cordial in a large container. Add prepared fruits and juices. Set aside in refrigerator until needed.
2. Add lemonade, ginger ale and spumante, all well chilled.
3. Pour into a punch bowl or jugs.
4. Add ice cubes.

Tropical Punch

2 litres lemonade

2 litres ginger ale

2–3 litres fruit juice (pineapple or orange)

1–2 cups diced fruit (peaches, apples, banana, passionfruit) or 400 g can fruit salad

2–3 trays ice cubes

Combine in a punchbowl.

(*Makes approx. 30 glasses*)

Pineapple Punch

2 litre can pineapple juice

2 litres ginger ale

mint, chopped

ice cubes

Combine in a punchbowl.

Mint Tingle

1 cup sugar
3 cups water
1 cup lemon juice
2 tablespoons chopped mint
green food colouring
1 large bottle lemonade

1. Place sugar, water and mint in a saucepan and stir over heat until boiling.
2. Remove from heat and allow to cool.
3. Strain and add lemon juice.
4. Colour mint green and chill.
5. Just before serving add lemonade, ice cubes and sprigs of mint.

NON-ALCOHOLIC COCKTAILS
Apricot Fluff

¼ cup ricotta cheese
½ cup plain yoghurt
1 tablespoon honey
1½ cups apricot nectar
ice cubes

1. Place ricotta, yoghurt, honey and nectar in a food processor and process until smooth.
2. Pour into glasses over plenty of ice and serve immediately.

(Serves 4)

Pineapple Crush

1 450 g can crushed pineapple
1 cup pineapple juice
200 mL coconut milk
ice cubes

1. Combine pineapple and juice in a jug and whisk in coconut milk until well blended.
2. Pour into glasses over plenty of ice and serve immediately.

(Serves 4–6)

Fruit Frappe

1 cup rockmelon, chopped
1 banana, chopped
1 cup pawpaw, chopped
1 cup pineapple, chopped
1 mango, chopped
1 cup pineapple juice
ice cubes, crushed

1. Place chopped fruits in a food processor and process until smooth.
2. Add juice and ice and process until mixture becomes slushy.
3. Serve immediately.

(Serves 4)

Spiced Mango

3 ripe mangoes, chopped
1 teaspoon honey
1 cup plain yoghurt
1 teaspoon cinnamon
250 mL milk

1. Place all ingredients in a food processor and process until smooth.
2. Serve immediately.

(Serves 4)

Sunset Mocktail

50 mL apple juice
50 mL apricot nectar
30 mL coconut cream
½ banana, sliced
¼ teaspoon cinnamon
¼ teaspoon nutmeg
1 scoop ice-cream

1. Place all ingredients in food processor and process until smooth.
2. Pour into cocktail glasses and serve immediately.

(Serves 2)

Category Index

Note: ✳ indicates a microwave recipe; ✗ represents gluten-free recipes.

General Index

Note: ✳ indicates a microwave recipe; ✕ represents gluten-free recipes.